POLITICS
AS COMMUNICATION

COMMUNICATION AND
INFORMATION SCIENCE

A series of monographs,
treatises, and texts

Edited by
MELVIN J. VOIGT

University of California, San Diego

POLITICS
AS COMMUNICATION

Robert G. Meadow

University of California, San Diego

ABLEX Publishing Corporation
Norwood, New Jersey 07648

Printed in the United States of America.

Library of Congress Cataloging in Publication Data

Meadow, Robert G
    Politics as communication.

    (Communication and information science)
    Bibliography: p.
    Includes indexes.
    1. Communication in politics.   2. Political
sociology.   I. Title.   II. Series.
JA76.M4   301.5'92   79-25176
ISBN   0-89391-031-7

ABLEX Publishing Corporation
355 Chestnut Street
Norwood, New Jersey 07648

For Carrie

with whom communicating is a joy

CONTENTS

III   COMMUNICATION IN POLITICAL INSTITUTIONS

8

9

10

IV   COMMUNICATION AS A POLITICAL ISSUE

11

12

PREFACE

Once again, as politicians, journalists, voters and scholars gear up for another U.S. presidential election, attention turns toward the role of mass media in politics. Aspiring candidates will seek to present their best side to the voters. Indeed, professional media consultants will offer advice, including literally which side of their candidate's face to present, while other advisers will offer wisdom on issues to raise or sidestep. Following the candidates will be journalists, all determined to be on hand for campaign eventualities ranging from new policy pronouncements, to gaffes, to fund-raising dinners at which chicken is *not* served, to assassination attempts. Whatever occurs will be presented to the editors, and, hopefully, the readers. Voters, too, will have to be prepared as campaign events eat into the dinnertime news, political ads replace ordinary commercials, and special reports or debates are substituted for prime-time entertainment television.

Finally, doggedly following candidates, journalists and voters, will be scholars trained in political science, sociology, psychology, mass communication, journalism, linguistics and even biology, all doing political communication research. For the most part, scholars from these disciplines will be investigating what political communication researchers have been looking at for the past thirty years. Without doubt, methods have changed, quantitative techniques improved and knowledge has been accumulated since the first election based political communication research of the 1940s. But directing political communication research projects to electoral and associated activities only has constrained the study of political communication.

Serendipitous findings in the early voting behavior studies gave the discipline an empirical focus before we had a theory of the politics/communication interface. Thus, for all practical purposes, political communication research was mass mediated messages about politics. Researchers developed strategies to look at the "effects" of messages on a range of political variables from party identification to information about candidates to voting choice. In each case, the results were the same: direct effects of exposure to campaign information were limited because voters would selectively expose themselves to information from candidates toward whom they were favorably disposed. Although other important concepts such as the two-step flow of opinion emerged from these early studies to spur communication research, the investigation of mass media effects during elections defined political communication research for over a decade.

Even in more recent research, the dominant focus has been on the mass media/election linkage. Agenda-setting, uses and gratifications, and media dependencies research which have dominated the literature for the past ten years still focus on election periods, press performance during elections, or single communication events such as debates during elections. Political communication research in Europe during the same period has similarly focused on elections.

No doubt many of these studies offer valuable insights into political communication insofar as the study of political communication is limited to the effects of mass communication on political behavior. But when we consider political communication more broadly and introduce conceptual and theoretical questions, knowledge of the linkages between mass media and elections does not take us far enough in our understanding of political communication phenomena. Problems such as the communication relations or information flow between third world nations and developed nations, while clearly political communication issues, are untouched because of the election oriented approach. Interpersonal communication issues such as those raised by bilingualism conflicts often have political roots. In the United States, constraints on the flow of information resulting from judicial decisions are political communication issues. Overall, there are many issues in political communication untouched because of the election emphasis.

My motivation in writing this book is to move away from election based research and toward a broader view of political communication. In so doing, I am not as certain that I have sown new seeds as I am of having found new ways to harvest old fruit. First, I have reconsidered the theoretical literature in political communication. It has drifted in a number of directions. I have sought to integrate this literature and impose order on it while offering my own model in which political communication phenomena are shown to appear both within political institutions and groups as well as to link these institutions. Second, I have directed much of my attention to general political concepts, arguing that concepts such as power, conflict, political participation, political development, political integration and political socialization can be seen as communication based and thus considered by political communication researchers. Although these concepts are not new, focusing on their communicaion dimensions is. Third, I have isolated those aspects of political institutions and processes in the United States in which communication phenomena play crucial roles. Finally, I have looked at how the centrality of communication has made communication itself an important political issue in political systems.

What this required was that I propose political communication be viewed two ways: first as the role that communication plays in political institutions and processes, and second as the role politics plays in shaping communication processes. The former issue has been well considered, the latter less so. One of my aspirations for this volume is that it may help put the two in better balance.

La Jolla, California
October, 1979   R.G.M

ACKNOWLEDGMENTS

Writing this book was far more difficult that I anticipated for two reasons. First, I have reported no data. Most of my earlier publications provided me with an opportunity to avoid extensive grappling with my vision of what political communication research ought to be. I hypothesized, collected data, and reported findings. Without quantitative findings to hide me, I feel more vulnerable to criticism from colleagues who undoubtedly will have differences with my conceptualization. Second, because this volume draws on materials from a variety of disciplines that have something to offer political communication researchers, I have often tread in unfamiliar areas. The result, of course, is that I may appear naive in my support of controversial theories, or perhaps even out of touch with emerging areas of these disciplines. I recognize this as a risk of interdisciplinary writing, and can say only that I am willing to bear the chuckles of experts in other disciplines if the end result is that political communication scholars widen their research and view the field as more multidimensional than in the past.

There are a number of individuals to whom I am indebted, some of whom are unaware of the contributions they have made to my thinking, others of whom helped by offering specific comments and suggestions. Among those of the two groups are Charles Elder, Roger Cobb, Jack Nagel, Neal Cutler, Doris Graber, Marilyn Jackson-Beeck and Dan Nimmo. Students in my graduate seminars in Political Communication and in Mass Media and Politics while I was on the faculty of the Annenberg School of Communications at the University of Pennsylvania were exposed to my first hazy thoughts on the topics in this volume. Their comments were quite helpful. Where the book sparkles, I give all of the above some credit, where it loses its luster, I accept the responsibility.

Institutional support came from a variety of sources as my mobility required. Early secretarial support came from the Annenberg School of Communications, University of Pennsylvania. The final manuscript was typed by Kathy Nguyen and Betty Marshall at the University of Kentucky. The Communications Program at the University of California, San Diego provided support at the concluding stages. I might add that when I joined the faculty at UCSD, Mel Voigt, editor of this series had his burden of prodding me to conclude made easier. He no longer had to call me long distance. His patience and support are appreciated.

Finally, there is my wife, Carrie, who contributed little to the manuscript in the traditional sense. Neither did she do things for the upkeep of our home that so many authors claim sustain them. Moreover, she had little tolerance for my banging at the typewriter late into the night; in fact she wanted it for her own research and writing. Her contributions to my life, however, pale those she could have made to the manuscript. It is to her, with love, that this work is dedicated.

POLITICS
AS COMMUNICATION

I

AN OVERVIEW
OF POLITICS
AS COMMUNICATION

1
DEFINING POLITICAL COMMUNICATION: AN INTRODUCTION

Disciplines running the alphabet from astronomy to zoology all deal with communication. As an emerging scholarly discipline, however, communication has encountered some difficulty in carving out its own identity distinct from the substantive areas to which it is most relevant. Now that communication has gained some recognition as an important discipline, its own subfields have to establish their own legitimacy. Political communication is one of many such fields.

Why does political communication stand out on its own? At least two reasons can be cited. First, it can be argued that political analysis is a mode or method of analysis. Moreover, politics is not a substantive area, but instead is a process. Social systems ordinarily have political subsystems designed (or functioning) to allocate values, make decisions, or compel action, the activities that political systems usually perform. Rather than concern ourselves only with the relationship between politics and communication, we are concerned with how the tools and techniques of political analysis can yield a greater understanding of the interface between empirical political systems and communication. In this volume, a process oriented view of politics is emphasized, making political relationships and concepts dependent on communication.

This politics-communication relationship hints at a second and perhaps more important reason why political communication stands on its own. It offers an opportunity to explore communication, both as a dependent and independent variable. On the one hand, political communication is concerned with the way in which the political world is shaped by the communication environment. In other words, to what extent does politics, as a dependent

3

variable, vary with changes in communication, either within, or across cultures? On the other hand, we know that the political environment can shape the quantity and quality of communication. As a dependent variable communication is argued to vary with the constraints imposed by political environments. These reciprocal relationships are unusual and underscore the pervasiveness of politics and communication as a justification for research.

The reciprocal relationships create some difficulties in constructing a working definition of political communication. Those scholars concerned with the communications (as independent variable) perspective have researched the role of language in political systems and the relationship of mass media technology to national political development. Others, with a political perspective, look at control of communications in varying political relationships, propaganda, or persuasion. Both of these approaches are deserving of further treatment as subjects within the scope of political communication, hence the definition must be suited to both.

For the purposes of this book, political communication refers to any exchange of symbols or messages that to a significant extent have been shaped by, or have consequences for, the functioning of political systems. Definitions, of course, can never be correct or incorrect, they are merely the premises from which logical analysis proceeds. They can, however, be evaluated in terms of their utility for clarification of disciplines and for promoting research. In brief, communication is considered as an exchange of symbols without specification in that it applies to verbal or nonverbal, interpersonal or mass, animal or human communication. Suffice it to say that in this volume, the bulk of research focuses on human, verbal, mass communication, but only because the political environment in modern societies operates thusly. There is no logical reason why nonverbal communication of social and political relationships in the animal kingdom could not be considered. However, our notion of what are political relationships and systems may circumscribe the wide applicability of the definition. Thus, a second crucial aspect of the definition is that the message exchange must be in relationship to political systems. Political systems broadly conceived are systems whose components interact with respect to power and authoritative resource allocation for the purpose of making decisions. To be sure, families, businesses, and other groupings have political aspects that could be considered, but again, our emphasis is on macropolitical systems as commonly understood.

The most troublesome aspect of the definition is that the symbol exchange must have been shaped by, or have consequences for the political system. In other words, not all communication is political, nor does all communication involve political actors. Whether or not communication is political depends on the extent to which the system is altered or communication patterns changed. Because there is no specific point at which consequences are significant to make a given communication "political," intuitive judgment must rule. In some circumstances, with this definition, a similar event can be considered political communication at one time, but not at another. Consider a conversation between the President and his wife. Indeed the President is a significant political actor, but domestic discourse with his wife will rarely have impact on the system. Were she, however, to discuss with him her impressions of foreign countries on a goodwill trip and the President in turn to consider altering policies toward those countries, the conversation can be considered political communication. As an alternative example, a parent may discuss moral principles with his or her child. At some point, this discussion may be translated into political action by the child. But for any single child, its significance to the system is too remote and too limited for the conversation to be considered as political communication. However, a mass political education campaign or the macro-concept of political socialization could be considered political communication in view of their potential system significance.

As can be seen in these examples, there is no absolute point at which message exchange is either political or has certain significance. The purview of political communication is relative and arguable. But establishing its parameters for our inquiry is important to guide our understanding.

The question still remains: why is not political communication defined and treated as a subset of the widely recognized and researched (if not understood) discipline, political science? The answer lies partially in the fact that political science deals with human interaction and political institutions, but generally in terms of processes and outputs. The exchange of messages *per se* in the processes is of less importance than the social and institutional framework, which allows the communication relationship to be established or the policy outputs to follow from the exchange. Of course, political scientists have considered the extent to which political systems shape the communications environment usually as philosophical questions (e.g., the right to free speech) or as a subset of regulatory questions. There are many exceptions to these general statements, indeed several interdisciplinary minded political scientists have made major contributions to communications theory and research. But on the whole, the discipline has not considered political communication adequately. Logically, there is no reason why political communication cannot achieve the status within the discipline achieved by political socialization, political sociology, political economy, or any of the other political compounds. But it requires a greater understanding of communication processes than political scientists thus far have been willing to muster. To this end, this book is addressed to political scientists seeking a foothold in the analysis of political communication.

At the same time, this volume is addressed to communication scholars and researchers who have something to learn from political scientists. In particular, the application of communication concepts to larger systemic social phenomena studied by political scientists is illustrative of the wider use of communication.

Students of mass communication, of course, recognize the system implications of communication, but in a political context, interpersonal communication scholars, sociolinguists, and semioticians similarly can contribute to understanding and explaining political phenomena. Political outputs are the result of human interaction, and the medium through which this interaction occurs is communication. Regardless of what perspective one takes on what is the essence of communication: information, symbols, language, meaning, and so forth, all are equally a part of politics.

POLITICAL OUTPUTS

What are the outputs of political systems and processes? Perhaps the question should be what is the output of political systems, for arguably there is only one end product—decisions. These decisional outputs are oriented toward a variety of goals, including the regulation of conflicts, the distribution and allocation of resources, and the maintenance of social control. To attain these goals, political systems must have the capacity to disseminate information about these goals, and mechanisms to determine the extent to which the goals are reached or not.

A part of political communication, as defined earlier in this chapter, is the study of the total communication environment in which these decisions are made and goals reached. As a result, there is no central thesis to this book confining political communication. Political communication is not merely the study of social control, or language use, or information gathering. Nor is it a property of only individuals, or only groups or government institutions. It is all of these, and involves the full array of political actors. Thus, political communication is construed broadly, encompassing the most important aspects of politics. Those aspects of politics involving information exchange are considered—but because most political action (ranging from expressing desires by voting, holding a press conference, lobbying, mounting a propaganda campaign) involves information exchange, nearly all political action can be viewed, and viewed fruitfully, through a communication perspective.

Defining the scope of political communication implies a conceptualization of the nature of human communication. Definitional inventories have been accumulated elsewhere and need not be repeated here. Yet the most valuable conceptualizations are those that allow for intrapersonal, interpersonal, and mass communication; those that recognize the political potential of almost all communication. In other words, communication with the self or others is ultimately linked to social control or social stability. As an example, one useful conceptualization of how systems or individuals operate has been offered by Herbert Blumer (1969) in his work on symbolic interaction.

In his view, closely linked to that of George Herbert Mead (1934), there are three possible roots of meaning—in the psyche, in social action, or in interpretation. With a somewhat different vocabulary, Dewey and Bentley (1949) argued that knowledge in a variety of situations stems from self action (i.e., the psyche), interaction (social action), or transaction (interpretation). Regardless of which vocabulary is used, the symbolic interactionist approach argues that meaning in a variety of situations—including the political—is interpretive and results from ongoing relationships between individuals and/or groups, stepping into the roles and perceptions of others. Thus, political communication is fluid: differing across social systems and individuals, or across any environment or individual framework in which meaning is attributed to messages and upon which future action is based.

There are always a variety of explanations that may be offered for a given phenomena or event. Sociological explanations of events or attitudes are rooted in meanings attributed to social role, social status, norms, etc., whereas psychological interpretive categories include stimuli or motives. Similarly, there are political explanations of phenomena, which rely on theories of power, control, authority, conflict, or other political concepts. For a variety of communication phenomena, political explanations offer more purchase than other explanations, leading to a need for politically based communication analysis.

Unlike other communication serving individual needs and drives for expressiveness (psychological, self-action), or phatic functions (sociability), political communication is necessary for decision-making. In particular, political communication results in the development of political symbols (or their demolition), which give people a sense of community and belongingness. Indeed, scholars have recognized this, ranging from Malinowski (1945) in his argument that communication is necessary only for unified social (i.e., political) action, to Duncan's (1962) argument that human communication is an attempt to create symbols, the use of which is believed to uphold the social order. Regardless of whether or not communication is created to perpetuate a society or shape it, the crucial belief is that the cement of many societies is political communication.

We have already noted that decisions are outputs of political systems. Decisions are made over issues or controversies, the resolutions of which are often beneficial to competing sides of the controversy. Such issues include the distribution of wealth, level of government services provided, the choice of decision makers, and others. In many political systems however, communication itself is a political issue on the agenda. Controversies over allocation of broadcast spectrum space, rights to employ unofficial languages, access to information, rights to privacy, and a host of related issues come before political decision makers. Thus, at a second level, political systems make decisions over communication—the exchange of symbols itself—in terms of which groups have rights, access, or can profit by communicatory activity. This, too, is political communication. For some, the politics of communication, and for others communication itself is no different than any other human activity. With this we disagree, for communication is at the very heart of our humanness. To constrain or otherwise limit the communication activity of one actor while expanding such activity for another places finite limits on human potential.

GOALS OF THIS BOOK

Overall, three intellectual goals motivated the writing of this book. The first was to clarify the dimensions of political communication as a subdiscipline. Undoubtedly, the perspective brought to bear on this issue from a communication researcher trained as a political scientist differs from that of a communication researcher trained in mass communication or journalism. Nevertheless, through careful and logical development, the parameters of a discipline satisfactory to all political communication researchers can be defined. In any event, an aim of this clarification scheme is to help focus on what political communication research is or can be. At the very least, this is a contribution beyond those essays trying to clarify what political communication is not.

Second, the book presents a process oriented political communication framework to enable researchers to shed new light on several major political concepts—power, conflict, integration, development, participation, and social-ization—that usually have been subjected to political analysis. A communication perspective on these issues, although substantively illuminating, should potentially spur other researchers to investigate other political concepts with communication variables. Looking at politics as a process and as a product of communication offers a different view of political concepts and institutions than that offered by many political scientists.

Finally, the clarification of research needs is a goal of this volume. One recent collection of essays with this goal (Chaffee, 1975) although fruitful, was constrained by a conceptualization of political communication as the political system/mass media interface. This volume is designed to raise research questions inherent in a larger view of political communication.

To these ends, the remainder of the book is organized as follows: Chapter 2 reviews political communication as a discipline. Although recognition as a sub-discipline *per se* is recent, earlier work was performed by mass communication researchers. However, much of the focus was on journalism and news, because the term "political" was perceived rather narrowly. The chapter goes on to explore the theoretical roots and empirical fruits of this research, and then examines the assumptions (and the limits) of the early work. Chapter 3 proceeds from the research review to present a model of political communication. After outlining the core issues of political communication—language and symbols—a systems oriented approach is developed. The research implications of this approach are suggested throughout the chapter.

The second part of the book links the primary communication concepts of language and symbols to major political concepts. In Chapters 4, 5, 6, and 7, it is argued that communication variables help provide a fuller understanding of what are generally viewed as political phenomena. The chapters in Part II focus on specific political concepts. Chapter 4 reviews conflict, integration, and development, advancing the notion that each of these is a function of information exchange and network establishment. The interface between communication technology and political processes is also developed in this chapter. Chapter 5 considers political participation as a type of political communication. Chapter 6 takes what has been called the core of politics—power—and examines the establishment and maintenance of power relationships as control systems through communications. Organizational hierarchies, information control, community power structure, and other power phenomena are discussed throughout the chapter. In Chapter 7, political socialization is offered as the final communication dependent major political concept. The role of interpersonal and mass communicators as socialization agents throughout the life cycle is examined, and particular attention is devoted to mass media in the political socialization process.

Part III of the book moves away from the behavioral concepts to take an institutional perspective on political communication. Chapter 8 looks at decision-making in U.S. political institutions, exploring communication uses and functions for each branch of government. In the following chapter, the focus is on news gathering and disseminating institutions. Particular attention is given to the relationship of these news organizations to decision-making institutions. In Chapter 10, the final chapter in Part III, communication in election campaigns is explored in detail. Although election news has long been the focus of communication research, recent evidence from both political science and communication researchers has shed new light on election phenomena.

The concluding portion of the book is devoted to the consideration of communication itself as an item of political controversy. Chapter 11 examines language as an issue on the political agenda with a particular focus on language use in multilingual states, and other examples. Chapter 12 is devoted to an analysis of the relationship between popular culture and politics. In recent decades, popular cultural forms such as television drama and popular music have been occupied with political subjects; the relationship of these to socialization is considered. The thirteenth chapter touches on the regulation of communication. Settings in which regulation occurs, and the philosophical implications of controlled communication in nontotalitarian political systems are investigated.

Finally, the government itself as a communicator is explored in Chapter 14. Distinct from political communication needed to function, this chapter looks at government as a producer of political messages.

Together these chapters paint a portrait of the scope of political communication as a discipline. Admittedly, many of the perspectives taken in this volume reflect my own concerns and definitions of the field, but it is my hope that the ideas presented have wider research and theoretical implications than any one scholar could possibly pursue.

2
EARLY APPROACHES
TO POLITICAL COMMUNICATION

Political communication as a field of social science inquiry is youthful, but, as with most subdisciplines, has roots in the social science revolution of the past fifty years. In this chapter, the history of political communication research in political science and communications is reviewed, and the assumptions guiding the pioneering work are examined. This analysis reveals the absence of continuity in political communication theory and research as well as a failure to develop a coherent discipline as more and more researchers began work in the field.

To examine only those works with political communication in their titles would limit the field, for there have been only four (Deutsch, 1963; Chaffee, 1975; Arora & Lasswell, 1969; and Nimmo, 1978), and each is very different. Using a less parochial notion of political communication, the review can include other theoretical and empirical efforts. At the very least, including works with some derivative of politics and communication in their titles would expand the list and the review to include works at the foundation of the conceptualization of political communication in Chapter 3, and reveal a rich and diverse body of literature.

Political communication as a concept distinct from other political analysis of communication phenomena or communication analysis of political phenomena is relatively new. By far the most common area of research in the past has been election studies. Although research along these lines prospered, theories of political communication never emerged. The classic voting studies (Lazarsfeld et al., 1948; Berelson et al., 1954) *defined* political communication research for nearly twenty years. For that period, political communication was composed of mass mediated messages about politics. Researchers developed strategies to look at "effects" of these messages on a wide range of political variables from party identification, to information about candidates, to vote choice. In each case, the results were the same: direct effects of exposure to campaign information were limited. Voters would selectively expose themselves to information toward which they were predisposed because of religion, socioeconomic status, or geographic location. Although important concepts (such as the two-step flow of information) resulted from these studies, the findings of limited mass media effects constrained political communication research for over a decade.

Besides the voting studies conducted by political scientists and sociologists, one other academic group developed a notion of political communication: journalism researchers. These scholars focused primarily on press (and later electronic) coverage of explicitly political events such as election campaigns. Although their early findings were oriented toward determining the relationships between editorial preference and disproportionate news coverage, later studies moving away from the questions of bias revealed much about press performance during campaigns.

Whether by political scientists researching elections or journalists evaluating press performance, political communication was without broad meaning. Only the growth of systems analysis led to a re-evaluation of political communication as a field with larger meaning.

EARLY WORKS IN POLITICAL COMMUNICATION

The most significant early work to use political communication as a part of its title was Karl Deutsch's *The Nerves of Government: Models of Political Communication and Control,* (1963). As the title implies, the work develops a series of models through which control in political systems is established. Deutsch's cybernetic approach, developed during the early years of the general systems movement, was inspirational for other systems oriented political scientists (cf., Easton, 1964, 1965), but had a view of political communication quite different from that espoused by communication researchers. In addition, Deutsch's book was most applicable and most effective in theoretically explaining power relationships, but less significant in its ability to draw a full picture of the scope of political communication.

A broader view of political communication than the cybernetic perspective is revealed in an introduction to the volume written several years after initial publication. References to works in political development, national integration, and policy formation pushed the boundaries of political communication one step further, and recognized the possibility of describing certain hitherto political concepts as communication phenomena. Still, the events of concern to Deutsch largely were those involving feedback, and those explicable as systems phenomena.

With Deutsch's work, political communication moved beyond evaluation of mass media in election campaigns. Research in comparative politics published about the same time as Deutsch's work (Pye, 1963; Lerner, 1959; Schramm, 1964) returned political scientists to a position of leadership in political communication research. But more important, for the first time whole political systems (rather than discrete events, such as elections within those systems) were considered to be influenced by communications. To be sure, communication to some political development researchers was still synonymous with mass media, but others began to look at communication more as a social process without which development or social integration could not occur.

The work of the development and modernization oriented political scientists was summarized by Fagen (1966), who in a volume titled *Politics and Communication,* sought to consider "a communication approach to the study of comparative politics" [p. vii]. Instead, Fagen went well beyond that limited goal, first, by describing the flow of politically relevant information as political communication in all political systems, and then by offering a functional definition of political communication:

> that communicatory activity considered political by virtue of its consequences, actual and potential, that it has for the functioning of the political system. [p. 20].

This all-encompassing definition (after all, there always are "potential consequences") certainly opened a wide range of areas to the purview of political communication researchers. Even narrowing down the consequences to be short term and direct—lest arguments suggest any communication event such as spanking a child on his or her exit from the womb at birth has important political consequences—just about all political activity is political communication if it involves information exchange or any other activity considered "communicatory." This is not to suggest that the scope of this definition is inappropriate if one is taking a communications perspective on political analysis. However, Fagen failed to consider the fuller implication of his definition because of his concern for macropolitical systems in a comparative framework. Key questions in the inquiry reveal the limits of the analysis. Fagen is concerned with communication processes in the selection of leaders, definition of the agenda, participation in decision-making, scope of permissible criticism, and socialization. In other words, political communication analysis is essentially limited to participation and socialization questions, particularly as related to questions of development.

Contemporary researchers were not beyond the "all political activity is communicatory activity" argument. Describing the functions of political systems —socialization and rule making, application and adjudication, Almond and Coleman (1960) argue all these functions are carried out through communication. With this notion, everything is politics and indeed is communication, or follows from communication processes. But their descriptive efforts considered communicatory activity to be a part of the political process and not to *define* the process. Moreover, in contrast to the approach taken in this volume, political systems are not described through communication variables, but instead as institutional settings in which political functions are carried out or disseminated through communications. In other words, altering the communications environ- ment would not, in all likelihood, alter the system, but only the specific way in which the system gathered or disseminated information for its functions. Fagen's approach was at least one step removed from the ubiquitous communication argument by considering the consequences of communicatory activity within a system rather than by defining a system.

These theoretical arguments and approaches were the last serious efforts. by political scientists to consider the role of communications in the political processes. In the first volume explicitly titled *Political Communication,* Arora and Lasswell (1969) pay little attention to broad notions of political communi- cation, instead considering it to be synonymous with the public language of politics as expressed in the elite press in the United States and India. This again is a mass media based notion of political communication.

Thereafter, all theory and most research in political communication by political scientists came to a halt. Indeed, the limited extent to which political scientists have kept up this tradition of communication analysis is revealed in the index to the recent *Handbook of Political Science* (Greenstein & Polsby, 1975). In over 2,000 pages of text, political communication, or even communi- cation, is not indexed once, although there is *one* reference to mass communi- cation. Journalism and communication researchers took over the field, but without the tools of political analysis and the perspective of political science. Only in the most recent years have political scientists become active in political communication research. The emergence of mass media in general, and television in particular, as a key variable in election campaigning, combined with new data on electoral behavior, has resulted in increased attention among political scientists to communication variables. Thus, despite the theoretical progress or at least the recogniton of communication as theoretically relevant during the early 1960s, the renewed research efforts considered political communication to be only a phenomena of mass media during election campaigns.

Despite the shortcomings evident in the studies of political scientists, communication and journalism scholars who have engaged in political communi- cation research in recent years have not developed a comprehensive picture of the field either. Isolated research projects look at media performance or candidate rhetoric, but rarely subtly analyze political communication phenomena of consequence to political researchers. Political relationships sustained through communications processes are all but ignored; definitions are still inexorably linked to mass media. For example, in a recent survey of the literature (Kraus & Davis, 1976), political communication is described as the "process of mass communication (including interpersonal communication) and elements within it which may have an impact on political behavior" [p. 7]. Again, as with Fagen, we are faced with something which "may" have an impact (i.e., consequences). But this time, it is on behavior rather than system functioning, and, moreover, is directly linked to mass communication processes. Thus excluded are virtually all intra and intergovernmental communication, as well as much interpersonal communication not linked to mass communication.

Other recent work fails to take into account the analysis of the role of political processes in shaping the communications process. Chaffee (1975) for example, in a volume entitled *Political Communication*, reflects the problem by conceptualizing political communication as a unidirectional discipline:

> What is sought is a set of research paradigms through which we can extend the depth and breadth of our understanding of the role of communication in the political process. [p. 15].

On some level, this is a difficult yet straightforward task. Assuming one can develop some parameters for confining the political process to some manageable and bounded system, one need measure or examine information flow as an input variable in political systems. For example, within this framework would fit the flow of news from public officials to citizens, intragovernment communication between various political actors, crossnational diplomatic and persuasive communication, expression of citizen demands, and similar activities. Excluded from this research approach would be more subtle yet equally important concepts, such as the role of communication in establishing political relationships, or, as indicated in Chapter 1, the importance of political systems in providing a framework for all communications.

Other researchers, although including the reciprocal relationships discussed earlier, still maintain a narrow view of the scope of political communication. Rivers et al. (1975), for example, outline four important political communication research areas. First, they note government's impact on the media, by which they mean the study of regulation law, economic control, news gathering regulations, censorship, and so forth. The second area is government information systems, including formal and informal information channels and government information personnel. The third area is the impact of media on government, including officials' use of the mass media, the impact of news on the behavior of officials, and so forth. The final area of research is focused on the news media and news content, institutional settings, social structure, and a host of other aspects studied by content analysts and sociologists of the newsroom. Unlike Chaffee's approach, these areas address the problem of political systems shaping communications environments, but only in a limited way. Only the impact on mass media is considered, rather than communication phenomena more generally (including that by non mass communication). Moreover, this approach, although comprehensive in terms of mass media analysis, ignores processes of communication. One goal of the present volume is to include more dimensions of communication (not just mass media) such as language and semiotics, to yield a more multi-dimensional view of political communication than that expressed by other researchers.

Blumler and Gurevitch (1975) began to address the issue of a more sophisticated notion of political communication. In their effort to demonstrate the theoretical linkage of communication to politics, they argue that if politics is about power, then this must be conveyed by power wielders. If politics is about participation, then the desires of citizens must be communicated to leaders. If politics is about legitimacy, then regime norms must be symbolically expressed. And, if politics is about choice, then policy options must be circulated. In this way, politics and communication are linked. Yet the research questions posed by Blumler and Gurevitch, comprehensive as they are, once again are limited to mass media. Appropriate research questions include examining the degree of state control over mass media in terms of regulation, financing, content, the extent of mass media partisanship, and the legitimacy of mass media. All of these are important issues, but reflect too narrow a view of communication, a view inconsistent with the range of communication phenomena that could be explored under the varying definitions of politics presented in Chapter 1.

Viewing political communication almost exclusively in terms of mass media content or the effects of mass media on certain participatory variables may partially be beneath the failure of political communication to establish itself as a recognized subdiscipline among political scientists and communication researchers. Yet this media emphasis is a comparatively recent development. Fifty years ago, social scientists began contemplating many sociological and political questions as communication problems. These exercises are still quite useful in terms of the potential they offer for reconceptualizing the domain of political communication. In the following section, these older approaches to communication are considered and their relevance to political communication updated.

SYMBOLS IN THE POLITICAL PROCESS

In the following chapter, political communication is viewed largely in relational terms, developed and maintained through symbolic information exchange in languages which in themselves are symbolic. Although recent work in political communication has for the most part ignored symbols and languages in favor of mass media emphasis, the pioneers of communication theory, (and, it may be argued political communication) relied heavily on an understanding of symbols.

Well before Lasswell wrote of communication as the study of Who says What in Which channel, to Whom and with What effect (Lasswell, 1948), he conceptualized communication as a largely symbolic interchange. Lasswell, considered among the first students of political communication, wrote of politics as largely symbolic (1935), and as a communication phenomenon. Much of his early empirical research (Lasswell et al., 1949) focused on symbols and their measurement and use in political contexts. Before Lasswell, social scientists were concerned with the relationship between symbols and social communication (Sapir, 1934) or even politics (Arnold, 1935). After him, Kenneth Burke (1945) more fully explored political symbols. More recently, other political scientists, employing fairly diverse literature, pursued the symbolic aspects of politics. Drawing from works in philosophy (Whitehead, 1927); psychology (Cassirer, 1944); anthropology (Malinowski, 1948); sociology (Himmelstrand, 1960; Duncan, 1968; Luckmann, 1967); and especially from aesthetic theory (Langer, 1953; Duncan, 1953; Beebe, 1960) Boulding (1956) and Edelman (1964) have been particularly instrumental in developing the notion of political symbols. But Lasswell's pioneering efforts joining political responses to verbal referents established at least one approach to political communication. However, as more and more political scientists discovered the relevance of considering political relationships and action (Friedrich, 1963; Edelman, 1971) as symbolic, the relevant communication aspects of symbol formation, maintenance and dissemination were lost. In other words, the existence of political dominance was explained in symbolic terms; processes by which the relationships were established were unexplained. Theory and research efforts in political symbol analysis (efforts have been relatively few, given the age of the concept) have focused almost exclusively on the meanings of various symbols, or the distribution of symbolic rewards for system maintenance. Examples of the latter include Gusfield's (1963) analysis of the Temperance Movement as a symbolic conflict, and theoretical statements by Zald (1966), Walzer (1967), and Mitchell and Mitchell (1969). Studies of the meaning of symbols in a variety of contexts include Prothro and Grigg (1960), Aberbach and Walker (1970), and Cobb and Elder (1972). These studies reveal symbols to be fluid and contextually dependent, but offer few insights into symbolic dynamics as a communication process or as the center of political communication.

Throughout the fifty years in which symbols have been recognized, they have been linked to language. More recently, political communication researchers have considered language as a central concern, particularly in view of theoretical developments in sociolinguistics. Beyond the omnipresent linguistic question of meaning in a natural language (Rubinstein, 1973), as it is shaped by psychological (Bloomfield, 1933), personal (Osgood, 1966; Blumer, 1969), and situational contexts, there exists the issue of language itself as a symbol. Language, of course, is used to exchange both general information (the "meanings" of which may vary contextually), and political information. Language, in a political environment, not only is a carrier of content, but in many ways is content itself, indicating social status and values, and serving as a symbolic referent for loyalties and animosities (Fishman, 1970).

Sociolinguists have long argued over the relationship between language and social status; similar arguments exist in political relationships. Again, Lasswell, Leites, and others (1949) played an important part in heightening awareness of language in politics, but their perspective stated that language is relevent in political relationships insofar as it results in the creation of certain myths and symbols. With the growth of sociolinguistics in the decade that followed, language itself was the focus of certain researchers. In particular, studies of language conflict in Norway (Haugen, 1966), India (Harrison, 1960; Kelly, 1966; McCormack, 1967; Das Gupta & Gumperz, 1968; Das Gupta, 1969, 1970); and elsewhere demonstrated the problems of linguistic chauvinism for political development.

In another volume titled *The Politics of Communication* Mueller (1975) suggested that even in developed systems, language use and linguistic "competence" distinguish groups and actors in the political system, and maintain the dominance of certain groups (or the importance of other groups) in most political systems. Turning the causal ordering around, Mueller goes on to argue that language is determined by political contexts and institutions. Indeed, he argues, certain political environments are characterized by so much noise that communication is distorted and that political communication is ineffective unless languages are altered.

Mueller's line of theory, and the research it may inspire, offers considerable purchase in explaining relationships in certain political environments. But the linguistic approach has not been well integrated into a broad conceptualization of political communication. Mueller's theory certainly is a step in this direction. Unfortunately, political communication is narrowly conceived of as "discussion of problems, issues and ideas that have public relevance" (Mueller, 1975, p. 19), whereas nondiscussion, or mass media news gathering, or the effects of those discussions are not considered.

The only theorist to link language to a broad notion of political communication is Dan Nimmo. In his most recent work (Nimmo, 1978), he conceives of politics as comprised largely of "talk." He argues that to understand the content of political communication, one must explore the nature and use of political language, and the symbols in which it results. This linkage of language and symbols, implied by others but never fully argued, is an important step toward a theory of political communication. But Nimmo applies his analysis only insofar as individuals attribute meanings to political messages to produce images. Elsewhere, Nimmo (1974) views political images as a largely individual level phenomenon, inasmuch as they result from language symbols and the context in which they are received. Hence, although symbols and language apply to political communication, systemic political communication phenomena and concepts such as power, conflict, and decision-making are underplayed. Nevertheless, Nimmo, through integrating diverse literature, has taken steps toward a symbolic/linguistic view of political communication.

When we consider the work done on voting behavior in the various disciplines (by sociologists, journalism researchers, cyberneticians, semioticians, or linguists), the notion of political communication is quite narrow. In each of the scholarly disciplines represented by these researchers, one aspect of commonly held definitions of communication as it relates to politics is considered. Taken together, they represent a very comprehensive view of political communication. Yet nowhere are these various approaches assembled, least of all in political science.

It may be the case that political scientists feel no need to develop theory in political communication because all along they have recognized politics as a communication process. Empirical research studies implicitly, though rarely explicitly, make repeated references to communication variables and processes as a natural part of political processes and even political institutions. Only by sifting through these studies is the communications perspective of political scientists presented. Their research can be classified largely through a framework evolved from a simplified Shannon and Weaver (1949) vocabulary. Communication political research is oriented toward actors, messages, and channels.

First exists what may be termed the actor oriented approach to political communication. Taking a page from the literature of political participation (Milbrath & Goel, 1977), this approach has as its focus gladiators, transitionals, spectators, or apathetics. Gladiators are those actually involved in political life, including office-seekers, campaign activists, decision makers, lobbyists, news gatherers, and disseminators—or others devoting full efforts to political activity. At the transitional level are those involved in partisan politics, including participation in events or fund raising campaigns. Spectators comprise a very large share of the population, including those who engage in political discussions, or vote. Apathetics, of course, engage in almost no political activity, and only with difficulty can they be considered political communicators. In some circumstances non-participation itself is a symbolic political message, but on other occasions it reflects indifference.

Political scientists have recognized the role of communications in the political activities of gladiators, transitionals, spectators, and even apathetics, although rarely explicitly. Thus, in terms of one of our views of political communication as concerned with the role of communication in the political world, there has been some recognition of political communication by political scientists. Often, however, the role of political participants as communicators is inseparable from (or even defined by) their role as politicians. Studies of the presidency, Congress, the Supreme Court, without focusing explicitly on communication variables, describe political activities as largely communicatory.

At the gladiator level, research and theory have considered communications activities of high government officials. Neustadt (1976), for example, says that presidential power is largely defined through his vantage point, his access to information, or his ability to control the flow of information. Studies of communication patterns of Congress by Kovenock (1973) and others reveal the wide range of information to which members of Congress are exposed. Still other research on the decision-making processes (Kennedy, 1968; Allison, 1971; Janis, 1972) reveal how communication patterns in gladiator level decision-making bodies are largely dependent on communication networks. These studies focus primarily on communication as a flow of information in political offices and organizations, but do not consider political relationships themselves as communication relationships.

Between the gladiators and the apathetics at the other end of the spectrum, who receive little (or are inattentive to) political information, are the moderately active participants. Research studies have described the sociological and psychological characteristics of these individuals. But also at this level are found second level transitionals such as lobbyists, news gatherers, and disseminators. These individuals have access to gladiators and to spectators who depend on them for news of the gladiators. Political scientists have studied these transitionals (Nimmo, 1970, Milbrath, 1960, Sigal, 1973), and these newspeople have often been the heroes of anecdotal or insider reports.

Political scientists have also looked at explicit communication by focusing on messages. Analysts taking this perspective look at political communications, i.e., the messages and information disseminated by political actors. The earliest work in political communication, or more appropriately propaganda analysis, considered the substance of messages rather than actors disseminating or receiving such messages, or the processes by which they were generated. In recent years, the renewed popularity of content analysis has once again increased the adherents of message oriented political communication research.

Message studies by political scientists have focused in several areas: diplomatic messages and propaganda (Lasswell et al., 1949; George, 1959; Holsti et al., 1965); political speeches and writings (Eckhardt, 1965; Eckhardt & White, 1967; Runion, 1936; Ellsworth, 1965; Wolfarth, 1961); and general news content (Lasswell et al., 1952). But most recent research by political scientists has focused on campaign messages (Graber, 1971; Frank, 1973; Meadow, 1973a; Hofstetter, 1976; Patterson & McClure, 1976; Bishop et al., 1978). The fact that these studies have been conducted by political scientists rather than communication researchers, however, is of little consequence. Message oriented research and, indeed, the actor oriented research noted earlier, ignores the essence of political communication as a process involving interchange among political actors, occurring within a political context, and as a largely symbolic exercise.

Channel of communication research by political scientists is usually seen as such. Deutsch (1953), of course, recognized the establishment of channels of communication as a precursor of social integration. Later, research on news gathering organizations (Nimmo, 1964; Cohen, 1963; Sigal, 1973) recognized mass media as the central channels through which political messages flow, not only to individuals outside the government, but inside the government as well.

But other research, which focuses on the channels used by those inside government, fails to recognize the processes described as communication processes. Studies of social protest (Turner & Killian, 1957; Lang & Lang, 1961; Toch, 1965), revolutionary behavior (Gurr, 1970; Davies, 1971), and even voting studies (Campbell et al., 1954, 1960; Nie et al., 1976) contain many references to communication within these contexts but pay only the slightest attention to elections as channels through which outsiders in politics may make their positions known to insiders. Only students of social conflict (Coser, 1956, 1967; Coleman, 1957) have recognized one of the functions of social conflict to be the creation of channels of communication to bridge communities. Overall, then, one of the most important aspects of communication channels has not been widely considered by political science researchers.

As noted at the outset of this chapter, political scientists have tried to research the "effects" of political communication, but again these studies focus largely on the direct impact, in terms of empirically observable behavior; of exposure to political information. Work on the "effects" of exposure to mass media by political scientists (Lazarsfeld et al., 1948; Berelson et al., 1954; Converse, 1962; Key, 1966; Kraus, 1962; DeVries & Tarrance 1972; and Patterson & McClure, 1976) have dealt with the use of mass media in election campaigns and found varying relationships of exposure to voting choice. With rare exceptions, political orientations (and behavior other than voting) as a result of exposure to mass media during nonelection periods (Robinson, 1976) and exposure to information from nonmedia sources have not been researched. More important, the definitions of political information exposure in such studies have been quite limited, and ignore broader questions of effects—long term effects for the political system that extend beyond the implications of voting in one election campaign. Specifically, political scientists have not considered the political effects of exposure to fictional media empirically, nor have they widely conceptualized much of political socialization research from a communication perspective. And, in any case, political scientists did not consider effects as political communication analysis.

The shortcomings of political scientists in conceptualizing political phenomena in communication terms (as has been noted previously) occasionally has been minimized by the insights and contributions of other social scientists. At the same time, one result is that political scientist's tools of analysis and conceptual approaches to politics have not been applied as frequently as possible to political communication theory and research. Missing from many research designs, and even theoretical conceptualizations of nonpolitical science communication researchers, are comparative and cross cultural questions. Concern for the communications relevance (or interpretation) of fundamental political variables such as power, conflict, decision-making, development, and the classical questions of political philosophy, freedom, participation and a host of others has at best been minimal.

Despite the exciting potential for political communication research offered by theories of symbols, language, and human interaction offered as possible Rosetta Stones, political scientists and others have not developed a full notion of political communication. Researchers in particular, in an effort toward immediate empirical research gratification, have chosen to conceptualize political communication largely as a result or an end product rather than to consider the essence of political communication as a process involving interchanges among political actors, taking place within a political context, and involving the exchange of symbols (rather than fixed messages) to some political end.

To be sure, this view of political communication as a process involves a conceptualization of communication itself as a process. Definitional inventories of communication have been accumulated elsewhere, but above all, communication is largely symbolic. But, among other things the ways in which meaning is given to political symbols, the effects they have on political relationships, the implications they have for government, separates political communication from ordinary communication.

Developments in political science over the past fifteen years have provided a framework for analysis of political communication phenomena. In particular, systems theory (and its derivatives) as sometimes used in political analysis offers a perspective useful for political communication analysis, because it offers a process oriented view of the political world, each stage of which is described in communication terms. In the next chapter this perspective is more fully described and posited as a paradigm for analysis of politics as communication.

3
THEORY AND MODEL
OF POLITICAL COMMUNICATION

So many different approaches to political communication have been offered in the past that the larger question of the utility of communication analysis for comprehending political relationships has been overlooked. In this chapter, theories and research paradigms for political communication are presented with an eye toward developing a model of political processes sensitive to communication variables and relationships.

Each of these approaches in one way or another suggests that politics is largely a communication or at least an information phenomenon. Citizens are linked to one another as individuals and in groups, groups are linked to government decision makers who have their own communication networks. Decisional outputs are communicated back to citizens through mass media or groups, and new demands may (or may not) be formulated. Overall, the processes are orderly in most systems (indeed the absence of orderly processes suggests a communication breakdown) and result in stabilized, controlled systems. Indeed, most political communications (i.e., messages) are designed to assure this stability.

In any event, whether successful or not in assuring stability, communication is the lifeblood of politics and political relationships. As the following sections suggest, regardless of the approach taken, the centrality of communication to politics is at the core of each theoretical orientation.

RESEARCH APPROACHES TO POLITICAL COMMUNICATION

In summarizing political communication research, it appears that there have been six fundamental research approaches that have been or can be offered as guides to research inquiry. These six approaches are termed the systems, linguistic, symbolic, functional, organizational, and environmental approaches. They have fundamentally different research premises and assumptions, but still attack the core issues defined within the parameters of political communication. Each of these approaches is described briefly and explored in more detail in the following sections.

The systems view of political communication is one taken primarily by cyberneticians. Communication is not used as much in the sense of message flow, but instead in general systems language to explain the interaction among elements in the system. Communication is linked to control in general. More specifically as it relates to political communication, communication is for social control. Political power is at the core of the cybernetic-systems conceptualization. Processes for describing patterns of social control, system responsiveness, and other mechanistic social forces are described through the systems approach. The most important contributions to this approach have been made by Deutsch (1963), although the work of Easton (1965) has been influential as well.

The linguistic approach, like the systems approach, is concerned with social control. Fundamentally, language is viewed as a vehicle through which social control in general, and limited access to political processes and institutions in particular, is exercised. Proponents of a language based theory of social control such as Mueller (1975) argue that decision makers in society carry out their activities with unique languages. Elites outside of decision-making circles speak these same languages, hence their demands are heard and understood by authorities. Nonelites, however, have no access to decision makers because they are politically inarticulate, unable to express demands. As a result, political systems and political relationships, are stabilized and biased toward the maintenance of the status quo.

The third major approach is the symbolic approach. Politics, like communication, is viewed largely as symbolic interchange. The social fabric is woven by the identification that system members have with the threads—the symbols. Leadership is maintained and exercised largely through the manipulation of symbols and the distribution of symbolic rewards. The processes through which these symbols are created and disseminated serve as the focus for this perspective on political communication.

The functional approach to political communication shifts the focus away from only social control toward analysis of the broader consequences of communications, particularly mass media, to the political system. Of course, one latent function is maintaining some degree of stability. But other functions include enhancing awareness of policy options, socialization to regime norms, or even certain dysfunctions, such as narcotizing (Lazarsfeld & Merton, 1948) or privatizing.

The fifth view of political communication is from an organizational perspective. Governments are seen as large, bureaucratic organizations with many of the same limitations and problems as other organizations. Political communication in this approach focuses on intragovernment information flows and emphasizes the organizational parameters constraining information flow. Political relationships are maintained through control of information and differential access to information.

Finally, there exists what may be called an environmental view of political communication. From this approach, political communication is viewed in terms of the ways in which the political system shapes communication processes. In other words, the political system is seen as creating an environment in which communication institutions are formed or processes established. Examples of this environmental approach are plentiful: the regulation of broadcasting by the F.C.C. in the United States, the surpression of minority languages in bilingual or multilingual systems, are two of the many instances that can be cited.

All six approaches to political communication offer some explanatory power. At times, the approaches overlap, but for the most part each offers a different way of viewing political communication. They differ most widely in their ability to provide a unique paradigm in which political communication, and only political communication, can be explained and distinguished from other communication. More important, only some of the approaches are appropriate for developing new ways of looking at political relationships in communications terms. Specifically, the functional, organizational, and environmental perspectives offer a limited view of political communication and are of less value in explaining political concepts described in Part III. The linguistic, symbolic, and systems approaches, however, form the bases for the treatment of political concepts, hence are given fuller treatment later in this chapter.

FUNCTIONAL PERSPECTIVES
ON POLITICAL COMMUNICATION

Previously, it was noted that functional definition of political communication has been offered by Fagen (1966) who suggested that it incorporate:

> communicatory activity considered political by virtue of its consequences, actual and potential, that it has for the functioning of the political system. [p. 20].

In many ways such a definition is tautological, not defining communicatory activity. At the same time, there is no knowledge of who considers the activity to be political. Finally, there is some implication that the greater the consequences, the more political any communication can be.

This functional approach emphasizes system consequences of communication; and at least for Fagen, provides a basis for comparative political analysis. The role of communications and communication processes with respect to the selection of leaders, the definition of the political agenda, participation in decision-making, receptivity to criticism, and socialization can be considered from this functional perspective, but only as end products of message exchange. In other words, analysis of consequences of communication ignores the establishment or initiation of political relationships. Questions such as who has power in society (rather than what are the implications of the division of power), how are conflicts resolved, and who controls political information are ignored by a functional approach. To be brief, the functional approach is useful for comparing political systems, but not very useful for looking at communication processes across levels *within* systems.

To some extent Charles Wright (1975) has analyzed the functions of mass (but not necessarily political) communication. Extrapolating from his work, it can be argued that the functions of political communication include conferring legitimacy on political actors, socializing members of a culture to regime norms, providing decision makers with information about the demands of constituents (and vice versa), providing an agenda, and others. But again this result oriented approach to political communication overlooks the processes through which these functions are established and is only of limited value in explaining political relationships.

ORGANIZATIONAL ANALYSIS
AND POLITICAL COMMUNICATION

From an organizational point of view, governments are not entirely different from other large organizations. They are hierarchically structured, with numerous divisions, responsibility centers, bureaucratic regulations, and so forth, and have decisions as their primary output. Organizational theorists have studied organizations from a variety of sociological and psychological perspectives much as governments have been studied. Since the development of sociometric techniques and other methods, communication patterns within organizations have also been analyzed. These same methods can be applied to governments. When they are applied, analysts perceive themselves to have measured political communication.

Primarily, organizational approaches to political communication are concerned with intragovernment communication. Governments are viewed as partially closed systems receiving some input (and transmitting some output) from *outside* the system, but ordinarily preoccupied with their own, internal communication. Thus the flow of information among branches of government (in the U.S. context), or even within one branch, from recognition of a problem, to gathering information for a decision, to the decision process itself are all part of the political communication process. Analytically, political communication analysis is not different from other organizational communication analysis, except it is over the range of organizations termed political.

Thus, without any other analytic approach, the organizational perspective would be quite limiting. However, used in conjunction with other approaches, it can expand political communication analysis to include intragovernment communication, which usually has implications outside the system.

POLITICAL COMMUNICATION AS AN ENVIRONMENTAL PHENOMENON

As noted in Chapter 1, not only do communications shape political processes and institutions, but politics shape communications as well. The environmental approach is so named because it suggests that the political system, its institutions and processes, shape the environment in which all communication takes place. Stated differently, political phenomena serve to constrain or promote communication.

A full range of political phenomena may illustrate this point. We know, for example, that in a variety of circumstances where the relatively free flow of information is surpressed, extraordinary channels of communication arise. In correctional institutions, for example, prisoners often develop elaborate signaling systems that range from eyeblink codes to tapping on walls to rapidly exchange information. In the process, practitioners of these codes develop extremely sensitive message reception facilities. As a second example, in the Soviet Union a rather large underground publishing network flourishes, the *samizdat* (literally self-press), where officially unapproved literature is typed, copied, and circulated to large numbers of readers. Again, political conditions lead to the formation of this unusual channel.

Even without the formation of new channels, political conditions constrain communicatory activity. In particular, public policies are often promulgated placing parameters on communications behaviors or institutions. In nearly all political systems there is government support, regulation, or control of broadcasting, and the placing, at least indirectly, of political constraints on programming or content. Even in areas where there is presumably little government control, such as the domain of free speech, there are judicially determined limits to the range of expression to prohibit slander and libel or proscribe the proverbial yelling of "fire" in a crowded theater. To be sure, only the extreme cases are politically controlled (after all, one can yell "movie" in a crowded firehouse) but they do represent the potential for political regulation of message content. Recent legislative and legal activity in a number of areas, such as freedom of information, rights to privacy, and sunshine laws all suggest increasing political involvement in information, if not communication processes, even in relatively unregulated countries where there is a premium on free speech.

In other political environments, control of communication may be even more pervasive. Beyond the limitations to free press and its accompanying censorship, or political control of nationalized communication industries, there are political controls on even interpersonal communication. For example, in several political systems bi- or multilingualism is suppressed in favor of one official language. Fear by governments that the use of unsanctioned languages will lead to demands for linguistic, cultural, and ultimately political autonomy results in outright bans on the use of languages.

These aspects of the constraints on communication, in conjunction with public policies directed toward the flow of information demonstrate how the political environment can shape communicatory activity empirically. Theoretically, the relationships between language and politics, for example, can be much more subtle, as the next section demonstrates.

A LINGUISTIC APPROACH
TO POLITICAL COMMUNICATION

Politics, it has been argued, is largely a matter of words (Graber, 1976b). Negotiations are held, speeches are made, debates take place, bargains are struck. Beyond these oral discussions are other forms of political talk, wherein written communications such as laws, proclamations, treaties, and other political documents are created. And, given that communication is increasingly recognized to be nonverbal, we may even consider many a physical gesture or facial expression to be a form of political talk.

All such political talk takes place through one or more languages, which are media through which ideas can be symbolically expressed. Although languages are both verbal and nonverbal, generally verbal languages—even in politics—transmit more universally interpreted symbols than nonverbal language. Each, however, contains sufficient ambiguity, so that situational contexts are quite important. Edward Sapir, for example, has raised one of the crucial questions of language and context that has important implications for political communication. Sapir (1962) asked whether concepts such as time, space, or matter are given the same meaning across contexts because they are based on experiences common to all, or whether these meanings are conditioned by the structure of language. In other words, our thinking may be determined by the language made available to us.

Two examples can help to illustrate this point. First, we can argue that much nonverbal behavior is either not understood or misunderstood because we have not been uniformly trained in nonverbal languages. To be sure, a frown or smile is widely recognized and uniformly interpreted. But what about more subtle facial expressions or body movements? Trained U.S. Government observers of the Soviet government leadership, for example carefully scrutinize photographs of Soviet leaders reviewing military parades or, at other public ceremonies, look for the distance of secondary officials from the chairman of the Communist Party. Kremlinologists argue that one can predict changes in leadership, demotions, and promotions by closely reading photographs. Stated another way, leadership roles are communicated nonverbally.

A second example of the relationship between language and constraints on thought was effectively provided by George Orwell. In *1984*, "Newspeak" as a language is molded to impose certain thoughts on speakers. Indeed, throughout the novel, Orwell argues that to control language is to control thought. The abolition of certain terms—freedom, liberty, honesty, and so forth—presumably eliminates them as values, and raises the question of whether or not it is possible to recognize concepts if there are no terms for them.

Commonly, the vocabulary of North American Eskimos is cited as an empirical example. Over a dozen nouns for snow of different textures, wetness, firmness, etc. are part of the vocabulary, as are numerous terms for shades of white. To the untrained, non-Eskimo eye, all snow is alike, and the absence of a specialized vocabulary (which skiers may develop) suggests that differences in snow may not even be perceived.

Not only can language constrain thought, it can also limit political action. Recent work by Mueller (1975), from which much of the following discussion is derived, has described the language/action relationship. It is a commonplace observation (think of Henry Higgins and Liza Doolittle) that social status is revealed in patterns of language use, vocabulary, accent, and so forth. Under most circumstances different language patterns have little meaning in the day to day lives of the users. In the political arena, however, these patterns take on a broader significance. Politics, for the most part, is conducted in a unique language. A certain specialized vocabulary, both literally and figuratively, is required in the political arena, but it can be argued that certain groups (the linguistically deprived) do not have the required vocabulary and thus, may be excluded from effective political participation. In other words, some groups in society are politically inarticulate; they are not able to articulate their demands to government decision makers. The speech of these groups simply prevents their expressing desires.

The groups more likely to be politically inarticulate are those already socially, educationally, economically, and otherwise deprived. Their limited vocabularies, needs for immediate gratification, insensitivity to generalization, and other characteristics of arrested communication, effectively preclude a dialogue with middle class politicians or more educated citizens who have the tools of middle class political articulateness. These include a broader perspective, an ability to provide illustrative examples, and beliefs in logical persuasion, all while stating demands in appropriately analytic, descriptive language. Overall, middle class participants have the capacity to understand the distorted communications of the political world with its qualifiers, obscurities, and ambiguities, and respond appropriately. The politically articulate cannot.

Differential access to the political world follows from different levels of articulateness. Moreover, political power is more easily maintained by those already in power because no voices can be raised to either press demands or challenge legitimacy. The inarticulate are systematically excluded from participation in a political world demanding expertise in political languages. Occasionally there are individuals who do speak the languages of both the articulate and the inarticulate and who serve at the interface between the two groups. However, it may be argued that those who are politically bilingual are more like the decision-making middle class articulates (through their educational training, socialization, etc.) than the inarticulates. Indeed, the very act of translating the demands of the inarticulate to the decision maker's articulated language may impose a structure on those demands not really desired by the inarticulate. And, the prospects for movement between levels are relatively small, so from generation to generation, groups remain divided into the two broad categories.

Occasionally, the inarticulate do make demands known without acquiring political language in the traditional sense. Indeed much nontraditional political participation (strikes, riots, demonstrations, and terrorist activity) may be viewed as the language of the inarticulate. Often, meaning can be transmitted only through direct action. However, the costs of these forms of participation are high because they often are illegal and/or repressed. Ultimately, in most cases, any successes are negotiated (unless there is total revolution) so the need for political articulateness still stands.

The uses and functions of language to maintain the political order has been suggested by Murray Edelman (1964). Specifically four types of language are used, each with a different political function. First, hortatory language is used to urge or convince the masses of the need for political support for the regime. Used during election campaigns or wartime propaganda, hortatory language introduced into the political dialogue has the effect of obscuring the underlying issues by raising a cloud of ambiguous slogans. Second, there exists legalistic language or legalese, a highly specialized language of legislatures, lawyers, and the judiciary that again forbids full understanding of the language to the politically monolingual masses. Found everywhere, from treaties to contracts to courtrooms, this formal yet ambiguous language cries out for judicial interpretation. Although precise in some ways, it is ambiguous enough in other ways to allow for fine distinctions. And, more important, this legal language serves certain symbolic functions that help maintain political order. For the masses, legalese means fairness, whereas even for elites who are otherwise politically articulate it suggests the presence of objective standards in the law and political process.

The third type of language is administrative language, a tongue fraught with ambiguity. Used chiefly to disseminate the work of government, it often hides the fact that government decisions are unfair. Rules and memoranda take on a false precision through administrative circumlocutions, such as "operation of considerable magnitude" (big) or "inoperative statement" (lies). The effect of many bureaucratic procedures requiring the use of administrative languages is to have some people throw up their hands in despair and forgo pursuing their demands of the government.

Finally, there exists bargaining language, the language of political negotiation used by political participants. It is this language that is notably absent in the politically inarticulate. Styles of negotiation are not learned by excluded groups, consequently as Edelman argues, they are excluded from social rewards.

These various languages have implications in a wide variety of political relationships. Indeed, often the very language used expresses political relationship or status. Lakoff (1974) for example, writes that men have maintained social dominance over women because of language differences which result from differential socialization. Furthermore, women who use "men's" language are perceived as threatening to masculine leadership, so its use is discouraged. Parallels exist between sex-role linguistic differences and more expressly political relationships. In developing nations (lesser developed countries, the third world, primitive countries, or backward countries—depending on the values held by the speaker) power is frequently exercised in the former colonial language, specifically to underscore educational differences between decision-making elites and local or other potential leaders.

Much can be revealed about political philosophies from the vocabulary employed in political relationships. On occasion, these differences create difficulties from translation of documents, or even roles, across culture. Consider the term "president" in a Weberian rational/legal system. In many cultures a leader based on other than kinship or traditional roles is literally inconceivable. Thus for many American Indian tribes, the president was called the "Great White Father," for they found no term in their languages for leadership positions independent of kinship.

Similarly, problems of translation in international documents are created by linguistic differences. English, for example, has often been considered to be a fact oriented language, in contrast to Russian, which is a category oriented language. Thus, if an English speaking diplomat intends "to discuss the matter before us," his or her Russian counterpart may intend "to discuss the categories into which the matter falls." Although these examples may be somewhat exaggerated, they clearly suggest a different perception of the agenda.

One final area of language has been pursued in political communication research. Styles of political rhetoric have been suggested to reflect varied aspects of the culture. For example, politicians may use metaphorical language and imagery, which is at the same time ambiguous, yet meaningful. A study by Frank (1972) looked at the references to bodies and physical health in presidential State of the Union Messages during crisis and noncrisis periods and found numerous references to a "sick" society, "feverish" economy, "healing national wounds." Similarly, Mebane (1977) looked at references to war and sports among metaphors of presidential candidates. Research on the presidential debates (Jackson-Beeck & Meadow, 1979a) showed references to the body ("hold out the hand of freedom," "off the farmers back"), sports ("reach the goals," "cruel blow," "kick-off press conference"), transportation and travel ("road to the presidency," "pay as you go economy," "these programs are re-treads"), or war ("kill a bill," "freedom will conquer," "freedom under attack") to be particularly prevalent in the debates. Comparative analysis of metaphorical use across cultures can yield considerable insights into political cultures.

Overall, there are a variety of linkages between language and politics, underscoring the importance of language in a comprehensive notion of political communication. To summarize; language use, first and foremost, is necessary to express political relationships such as power and authority. Equally important is its role in maintaining these relationships and contributing to social stability. Primarily through the development of specialized languages for political functions, political outsiders are denied access to much of politics. Language in a political context, of course, is a broad concept and includes the nonverbal languages, but inasmuch as politics is largely "talk," the subtleties of verbal languages are particularly meaningful in a political world. Perhaps most important is the symbolic aspect of language and language use. It expresses status, values, and hierarchies nearly independent of message substance. Indeed, the symbolic approach to politics is a major paradigm for political communication and one to which we now turn.

SYMBOLIC APPROACHES
TO POLITICAL COMMUNICATION

Much of communications analysis deals with symbolic behavior. The same is true of political analysis, perhaps to even a greater degree. We know that political activity takes place in a general symbolic environment, so contending meanings to the same symbols exist. The generality of symbols makes them applicable in a wide variety of circumstances, particularly when no one language is understood by all. In other words, where there is a language for decision makers and a second language for the politically inarticulate, symbols and their accompanying ambiguity can bridge the gap. As with language, symbols help to maintain the political order, so much so that one of the functions of political systems is to generate political symbols.

Symbols in the political processes and political communication have a lengthy history. Beginning from a psychoanalytic tradition, Lasswell (1935) said that symbols help to synthesize meanings for individuals, and further help them to attribute meaning to and provide a basis for social interaction. Similarly, they serve to preserve social stability. In particular, one need only consider why laws are ordinarily effective. In regimes with a rule of law, only the symbols of law are usually necessary for communicating commands of social order. One police officer can control a crowd of ten individuals by his or her presence, the implied threat of a jail sentence for legal violations, enhanced by our picture of a life behind bars, is sufficient to maintain order. In short, symbols can be viewed as effectively communicating power and authority relationships as much as or more than coercion itself.

Modern students of political symbols recognize the power of symbols and the mythology and rituals accompanying them. However, they have also drawn distinctions between referential and condensational symbols. Referential symbols are specific, empirically based symbols that merely serve as shorthand ways of identifying objects. For example, journalists may refer in a press report to the White House, which is a simple way of saying the president and members of his staff. With the words "White House," these elements are simplified. Condensational (or inferential) symbols have ambiguous, emotional meanings. Thus one can refer to the flag and see more than thirteen horizontal stripes and fifty stars. As a condensational symbol, one can think of patriotism, love of country, and those sets of values for which the flag symbolically "stands."

Political symbols have different meanings at different levels of analysis. First, a term such as "flag" (or "hippy," or "cop," or "Watergate") has value as a sign, meaning that it brings to mind a specific object. Secondly, the terms have symbolic values, whose precise meaning depends on usage context and, more important, the ideology of the audience. It is in these symbolic values that people find their meanings.

Ample evidence exists of the potency of symbols. One most interesting study was conducted by Prothro and Grigg (1960). In general, they found the symbols of America, such as free speech, majority rule, and minority rights to be highly cherished and valued as abstract principles by 95 to 98 percent of those sampled. This consensus, however, does not hold when people are asked specifically whether they would allow an antireligious speech in their community or would allow an elected communist to take office. In other words, when these abstract principles are solidified and people are forced to decide on issues rather than symbols, social consensus appears to break down. Thus, in terms of holding society together, symbols are extremely important.

The sources of symbols in the political system are varied. Some are derived from our ordinary socialization processes. Exposure to various symbols and their agreed upon meanings in school and at home provides a framework for comprehending long standing symbols. Exposure to mass media interpretations of symbols similarly provides meanings to symbols. The role of mass media in the symbols process is constrained at times in that media serve to present symbols created elsewhere in the political system. At the same time, it can be argued that symbols can not be created without the cooperation of mass media. During the 1976 campaign, for example, at one point on the campaign trail, Jimmy Carter referred to his desire to maintain the "ethnic purity" of neighborhoods. Although Carter may have meant he was concerned with maintaining ethnic pride and cultural opportunities for various ethnic groups, the phrase was widely reported (and interpreted) as antiblack, segregationist rhetoric revealing the feelings of an incorrigible Southern racist. As reported in the mass media, "ethnic purity" was viewed a symbolic representation of Carter's desire to see all-white neighborhoods remain. In such incidents, it is difficult to determine where the symbol began—with Carter (who denied its popularly reported symbolic meaning) or with the mass media, giving life to the expression through widespread reporting of the phrase.

In propaganda campaigns, symbols that emerge are essentially manipulative. However, this is the case only if symbolic meanings are narrowly interpreted and meet with widespread aggrement. Ordinarily, symbols are vague enough so that individuals can put their own meanings, their own interpretations to work. The wide appeal of symbols is that people respond to the symbols rather than to messages. The ambiguity thus allows symbols to serve any number of functions for various individuals. Fulfillment of needs for ambiguity, security, reassurance, reference points, identification, all can be found through symbols. More important, because people read in their own meanings to symbols—or at least are exposed to different media that digest symbols for audiences—it is often possible to mobilize large numbers behind any symbol. Moreover, even though individuals may respond to symbols for different reasons, the behaviors that follow such responses may be uniform.

Examples of political symbols sufficiently vague, but able to mobilize large numbers of adherents are numerous. In the mid-1960s, for example, "Black Power" was an important symbol in the civil rights movement. To some, it meant ethnic pride, to others armed conflict with whites, to still others black economic power and capitalism. But these meanings were not always articulated, hence black power had nearly universal appeal in the black community because of the variety of possible interpretations. Similarly it was perceived as threatening in large segments of the white community. As a symbol, the "communist menace" was equally powerful, rallying supporters from those anxious for military conflict to those who sought economic progress to avoid being "buried" by Kruschev's grandchildren. In general, these examples suggest the more abstract the symbol, the more meanings it is given, and the more massive is the responding audience.

Symbols have several dimensions by which they can be evaluated, some of which have been described by Cobb and Elder (1972). First, symbols can be evaluated in terms of their potency or ability to arouse groups or individuals to action. Second, symbols have varying degrees of efficiency. On the one hand, efficiency is maximized by ambiguity (within a limited range). On the other hand, if a symbol is used incorrectly, even its broad meaning is lost, and it no longer has general appeal. Third, symbols have saturation points. Overuse limits the utility of many symbols and results in meaningless cliches. Finally, symbols can be looked at in terms of their urgency. Some symbols have meanings limited by time and space, but have an urgency unmatched by time-worn symbols. Chanting for "peace now" at a peace demonstration, or "get whitey" during a racial demonstration, have an urgency that adds to their meanings.

The creation of symbols, of course, does not automatically guarantee the success of a political movement or policy. Indeed, many symbols generated to ease communication among movement sympathizers (a peace "V" sign) and to serve as badges of recognition (a black power raised fist salute) are coopted. The "V" sign, for example, taken by peace advocates to suggest a victory for move- ment goals was coopted by Nixon Republicans at the 1968 convention. Indeed the symbol was generalized to return to its original Churchillian meaning of victory rather than "peace." Overuse of symbols decreases their potency. In addition, symbols may be sufficiently vague, resulting in associations with the wrong objects. Finally, some symbols simply may be too concrete, and never have wide appeal.

In political communication processes, symbols have several functions, but perhaps most important, they ease the comprehension of politics. In the absence of symbols, politics can be seen as too complicated, too abstract, and too diffi- cult an activity in which to engage. Indeed, voting itself is often looked at as a symbolic act. Why, after all, do people participate in elections? Is it to choose leaders, or is to to reaffirm one's commitment to the political system? Regardless of why people participate, symbolically there is communication to political elites.

Symbolic processes in politics have been demonstrated by several typolo- gies, culminating in a description of political reality. From Edelman's (1964) perspective, for example, there are two types of political actors: the elites (the organized participants who perceive of political participation instrumentally) and the masses (unorganized spectators for whom politics is largely expressive). There are also two types of rewards or political outputs—symbolic and tangible. Edelman argues that the unorganized masses are offered largely symbolic rewards, ranging from pride in their country, to election contests, to medals when wounded in war. The organized elites, however, receive the tangible rewards of allocations of scarce resources, such as political power, economic prosperity, or other specific rewards.

Looking only to the communications industry for example, Edelman's thesis applies. Considering the Federal Communication Commission, one can see that much regulation takes place only with the approval of the regulated when economic issues are involved. Symbolically, of course, there is much regulation: the declaration of new rules, the protest by the industry, the F.C.C. response with a hard line, and other ritualistic posturing presents a symbolic reassurance to the public that the government is acting, whereas the organized, elite participants recognize that even the agenda of concerns is limited.

Other examples abound that demonstrate how simple it is for decision makers to render a group quiescent by offering symbolic rewards. Often the government declares a region a "Federal Disaster Area" to symbolically demonstrate commitment that may already be tangible. The creation of new cabinet departments such as Energy or Housing and Urban Development or Education often transfers functions already carried out by other departments, but offers purely symbolic rewards as often as efficient reorganization.

The final, but by no means least important aspect of symbols in the political process is that they replace instrumental politics. Groups that have no legitimate way of expressing and communicating their goals and needs often do so symbolically. Many a' social conflict has been a symbolic conflict. Gusfield (1963) wrote of the Temperance Movement, not so much as a movement to prohibit the sale of alcoholic beverages, but as the only method by which rural, WASP America could call attention to itself and its values in an era of freed slaves and urban ethnic immigrants, who were minimizing the total control WASPs had exercised in American political life. More recently, textbook controversies and sex education protests by parents have suggested not so much that parents are opposed to certain texts being used in schools or that sex education is immoral. Instead, these parents symbolically want to tell educational administrators that they wish to determine what is taught in school and reestablish parental dominance in an era of the demise of parental authority. Other controversies ranging from gay rights and Anita Bryant in Miami to the drive to see the Equal Rights Amendment enacted are largely symbolic exercises to communicate legitimacy and equality in the social and political worlds.

A SYSTEMS VIEW OF POLITICAL COMMUNICATION

The relationship of communication to the development of systems thinking is strong. Indeed, the very elements at the core of political communication—symbols and language—played special roles in the systems movement. Suzanne Langer (1942) argued for the generality of symbols, whose meaning was independent of their physical properties. At the same time, she noted a shift from elementary particles and events to symbols. Her work was later expanded by Morris (1946) who considered the central focus of study to be not symbols, but the languages to which the symbols belonged. The developments of Weiner (1948), and Shannon and Weaver (1949) moved systems analysis further by specifying the interaction patterns of communication among system elements.

Systems theorists working in the biological, engineering, and social sciences have sought to develop a general theory of systems applicable across a wide variety of fields and empirical referents. Thus, it comes as no surprise to learn that when political relationships and processes are viewed in systems analytic terms, the relationship of politics to communication becomes more visible than when these same political phenomena are viewed through individual, group, or institutional theories. Consequently, systems analysis would seem to be an appropriate mode of analysis for examining political communication phenomena. In many ways, a system perspective simplifies political communication analysis by presenting a general model of political communication applicable across levels of government within one system, or even providing a framework for analysis across systems.

Systems analysis is a mode of analysis that has had many meanings to social scientists. Functional analysts from sociology (Parsons, 1951); anthropology (Malinowski, 1945, 1948; Radcliffe-Brown, 1935); and political science (Almond & Powell, 1966) thought functional analysis to be the true systems approach. Concerned largely with elements that serve to maintain the system by performing certain functions, functional analysis has been criticized for assuming social systems to be static. Largely a descriptive mode, functional analysis in political science has considered the development of certain institutional structures to assure system maintenance. Political functions include socialization, recruitment, interest aggregation, and interest articulation; whereas governmental functions include rule-making, rule-application, and rule-ajudication. All of these functions involve communication processes or institutions, and thus might appear appropriate as a framework for political communication analysis. Indeed, taking off from this model, Kraus and Davis (1976) have (See Figure 3.1) refined the Almond and Powell (1966) approach by considering communication processes—mostly mass media use by publics and elites—which ultimately lead to system legitimacy and, presumably to maintenance.

The functional approach, even with the Kraus and Davis modification, still suffers certain weaknesses. Beyond its static nature, it fails to elaborate the interdependence and thus communication patterns of actors and elements in the system. Moreover, the Kraus and Davis model takes a rather narrow view of communication, considering only mass media. This perspective limits the model to developed societies, and does not consider communications processes in other political relationships. With a broader view of political communication espoused in this volume, other systems approaches might appear more useful. General systems theory offers a more appropriate approach.

Stated simply, general systems analysis is a logic for expressing the interdependence of variables in a relationship independent of empirical referents. As such, systems analysis is more a grammar than a theory, in which the interaction rules of two or more elements or components are specified within some temporal or spatial boundary. Examples of systems abound. Humans are biological systems whose components themselves are systems (i.e., the circulatory,

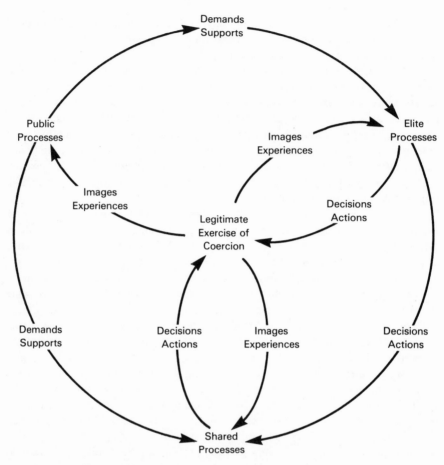

Figure 3.1 Kraus-Davis Model of the Political System. [After Kraus-Davis, 1976.]

digestive, and nervous systems) composed of further subsystems (individual organs) and yet more subsystems (cells). A mechanical wristwatch, too, is a system of elements (balance wheels, gems, minute and hour hands, etc.) interacting in very predictable ways to provide the owner with an output—the time of day. Similarly, there are social systems ranging in size and scope from families as social systems (defined culturally as nuclear or extended) to voluntary associations, to national political systems, each characterized by a set of components, interaction patterns, boundaries, and in search of certain goals. This teleological or goal seeking behavior of social systems (e.g., harmony and love in family systems, social welfare, order and stability in political systems) may distinguish social from mechanistic systems, but each may be described with similar terminology.

Regardless of the type of system, the elements or components have two major properties: (1) the properties, or behavior, of each component has an effect on the properties, or behavior, of the whole system; but (2) no component has an independent effect on the whole system, because the effect of any component depends on its interdependence with other components in the system. Thus, the components forming any system lead the system to have some characteristics that none of its components have. In other words, a complex system emerges from the interaction of its components with properties or behaviors not found in its elements alone.

Returning to the wristwatch as a mechanistic system, the first of the two major properties suggests, for example, that the extent to which the mainspring is wound effects the number of hours the system will operate. But at the same time, the effect of a wound mainspring in terms of assisting to yield an accurate time depends on the precision of the balance wheels, minute hands, and other components of the wristwatch. In the political system, the two limitations also pertain. Considering very simply the three branches of American government as components in the system, one can consider the effect of a Supreme Court decision on school desegregation. Clearly its effect depends on the extent to which the executive chooses to enforce the decision or if the legislature allocates funds for that purpose. The effect is thus filtered through interdependence of the branches of government.

General systems theory is not without its limitations. Criticisms range from the argument that systems theory routinizes, trivializes, and mechanizes complex social phenomena; and only describes rather than explains social phenomena. Moreover, in terms of its utility for capturing political variables, it neither describes key political concepts such as power or socialization, nor explains processes by which political goals are established. At the same time, general systems theory is a dynamic approach permitting us to clarify interaction patterns that in our view are relevant to political communication analysis. And, it permits establishing a framework for considering system maintenance without the rigid limitations of the functional approach. For our abstract consideration of a system of political communication we need not be limited to an empirical system using a general system approach (even though examples are drawn largely from U.S. politics in Part III).

Beyond the functional and general systems approaches lies the third method, input-output analysis. Proposed and developed for political science largely by David Easton (1964, 1965) the input-output approach deals with the more concrete, day to day operation of political systems. Easton's model of a political system is presented in Figure 3.2. Like the functional approach, it is oriented toward system maintenance, containing a number of regulatory mechanisms to handle stress. At the same time, the model emphasizes the processes of conversion of demands in a political system to policy outputs.

In many ways, the input-output approach has the advantages for political communication analysis of general systems theory and functional analysis without their problems. Although there is emphasis on maintaining the system,

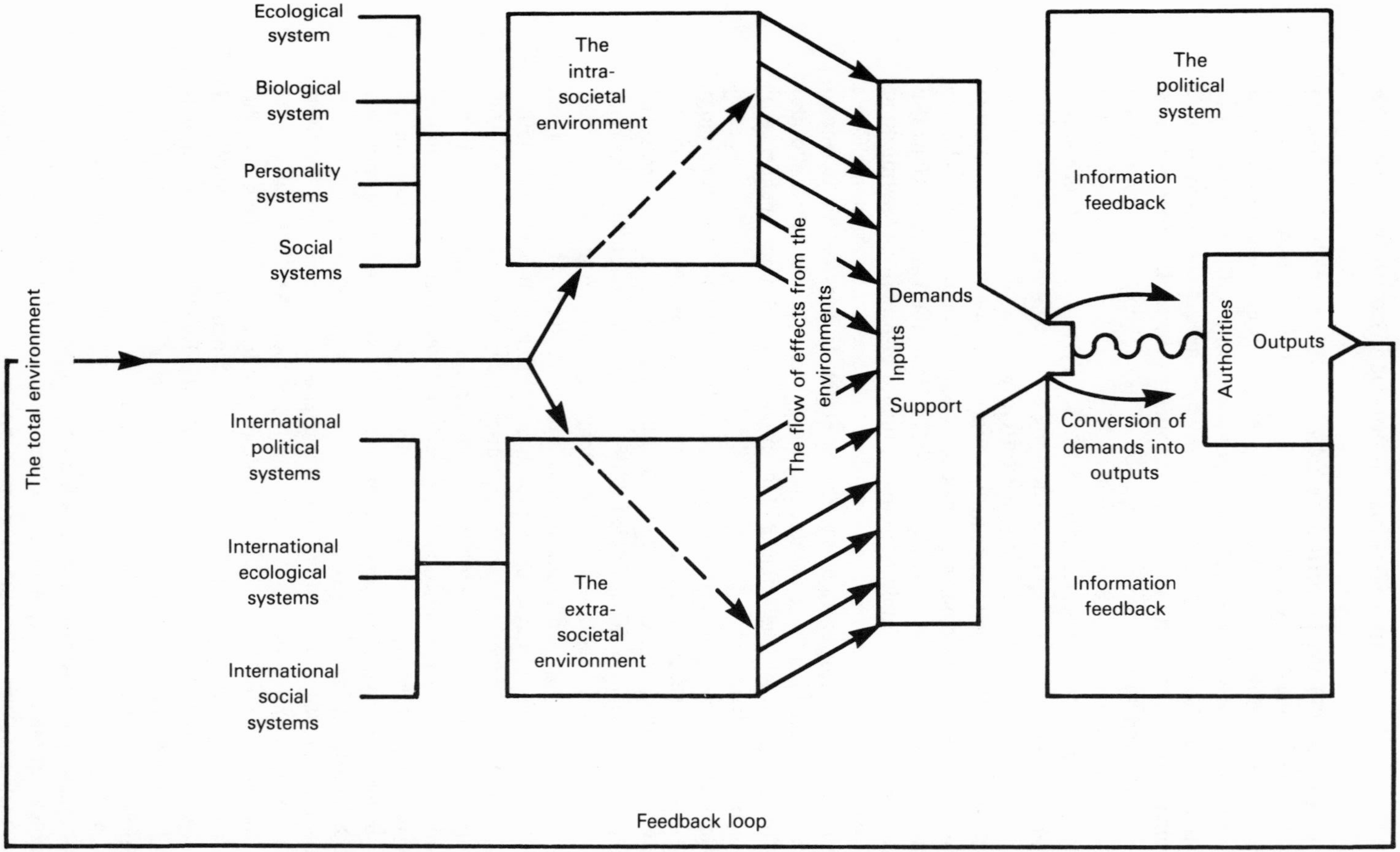

Figure 3.2 Easton's Dynamic Response Model of a Political System [After Easton, 1964.]

it is a dynamic system maintenance, allowing for changes of the demands and supports through continuous feedback mechanisms. Interrelationships of functions rather than elements are stressed, but the focus is on a whole, bounded system. As with general systems theory, the approach is applicable over a wide range of systems, and thus offers possibilities for cross system comparison. Most important, Easton considers communication channels to be integral parts of the model by regulating the flow of information within the system. What Easton does not consider in the diagram or elsewhere is that there are communications processes within each of the system processes such as the formulation of demands, the conversion processes, and so forth. Moreover, the political system is viewed largely as conversion process and includes only the authorities rather than actors giving rise to demands and supports.

Easton's primary concern with the persistence of political systems leads him to focus largely on the erosion of support from the failure of policy outputs. However, one may look at the components and the interactions within the system at all levels to find the roots of system problems. At the very least, the strength of filters (such as mass media or gatekeeping groups) in the system, the failure of citizens to effectively communicate either demands or supports, and the barriers to communication within each system component are equally important. To put it another way, demands, as well as policy outputs, are always being reduced, distorted, or otherwise changed, and system components are not always gratified. Therefore, we might want to consider examining the communication processes within and across system components.

In an expanded, slightly modified version of Easton appropriate for political communication analysis, the political system is viewed first as a closed system (Figure 3.3). In other words, the assumption is that politics can be largely isolated from other facets of the culture (such as religion) but only for analytic purposes. Certainly there are interrelationships, and the openness of the system has implications for the kinds of issues that yield demands or shape the extent of support. But these prior experiences can be considered included in the demands or supports.

Considering the diagram in terms of fundamental communication variables, one of the sources of political communication, as well as the object of system control (entering the model from the demand side), in both democratic and nondemocratic contexts is the citizenry. In other words, rather than considering only "authorities" to be relevant actors, the objects of authority action are fundamental system elements. Indeed, one revision is that the focus is on actors rather than messages, i.e., on political communication (processes) rather than political communications (messages).

At the second level are the filtering and control mechanisms. Groups, secondary associations, and similar organizations aggregate some demands, but screen out others. Independent of these groups are mass media that serve to transmit messages to, and especially from, the fourth set of actors in the decision system—the government.

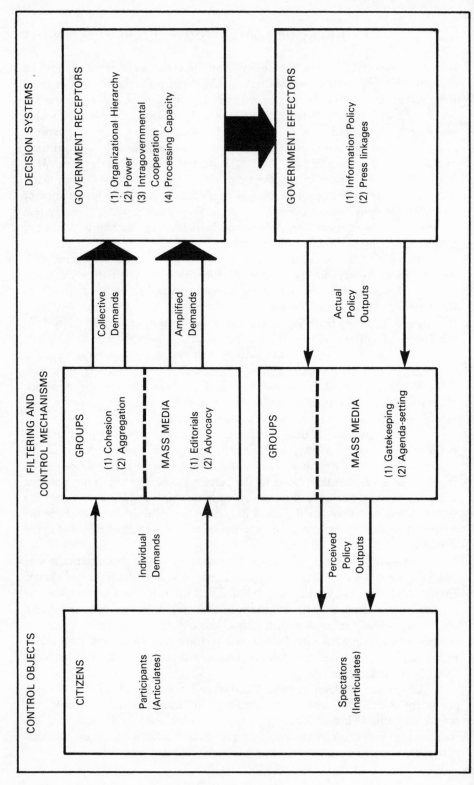

42

These actors transmit or receive two types of communication. First there are internal communication processes in groups, mass media organizations, and government. Secondly, each actor transmits to the other actors. In general systems terminology, the components of the system—the actors—are interdependent through their patterns of information exchange.

The processes suggested by the model can be briefly explained. There are large numbers of citizens potentially expressing political demands. Rarely can these be articulated directly to government, particularly for the linguistically incompetent. Instead they must be aggregated (and reduced) through groups, associations, political parties, and so forth. At this point, the demands of those without secondary affiliations will be eliminated from the system, as well as those of citizens unable to articulate their demands. For some individuals, however, demands can survive without secondary associations, provided the individuals are sufficiently capable of expressing their demands and have the ear of either decision makers (rare) or are capable of capturing the attention of mass media directly (more common). Media-based demand presentation occurs through letters to the editor, human interest stories of problems with the bureaucracy, or advocacy type "action line" services.

Groups and secondary associations channel these aggregated demands through mass media or occasionally directly to government leaders. Mass media then forward some of these demands to government decision makers, but gatekeep other demands. Once these demands have reached government decision makers, action is taken (or not taken), and outputs in the form of decisions are made known to citizens through the mass media or directly, in the case of private demands that bypass filters.

The process seems simple and straightforward enough if viewed as a decision system in its entirety. The model only becomes interesting for political communication researchers when we consider each of the identifiable subsystems where communication activity is of particular concern. The first subsystem is the citizen/interest group interaction. Communication questions arise first when considering how groups form, and then how these political groups organize their own communication patterns. Questions in this subsystem include detailed analysis of demand filtration: why some demands make it on to the group agenda, how conflicts may expand to new publics, how social movements begin, and how requisite articulation skills are developed to enter into the group process.

Second level interactions include mass media/group interactions. To which groups do mass media attend? What are the economic and social variables orienting mass media to some participants rather than others? Specifically how do groups communicate with each other. Then, of course, continuing to explore questions at the group level, the analyses of media themselves as organizations is appropriate. How are they economically and bureaucratically structured to report or transmit demands? What role do media play in terms of gatekeeping demands or decisions?

At a third level, of course, are media/decision maker interactions, focusing on the extent to which decision makers attend to mass media as sources of demands, or employ mass media for other purposes such as disseminating decisions or even intragovernment decisions.

Each of these systemic relations falls within the domain of political communication research. At the same time, each actor raises important political communication questions, as do the relationships the whole political system has to other systems (i.e., the communication system). We have already mentioned some of the questions (organizational communication, bureaucratic structures, and so forth) for groups and mass media; the same questions apply for government decision makers. In terms of the whole system, our definition of political communication also indicates a role for the political environment in shaping communication. In conjunction with other systems (e.g., technological systems, biological systems, educational systems) the political world is a component in a communication system.

All of this is simultaneously straightforward and abstract. On the one hand, it is simple: elements expressing their interaction through communication with respect to political phenomena. But within each element or across each component dyad, many pertinent political communication questions exist. Even so, in our search for generality, we seek only an understanding of processes common to all system elements.

The view of political communication processes and variables expressed in Figure 3.3 is not the only one to be offered through a revision of Easton's approach and vocabulary. Steve Chaffee (1975), for example, emphasizes the support and authority orientation of Easton and suggests that ideological political systems cognitively have as their goals the understanding of system functioning, and affectively, the development of outputs to maintain the support of members. These goals are contrasted with communication system goals that Chaffee argues from his coorientation view, which is the development of value consensus among members and accuracy of members perceiving system inputs. In other words, Chaffee argues that political systems analysts are concerned primarily with system persistence, whereas communication analysts are more interested in seeing that system members understand how the system operates. Chaffee suggests the core question in evaluating a communication system within the context of a political system is one of the diffusion of political information. In terms of the model in Figure 3.3, the only question is, do the citizens with demands learn how the system operates and what the decisions are?

Chaffee's information based approach is somewhat limiting, largely because the whole process by which demands are raised, aggregated, brought to the attention of decision makers, decided, and information returned to the citizens is a communication process. Each actor, each step has its own communication variables, hence a comprehensive view of political communication must include the workings of the whole system as well as an understanding of the communications processes in each of the component parts. Without doubt, understanding the political socialization process is part of political communication analysis—but it is not the only factor.

SYNTHESIZING POLITICAL COMMUNICATION

Each of the six approaches to political communication discussed in this chapter has something to contribute to the model developed in Figure 3.3. Taking each perspective separately, the functional approach indicates the stability of the model; the political functions of mass media are to assure a filtration of demands to manageable numbers, and at the other level, to assure a citizenry informed about government undertakings. An organizational perspective operates at several levels, focusing on the group level at which demands are filtered, and describing the communication processes within government organizations. Without an organizational analytic framework, the important system components—groups, mass media and government, would be black boxes. From an environmental point of view the feedback loop in the model is considered. Government decisions establish the parameters under which citizens operate; citizen communication occurs within these parameters. Linguistic theories partially describe the origins of demands within citizens, and ultimately their expression to decision makers. At the same time, social control is exercised through manipulation and creation of symbols by government and mass media feedback as well as through the creation of demands. Finally, a systems view places each of the political actors in relationship to one another, and yields an overall vantage point from which to consider political communication. Taken together, all of these perspectives generate insights into the political communication interface, and provide the vocabulary with which the political concepts in Part II can be explored.

Some of the questions raised by interaction and communication within and across system components provide the basis for the discussion of the political concepts in Part II, as well as the empirical examples of Parts III and IV. Looking at the description of the revised Easton model, concepts are raised: how conflicts are initiated or expanded within and across groups, how the requisite degree of political articulation skills are developed, what modes there are of participating to communicate with decision makers or how strategic location within an organization can effectively control communication certainly raises questions for conflict, socialization, participation, and political power, the concepts discussed in Part II. Similarly, the examples used in Parts III and IV to illustrate these concepts are suggested by the model. Taking just two examples, why media attend to only some messages or are forced to limit their coverage, or how governments use mass media to enhance system persistence and support, are derived as much from the model as from the concepts they empirically illustrate.

II
COMMUNICATION PERSPECTIVE
ON POLITICAL CONCEPTS

4
CONFLICT, INTEGRATION, AND DEVELOPMENT

If politics as a whole can be viewed in communications terms, so too can many of the major concepts which define the parameters of those aspects of the culture we call political. Conflict, integration, development, participation, power, and socialization are but six important concepts in which communication-based explanations can be offered of political phenomena. Each major concept refers to a concrete range of phenomena, but is unbounded by a particular political system. Thus the major concepts are applicable across systems, although most examples are drawn from the U.S. political system.

In this chapter three political concepts are explored: conflict, political integration, and political development. They are distinct from one another, yet at the same time related because of their common linkage to communication variables. For the purposes of this chapter, conflict refers to a competition or disagreement over values, leadership, resource allocation, or any other important item within a political system. Integration refers to an amalgamation of communities or individuals such that they share a common identity. Finally, political development most generally refers to an increasing complexity of a system and the interaction among its components as it moves toward system goals.

Each of these concepts is defined more completely and examined thoroughly. Specific attention is paid to the concepts as artifacts of communication processes and in demonstrating these political concepts as communication.

CONFLICT

In Chapter 3 we refer to Easton, who defines politics as the allocation of values. On the one hand, the allocation is authoritative, implying the significance of power in politics. On the other hand, the underlying reason an authoritative decision is needed is that there is disagreement—conflict—as to whom the resources should be allocated. Thus, conflict, along with power (see Chapter 6) is at the core of politics. Many of the institutions of politics (parties, interest groups, legislatures, judicial systems) have conflict or the resolution of conflict as their raison d'être.

Conflicts of all kinds ordinarily pass through four stages, each of which has communications linkages. Although students of conflict from Simmel (1955) and Coser (1956), through Coleman (1957), and Schattschneider (1960), have not always taken a communication perspective, the stages of conflict they cite, regardless of the substantive focus, can be explored through communications. First, of course, is the origin of conflict. Two or more actors possess different values or goals, or seek the same scarce resources (economic or political), and become aware of each other's existence. This latter phase is crucial, for in the absence of awareness of each other's existence, there is no social conflict. To be sure, an actor may not reach a goal, but may perceive of this failure to be one's own shortcomings, inadequacy of resource or effort, or some other limitation. Once there is awareness of other's search for the same resources, the *sine qua non* of conflict is present.

Second, conflicts frequently pass through an expansion phase. Schattschneider (1960) best explains conflict in dynamic terms, arguing that it continually grows to include both new issues and more actors. Coleman (1957), too, has recognized this phenomenon, focusing on issue transformation during conflict expansion. Social conflicts move from the specific to the general, new and different issues arise, and disagreement moves toward outright antagonism. And, along with the expansion of issues, new individuals become involved, polarization with the community increases, leading to the outbreak of more and more conflicts and permanent cleavages.

Because of the destructive consequences of social conflict, there is usually a drive somewhere in the community to manage the conflict to prevent cleavages. Authorities may seek to provide a forum for conflicting parties to air their differences, issues are clarified and isolated, and depersonalization of the conflict is encouraged. Conflict management leads to the final phase: resolution. In this phase, agreements are concluded, a presumably authoritative and binding decision is rendered in accordance with previously agreed upon rules. Ultimately, the preconflict level of social harmony is reached, although on occasion bitterness lingers.

Each of these conflict phases manifests important communication variables. In terms of conflict origin, awareness of competition for the limited resource is essential. In the absence of such information, adjustive behavior within the social unit seeking the resource is internally oriented, i.e., the failure to reach the goal is a result of incompetency, poor organization, or lack of desire, rather than externally imposed by a competitor so the unit can direct its conflict behavior toward the enemy. In the absence of a well-identified opponent, conflict behavior is likely to be random and aimless. Whereas there are a number of ways parties in conflict may become aware of one another, mass media may play as significant a role as interpersonal communication.

In fact, mass media may initiate an otherwise latent conflict by reporting opposing positions or even the existence of alternative actors interested in the same resources. Decision makers who may later aid the resolution of conflict may first be apprised of a conflict through the eyes of mass media. Interpersonal communication, too, may be significant in conflict recognition. In particular, individuals with crossmemberships in organizations on either side of the controversy are often the first to recognize a potential conflict. At the same time, their multiple loyalties serve to minimize tensions across conflicting parties.

During the conflict expansion stage, widespread dissemination of conflict information results in the inclusion of numerous actors with no direct access. Such individuals perceive their interests to be effected, or may join simply because of value preferences. Issue transformation occurring during this stage may be a direct result of conflict reporting: journalists may focus on only one dimension of a multidimensional conflict or may perceive the conflict differently than the original participants. Thus the new participants are operating under different issues. As a simple hypothesis, it could be argued that the greater the role played by mass media in a conflict, the more diverse the actors and perceived issues. During this conflict expansion phase the potential for condensational symbol development (see Chapter 3) is greatest. Indeed as symbols emerge, the potential for both actor and issue expansion is heightened considerably.

During the management and resolution phases, it is essential that channels of communication be provided for the parties in conflict. Arguably, a conflict may be snuffed out by a failure to publicize it during the expansion phase; it is equally likely that in the absence of an arena providing a forum for the resolution of differences, a conflict will continue almost indefinitely. The legitimacy of parties in conflict is established by providing them with a forum for the interchange of views. Ultimately, the resolution of conflict is incomplete without the wide dissemination of information that hostilities have concluded.

There are many arenas for managing and resolving conflicts. Depending on the substantive conflict, they may range from violent aggression (generally viewed as the last resort after a failure of other resolution mechanisms), to the more frequently used bargaining table where the rules are well defined. More formal institutions also exist for parties in conflict. For those with sufficient political clout to rate a position on the systemic agenda, there is a legislative resolution. For others, litigation offers an opportunity for an impartial hearing of conflict merits and well established procedures for implementing decisions.

The importance of information dissemination during the management and resolution phases is made clear from a number of examples. Among the most interesting are the accounts of the capture or surrender of Japanese soldiers from World War Two in Philippine jungles. As recently as the mid-1970s, soldiers separated from their units in battle, have been found in the bush still fighting the war despite its termination thirty-five years ago. Without knowledge of the resolution of the conflict in their minds, it continued despite no contact with the enemy (or friendly troops for that matter) for decades.

Another example is drawn from labor disputes. Workers about to strike or already on strike must keep abreast of union action during the final negotiating sessions. However, frequently these sessions are closed; hence it is impossible to find out what agreements are being made to resolve the conflict. So, occasionally workers adhere, in the absence of alternative information, to the strike deadlines despite the fact that an agreement has been made.

Finally, when conflicts are depending on court dockets, those with similar cases or controversies suspend action while awaiting a decision. Court decisions are rendered in either broad or narrow language; broad rulings effectively resolve a variety of similar conflicts, more narrow rulings encourage litigants to continue to use the courts as a conflict arena.

Davison (1974) has devoted considerable effort to analyzing the role of mass media in minimizing the frequency of social conflict and assisting in its resolution. First, the quantity of information available to potential parties in conflict will, if great enough, minimize conflict. With information, parties are less likely to resort to violence, particularly if they have built up a reserve of good will. Mass media can contribute in this regard through dissemination of cross cultural information, leading to the proverbial "better understanding between peoples." In addition, smaller scale actions such as the establishment of hot lines for immediate clarification of uncertainties, or student exchanges for long-term understanding of potentially opposing cultures, scientific exchanges, or even tourism further promote these goals. Finally, contrary to common censorship practices, constraining the flow of information does not contribute to security or conflict minimization, instead it may enhance the prospects for misunderstanding, as well as undermine crosspressures for tension reduction emanating from nonofficial channels.

Davison also argues for increasing the quality of communications as a method of conflict management and resolution. In particular, he cites the importance of accurate transmission of information. In turn, this requires there be two-way, interactive exchanges with sufficient channel capacity for many simultaneous messages. Avoiding loaded and/or vague terms and especially circumventing arousing emotion laden symbols can be important. And last, message transmission in which both translation and semantic problems can be avoided are most likely to prevent conflict expansion and enhance resolution.

A particular role for the mass media can be played by serving as early warning mechanisms in potential conflict situations. As a crisis emerges, steps can be taken to work out a solution, or at least understand the depths of the problem. Moreover, because much government (or bureaucratic) action is reaction to emergencies rather than long-term strategic planning, early warning provides an opportunity for decisions based on deliberation rather than muddling through. Speculation in the mass media about the consequences of conflict may also result in pressure to seek satisfactory resolutions before a conflict expands.

For conflict resolution, mass media may play an important role by encouraging resolution through words rather than through violence or other hostilities. News organizations in particular (see Chapter 9) have the capacity to assist in the negotiation process by serving as intermediaries between parties in conflict. Information released to news organizations by one side is heard by the other side. A willingness to negotiate or a subtle change in negotiating position may not be declared at a bargaining table, but will be discussed "off the record" with journalists, or raised in a backgrounder or through a trial balloon. Even in the intense conflict in the Middle East, "Cronkite diplomacy" was able to contribute to the peace process. By proceeding through news intermediaries, invitations to negotiate were offered.

Not only do mass media play an intermediary role, they are also in a position to contribute to resolution by voicing editorial opinions and providing forums for the introduction of new ideas by those not in conflict. For low level conflicts, mass media may provide maximum amounts of information, and bring items to the attention of negotiators or mediators. Overall, the prestige of mass media may play a positive role in conflict resolution through the actual content of media.

Davison goes on to suggest that content alone is only one possible avenue of aid from the mass media in conflict resolution. Perhaps as important is the mood created by mass media conducive to harmony rather than conflict. Both government decision makers and citizens have moods influenced by mass media, particularly in terms of trust, values, perceived hostility, and so forth. The tone of a crisis (or even the fact that it is a crisis) can be altered by mass media reporting. Of course, it is assumed that there is a degree of independence exhibited by mass media, otherwise media moods reflect official policy.

The final role for mass media in conflict situations is to mobilize. Although Davison emphasizes mobilization for peace and conflict resolution, the result may be mobilization to join the conflict. Overall, however, actions for the resolution of conflict may be coordinated through wide attention to a conflict.

Substantive examples to illustrate these points are drawn from the role of mass media in conflict resolution in the Middle East. Davison cites modern events intermingled with historical animosities. Arab-Israeli communication, for example, has been relatively low. As a result of the insufficient quantity of information, historical fears, ill will, and hostility have thrived, accompanied by mutual misunderstanding of regional goals. So little information is provided on opposing cultures that there is even relatively little knowledge of technical advances made in the opposing country. Consequently, feelings of social/intellectual/cultural superiority emerge, making resolution all the more difficult. Relations are further hampered by the absence of first hand reports in the media of the enemies. Instead, all actors rely on third-party reports in which they have little faith and perceive other interests. Extreme pressures exist within each culture to avoid virtually all contact or information exchange; limited mail, travel, and business exchange combined with no media reports prevent understandings.

Because of all these factors, the decision by Anwar Sadat to visit Israel, following a round of "Cronkite diplomacy" in 1977, was indeed historic on two levels. First, it opened directly the channels of communication between Israel and Egypt as an important step towards mutual understanding at an interpersonal level. In addition, Sadat's initiative led to a wave of follow-up visits to Egypt by Israeli journalists and others who would be in a position to widely disseminate their perspectives and first hand accounts of Egypt to domestic audiences. Overall, Sadat's initiative, despite its failure to lead to immediate peace, was an essential step in moving towards conflict resolution by March, 1979.

Second, Sadat's invitation to Israel underscored the potential of even third party mass media in conflict resolution. Originally, Sadat was asked in an interview with Walter Cronkite if he planned certain peace initiatives. Sadat responded that he was prepared to visit Israel if necessary for peace. At the same time, Prime Minister Menachim Begin, when interviewed, declared he would receive the Egyptian president. Thus, through electronic interviews with a third party correspondent, a match was struck. Once Sadat's visit began, news coverage was extensive in the United States as well as in Egypt and Israel, including person-on-the-street interviews with Egyptians and Israelis, an in-depth report on a kibbutz, descriptions of Jewish and Islamic rituals. Both officials and ordinary citizens were included in media reports and analysis; their expressions of optimism were mutually encouraging. Indeed it could be argued that so much enthusiasm and optimism was engendered that there was a considerable letdown when an immediate agreement was not reached. For third parties such as the United States, official policies shifted in response to the event to a more evenhanded approach. In large part, Sadat's personable style and media charm aided his efforts.

In many ways, the Sadat visit to Israel met many of the requirements for conflict resolution suggested by Davison. He argued that only expanded communications in the Middle East could prevent the generation or spread of stereotypes and that a top priority was to break ground for negotiations. Although this was accomplished, expectations for a settlement, which has yet to be met were also raised as attention was focused on the Middle East.

The significance of communicative interaction in the conflict processes has been examined more empirically than by Davison. Donohue, Tichenor, and

Olien (1975), for example, explore the relationships among levels of conflict, mass media and the "knowledge gap." Ordinarily, there is a considerable difference (i.e., a knowledge gap) between the highly educated and the less well educated, or between high and low media users in terms of their levels of information on a variety of subjects. However, in high conflict situations, there is a relatively low knowledge gap, suggesting that those on the socio/political periphery do gain access to information when significant issues arise. In particular, this finding has significance for power relationships within a community (see Chapter 6). A gap in knowledge leads to a deprivation of power, because possession of information is a key variable in power situations. Groups or individuals ordinarily excluded from power by a lack of knowledge of the issues are included in high-conflict situations. Donohue, Tichenor, and Olien hasten to point out that several variables may intervene in the status/knowledge gap relationship, among them the fundamentality of the issue in question, the homogeneity or pluralism of the community, patterns of media coverage, and the level at which the conflict occurs. Overall, local issues in homogeneous communities are characterized by a lower knowledge gap than national issues in pluralistic communities, but far more important is the conflict level of the issues. Interestingly, in general the patterns of media coverage were irrelevant to the knowledge gap.

In highly symbolic conflicts, of course, levels of information may be less relevant. Similarly, in intensely emotional situations rationality may be unimportant. Consequently, conflicts in many circumstances find their resolution independent of information despite Davison's arguments. However, interpersonal communication and interaction are sometimes cited as possible means of conflict reduction if not resolution. Business and pleasure travel, for example, have been argued to be important contributors towards international understanding. Addressing this issue, Salter and Teger (1975) suggest that international contact *per se* does not guarantee favorable attitudes (i.e., lessened conflict), but the *quality* of interaction is essential. Tourists, for example, having a fundamentally positive experience but little personal contact with foreigners, were found to have had their positive feelings enhanced by their travels. Individuals who worked with foreigners, however, had negative feelings reinforced by their experiences. Although not definitive, these data, too, suggest that interactions do not guarantee the wherewithal of conflict reduction.

As a final study linking communication and conflict, it is important to consider Singer's study (1972) of Detroit rioters. During periods of social conflict such as a riot, communication turned out (at least for the respondents— all of whom were riot arrestees) to be an important factor. Rioters, like decision makers, depend on both interpersonal and mass communication for their riot information. Essentially, how to riot is learned through awareness of activities in other locales; within the city during a riot, mass media (Davison not withstanding) enlarged the disturbance by indicating a riot was occurring and stating its location. Thus, for all the opportunity mass media have for conflict reduction, (including peacemakers pleading with rioters through mass media to return to their homes) there are significant chances to expand the conflict or increase the number of participants.

THE FUNCTIONS OF CONFLICT:
A COMMUNICATION PERSPECTIVE

Conflict is often thought of as dysfunctional to social systems because it introduces strains, tensions, and disharmony within communities. Coser (1956) demonstrated that a number of positive functions are introduced with conflict, ranging from the clarification of ideology through creation of wiser and more experienced leaders. From a communications perspective, there are at least four functions of social conflict.

First, social conflict may open lines of communication where none had existed before, or where the channels were clogged. Two opposing actors may even be unaware of each other's existence until a conflict arises in which each has a stake. Even actors with interests in common, fighting for the same goals, but also unaware of each other, may form a coalition when introduced to each other in conflict. Groups formerly in opposition over one issue and without communication as a result of their former conflict, may find themselves reestablishing linkages in agreement on the new issue. Overall, there is a creation of mutual interest from conflict, and a certain integrative function of conflict.

Second, social conflict is a valuable communication mode, particularly for the politically inarticulate. Moreover, for those in positions of political leadership, conflict may serve as a danger signal, i.e., that some within the systems are discontent. As explained in Chapter 3, the politically inarticulate do not have the resources or skills for participation in many decision-making arenas. Consequently, when they take to the street in protests, riots, or other nontraditional participation to have their voices heard, recognition by decision makers is assured, if not welcomed. For the disenfranchised, protest as a communication resource establishes a presence, coaxing those who would remain on the sidelines to join, and reassuring them that there are like-minded political inarticulates who have demands to make in the system. For decision makers, the absence of visible social conflict lulls them into a sense of complacency and false security, rendering them unprepared for the explosive potential of the inarticulate that is system threatening. Thus, for all parties, conflict serves as a functional signal.

Third, conflict may serve as a catalyst for otherwise considered but unimplemented change, particularly if the conflict is visible. Decision makers are forced to react to certain conflict activities, hastening a response. The response, of course, reflects on the success or failure of the conflict for the parties. A recent example might be the success of civil rights sit-in demonstrations, which often were met with force and violence, thereby escalating the conflict for only one side. By using such tactics, those using violence were condemned by external observers, and the successes of the protest were assured. Arguably, conflict may at times act as a negative catalyst as sympathy and support for violated people increase as result of extralegal activity.

Finally, conflict may serve internal communication functions for group members such as defining group boundaries or increasing group loyalties. To a degree, social conflict increases social communication among the members, who in the absence of conflict, lose touch with one another. In particular, propaganda campaigns within a nation are a good example of this phenomenon. As citizens are encouraged to rally around the flag in time of crises, they develop a new national purpose and reinforce their identity. Lesser social cleavages are dropped in favor of broad unity. Even in smaller organizations, similar principles apply as a conflict takes shape; either people must reaffirm group loyalties or withdraw. In the absence of conflict, peripheral identifiers are not required to make such a commitment.

CONFLICT VARIABLES

In the analysis of conflict from a communications perspective, there are five relevant variables: size, scope, intensity, visibility, and dynamism. Many of these concepts derive from Schattschneider (1960) through Cobb and Elder (1972).

Size refers to the number of individuals (or groups) involved in a conflict. The size of a conflict may expand through dissemination of information about its existence (or may decline from the lack of information) and inclusion of new actors. Long term conflicts may increase in size through population increases (e.g., consider the Hatfield-McCoy clan conflicts after several generations). The notion of size (sometimes called scale [Wilson & Wilson, (1948)]) is related to the modernity of communications within a society, suggesting that conflicts in modern nations are larger in size than those within less modern nations because of greater literacy, speed of transmission, and so forth. Indeed, a variety of environmental conditions may effect size: transportation, navigability of waterways, mountains, etc. Arguably, size of conflicts is one way in which one might differentiate between modern and traditional cultures.

Conflict scope refers to the range of phenomena over which there is controversy, how many activities, values, resources, and so forth are involved. Scope is particularly important with reference to the expansion of conflict. At the outset, a controversy may be limited to a single element. However, to attract more conflict participants (i.e., increase the size), actors may expand the scope of a controversy. A good example is cited by Gusfield (1963) in his study of the Temperance Movement referenced in Chapter 3. Rather than simply addressing the issue of the prohibition of the sale of alcoholic beverages, more issues were incorporated so that the conflict became a general one between the rural and urban, or between the old and new immigrants, or other basic social cleavages.

Even government actions such as the War on Poverty of the Johnson Administration expanded the scope of the "War" to include many fronts and greater general support. As a final example, Hacker's (1962) study of a trucker's conflict being redefined during the conflict, demonstrates a changing scope. At the outset, the issue was simple: how much tonnage is permissible. But the conflict grew in scope (and in symbolic significance) to include questions such as who sets policy for public safety, anti-trust regulation, and ultimately the issue of free speech and the right to influence legislators. Throughout, an expanding or changing scope requires continuous updating of messages and careful integration of themes during the transition from issue to issue.

The intensity of conflict refers to its significance and the extent to which it occupies agenda time. In many ways, the intensity of a conflict is revealed in the commitment for involvement exhibited by the parties in conflict. Often the conflicts of the shortest duration are the most intense, consuming all the energies of the parties in the conflict before exhaustion or ennui set in. From a communications perspective, intensity has implications for channel usage and crowding. Channels of communication between conflicting actors as well as within organizations in conflict may become clogged as messages exceed channel capacity. Intense conflicts, therefore, require special or unusual channels for message carrying to assure open channels.

Conflicts can also be considered in terms of their visibility. This is important on two levels. First, visibility is related to the number of outsiders aware of a conflict. Second, recruitment to a conflict depends on visibility. Visibility in turn depends on variables ranging from the power of the participants, location within the political system, desire of the parties to present or obscure the conflict, and especially, the decisions of news gathering and disseminating media to publicize the conflict once they are aware of its existence. To a large extent, conflicts can be smothered by a failure to publicize them and have new joiners sustain them.

Finally, conflicts vary in their dynamism. To be sure, there are long standing disagreements that smolder for centuries, but rarely flare up, and there are others of brief duration. But each conflict changes over time, though the extent to which they do so varies. Conflicts may pass through several stages, moving from a specific controversy, to a more general unease. Again the Temperance Movement serves as an example, as conflict moved from the sale of alcohol to a more general conflict of power and prestige in society. As conflicts generalize, symbols are involved, further generalizing and creating ambiguities in the conflict. Conflicts often become multidimensional as they evolve, moving from a general disagreement over a value or resource allocation to a personal animosity and antagonism. Many wartime propaganda campaigns include ethnic and racial epithets to personalize the enemy; even election campaigns often move from issues based on disagreements to personal mudslinging campaigns. Inherent in this process is the danger of a total collapse of communication channels between the parties in conflict as they refuse to deal with one another. At this point, mediators may be necessary to rechannel messages directed toward conflict resolution. Conflicts in which personal antagonism emerges may be resolved, but the seeds are already planted for future conflicts because of deep seated animosity. Finally, new issues emerge in dynamic conflicts. Over time, however, peripheral issues brought in as arguments for the issue are exhausted, or new issues are needed to sustain conflict interest.

Ultimately, of course, conflicts are usually brought under control, placing a finite parameter on their dynamism. First, if a conflict is within a system or organization, solutions may be imposed from within the organizational hierarchy. Established rules and procedures for resolving union grievances with management, for example, limit the extent and duration of a conflict. Under unusual circumstances, hierarchies fail to resolve the conflict and the resolution becomes unsatisfactory, leading to conflict expansion (i.e., in the union example, a wildcat strike or lockout). International disputes are hardly resolvable within an organizational framework; both the United Nations and the International Court of Justice have no severe sanctions to impose on those who do not willingly comply with their proposed solutions. In the international arena, therefore, conflicts, if they do not end by mutual agreement of the parties involved often have their solutions imposed from the outside, particularly when they involve smaller nations. A rebel uprising in Zaire may be temporarily suppressed by European paratroop forces; a conflict in the Middle East can be terminated by a failure of superpowers to ship arms; a minority government in Rhodesia can be virtually ousted by sanctions and less political support by South Africa. Although such solutions are not always satisfactory to the parties involved, they do terminate conflicts. Finally, in the international arena and elsewhere, cross pressures can lead to conflict resolution. Individuals (or nations) with access to information from both sides, by either joint membership or mutual trust, are in a unique position to find similarities in bargaining positions that lead to conflict reduction and resolution. In the international arena, shuttle diplomacy of Henry Kissinger provides a good example. Having earned the trust of both Egypt and Israel, Kissinger was able to help conclude an interim first-stage agreement for peace negotiations and troop withdrawals in the Sinai peninsula. Indeed, all mediators operate by finding those points of agreement available only to those with information from both sides.

CONFLICT AND COMMUNICATION:
AN OVERVIEW

Overall, the relationship of social conflict to communications processes is a complex one. Within groups, conflict need not be dysfunctional for it may serve to bind the membership together by providing an identifiable enemy around which to communicate and about which symbols may be developed. Group cohesiveness can be fostered through increasing internal communication linkages.

Across groups, social conflict does not necessarily disrupt the channels of communication linking social actors, but may instead create channels where they were dormant or nonexistent before. In conflict, actors are bound together as relationships are created and sustained to work toward a resolution (at least until antagonism has overwhelmed the desire for resolution). Even if there is prior interaction, an interesting paradox is presented. Arguably, the greater the level of prior interaction, the greater the size, scope, and intensity of a conflict. If channels of communication exist, presumably they will be utilized for the transmission of conflict information.

The channels for handling conflict in a given social system have significance for system longevity. In Figure 3.3 for example, sufficient capacity for demands to travel from citizens to decision makers as well as adequate capacity for the return of decisions to citizens, minimize system tension and stress. Similarly, systems providing channels for grievances (i.e., rights to petition or lawfully assemble) ordinarily exhibit little system threat. Of course, all systems potentially may experience channel overload when there are simply too many demands made at the same time.

When this occurs there is no time to separate cues or act on relevant information. Crisis decision-making results in less than optimal solutions. In developed systems, this occurs less than in developing systems because demands are fed into the system by queuing up, conflicts are sequentially introduced for resolution and conflicts over agenda priorities are worked out on the basis of strength and access. Moreover, those demands presented by the inarticulate, unless system threatening, are dismissed as illegitimate and are not introduced into the agenda. It should, however, be noted that frequently, because the cost of communicating with decision makers is so great (litigation, lobbying, regulatory agency rulings, etc.), conflicts are not put before officials for resolution. Conflicting actors therefore usually seek to establish channels for communicating without official participation by decision-making bodies. Only through direct negotiation can fidelity of communication be assured, and information imparted that is essential to conflict resolution.

All of this suggests, at the very least some degree of integration of actors is necessary as a precondition for conflict resolution. Some theorists have argued conflict and integration to be undimensional concepts at opposite ends of a continuum. Such, apparently, may not be the case, for some degree of integration is necessary to both cause conflict and resolve it, because of the communication aspects of conflict.

INTEGRATION

Although not on a continuum, conflict is similar to integration in at least two respects. First, both integration and conflict exist only through interchange and communication. Second, at times both concepts serve largely symbolic functions; our interest in symbols compels their consideration.

Integration refers to an amalgamation of groups or communities such that they share a common identity. Described in symbolic terms, these groups are oriented toward the same symbols and give a relatively uniform meaning to those symbols. Thus most modern nation-states are what may be termed politically integrated: responsive to the same government actions, laws, and symbols. Some states, of course, exhibit less national integration with regional loyalties or even kinship orientations being more significant. But in both cases, integration is defined through communications transactions.

Communication linkages as a basis for integration have been discussed in Deutsch's (1953) early work on social communication and nationalism. Rather than consider integration to be defined through geography, language, markets, or some other indicators, it is defined through integration of all exchange media. Deutsch argues that the world is actually a series of clusters linked by social communication, and indeed, a people or culture is defined by the complementariness and efficiency of communication (i.e., mutual understanding and commonality of language, be it natural language, symbolic language, or even commodity bartering). Where this efficiency breaks down, the cluster boundaries are established. Within a cluster, at least for Deutsch, power (see Chapter 6) is defined largely in terms of access to social communication facilities.

Social communication as an integrative concept is not limited only to language based message exchange. Arguably, there are three objects of exchange that link groups: goods, people, and messages. Goods exchanged include imports and exports; people exchanged may include students, business travellers, tourists, diplomats, or cultural groups; and messages and information may be exchanged through mail, telephone calls, telegraph, airline flights, books, radio, television, and film. Within nations these linkages are greatest; across national borders they decline.

Defining integration in these exchange terms requires that we assume a greater volume of exchange and means greater information exchange for increased understanding. Volume of exchange, however, is insufficient because the salience of exchanges as well as their symmetry make a difference. Deutsch and Singer (1964), for example, argue that there are integration thresholds below which exchanges have little salience. As volume increases and begins to occupy much or all of the total exchange, attention is commanded, and it becomes impossible to maintain exchange indifference. The symmetry of communication exchanges provides clues to the durability of relationships. In superordinate/subordinate relations, or in colonial relationships, one party dominates the exchanges and relational leadership while retaining dependence of the subordinate. In the long run, however, asymmetrical relations do not prosper as dependent parties seek more equitable relationships. Presumably, some asymmetrical relationships can be sustained if there is complementary asymmetry, with each side contributing to the relationship.

Integration has also been approached and conceptualized from a learning theory perspective. Teune (1964) and others suggest that a community is best understood in terms of responses to symbolic cues and the associated feelings of loyalty—"we-ness"—and attention to similar stimuli. In other words, political integration can be viewed in terms of people uniformly responding to stimuli and responding to each other as stimuli. For Teune, integration is thus a question of identification, where stimuli become significant through the socialization process (see Chapter 7). As an example, from an early age, children are rewarded for being identified as "American" and for responding to appropriate stimuli (usually symbols). This view even explains the political stability of prosperous countries. Because all rewards descend from government allocation decisions, identification with and responsiveness to the government is rewarded. Of course, fear of punishment may serve as a negative reward in some nations to encourage national identification.

Recognizing the importance of rewards and punishments in identification and integration, propaganda campaigns are often oriented toward shifting rewards. Whether it be greater freedom, material wealth, or an end to oppression, revolutionary forces promise new rewards to ensure that they will be responded to as significant stimuli. Overall, while a simple S-R paradigm may not fully explain political integration, it offers some insight into the importance of developing symbols to serve as widely recognized stimuli and the significance of publicizing outputs as rewards for successful participation in the game.

INTEGRATION AND CONFLICT

Previously in this chapter, it was argued that conflict may bring strangers together. But we also noted that where there already is some ongoing interchange, conflicts frequently arise. In other words, conflict is inevitable on many occasions. Integration theorists have argued that as transactions increase in intensity and extensity, there will be more connecting links, hence more bargaining, cross pressures, and other conflict reduction mechanisms to minimize hostility. Drawing from Meier's (1962) work on urban growth, some explanations for seemingly contradictory positions, and the accompanying inevitability of conflict can be offered.

In urban space, as elsewhere, frequency of communication is related to physical proximity, as expressed by Figure 4.1. At short distances, communication is very frequent, at greater distances it declines. Distance may be physical, social, or even political; those remote from one another in salient areas may have little cause for interaction.

In Figure 4.2, the relationship between cohesion and frequency of communication is charted. Where there is little integration, there is no communication. At middle levels of communication there is substantial integration, but then the curve bends backward and more communication is associated with declining integration and cohesiveness as a saturation effect is introduced. Familiarity, in a sense, breeds contempt, and too much interaction leads to conflict.

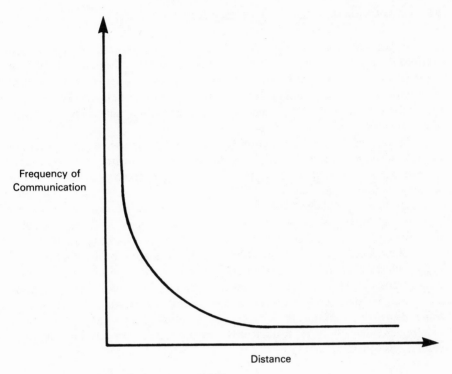

Figure 4.1 [After Meier, 1962.]

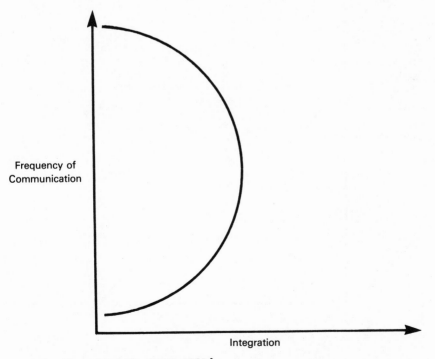

Figure 4.2 [After Meier, 1962.]

Figure 4.3 combines Figures 4.1 and 4.2, relating social distance to integration, suggesting that integration (or cohesion, or attractiveness) is highest at medium distances. This fits with the discussions of conflict, in that frequent transactions result in conflict (i.e., nonintegrative conflicts) because of the saturation effects, and, at the same time, low levels of interaction make conflicts easier because cohesiveness and comprehension is low.

Studies of political integration have focused on supranational integration as well as national integration. In particular, much research has emphasized European integration in such organizations as the Common Market (EEC) or security communities such as NATO. In each case, difficulties have been engendered by problems of multiple loyalties and what can be considered problems of homogeneity. As noted earlier, homogeneity is a minimum requirement for message compatibility, which in turn is required for integration.

Homogeneity requires compatibility, and mutual responsiveness to similar cues, including identification of common interests and intensive and extensive interactions. There must be, moreover, expectations of joint rewards, finite limitations to the parameters of conflict and conflict resolution, and, hopefully, some degree of ethnic and linguistic assimilation. Historically, these latter requirements have been most difficult to meet, even in fully integrated national federations (see Chapter 11).

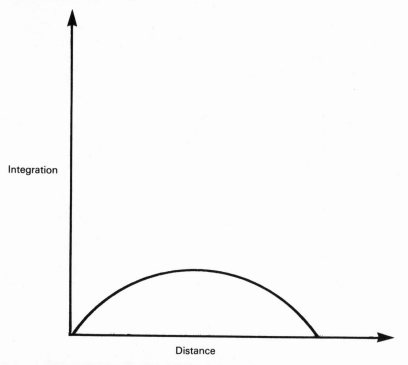

Figure 4.3 [After Meier, 1962.]

The relationship of integration to conflict is a complicated one. To be sure, conflict is descriptive of non-harmonious relations and creates certain animosities, but at the same time may bring parties closer together at its conclusion. And frequently, conflict emerges from substantial integration. Conflict with no interaction is impossible, so conflict and integration are not polar opposites. Indeed, they can be viewed as different variables on which interacting dyads are placed, as in Figure 4.4. Both conflict and cooperation (integration) can be found in any relationship. The Common Market, for example, is characterized by high conflict between its members; but conflict resulting from multidimensional cooperative agreements. At the other extreme, conflict hardly arises between two nations that have virtually no interactions, such as Angola and Fiji. Other dyads reveal elements of high conflict with low cooperation (China-USSR) and low conflict high cooperation (US-Canada).

The samples used in discussion throughout this section have been mostly of international integration, primarily because when occurring within a political system, increasing integration is one element of political development, a topic to which we now turn as another political concept with communications origins.

POLITICAL DEVELOPMENT

In a handful of pages, it is impossible to even hint at the complexities of political development, even when concentrating only on its communications relevance. All systems develop over time, but from such different levels that no single explanation fits all. This section, therefore, is limited to discussing only a single aspect of political development of new nations emerging from colonial pasts, and for which the modern nation-state is a new concept.

COOPERATION

		High	Low
CONFLICT	High	Common Market	China-U.S.S.R.
	Low	U.S.-Canada	Angola-Fiji

Figure 4.4

The goals of most political systems, regardless of the methods chosen for their attainment, are usually the same: order, stability, and prosperity, although not always in that sequence. The question for most analyses of political development from a communications perspective is how communications processes and institutions can help attain these goals. Traditionally, political development is defined as the process of integrating a nation so that the government becomes effective in serving as a source of policy output and efficient in gathering demands. Students of political development writing for the Committee on Comparative Politics of the Social Science Research Council (Pye, 1963; LaPalombara, 1963; Almond & Coleman, 1960; Coleman, 1965; Pye & Verba, 1965; LaPalombara & Weiner, 1966; and Binder et al., 1966) have offered notions, such as demonstrating effective control, increasing participation or efficiency in rule making, application, and ajudication, but each of these is tied to specific functions of a government.

A more general approach to political development is derived from general systems theory. System development is characterized by at least three phenomena. First, there is increasing complexity of the system and its interactions. In other words, the interrelationships of the components change. Second, not only do the component relationships change, but the level of exchange increases. Interactions are more frequent and qualitatively differ, and the range of phenomena subject to transaction increases. This, of course, closely relates to the concept of integration described earlier. Third, development is characterized by system movement toward the goal state—presumably order, stability, and prosperity.

Whether one uses a traditional or a systems approach, studied from a communications perspective, three major issues in political development emerge: (1) the relationships of communications institutions to the evolving political institutions processes; (2) the role of the political system in expanding communications networks; and (3) the role of mass media as a change agent in evolving systems. Some of these issues are significant at the individual level of analysis, others are more meaningful when considering the system as a whole.

In developing systems, communications institutions have the major burden of establishing nationhood and reorienting individual loyalties toward the national level. Interpersonal communication is less useful in this regard, because ordinary contacts are with those in already established relationships—kinships, tribes, or regions. Instead, familiarization with a higher level system must be established, as must a recognition of new institutions and modes of leadership. Recognizing this, political systems concentrate early on developing communication systems beyond the traditional interpersonal mode. More than anything, mass media are looked upon as important agents of social change—be it among peasants, (Rogers, 1962) or residents of Rovere (Merton, 1949). In a sense, what is being introduced is the diffusion of innovation, but of national concepts, not programs. Only recently have communications scholars (Rogers, 1976a, 1976b) begun to realize that mass mobilization and political development, rather than economic development, literacy, or unlimited media expansion were the real burdens of communication.

There are certain differences among the various media that have bearing on their utility in fostering development. Electronic media clearly are the most costly to initiate, yet are most effective where literacy rates are low. Community television and/or radio offer unusual opportunities for nation building orientations, as well as specific economic development projects requiring these media for instructional purposes. Print media, where comprehensive, are of less value because of a literacy requirement, and also because they require sacrifice in the form of a daily purchase. In addition, distribution costs of newspapers where transportation facilities are inadequate are too high to support national newspapers. New technologies, particularly through the introduction of satellites, can lower costs of electronic information sources considerably, hastening the national integration process. Of course, there are still a number of harmful media effects in developing systems. These result from raising expectations of citizens, which as Gurr (1970) and others suggest, leads to ever increasing levels of frustration and aggression. Rising expectations, created through exposure to the quality of life in more modern nations, (through demonstration effects) can rarely be met. Consequently, there is considerable censorship imposed to limit the demonstration problem.

This discussion of media introduction emphasizes only two aspects of development—national orientation and social mobilization. Some have argued, however, that social control is a much more important dimension of development. Frey (1963), for example, suggests power is at the core of political development, and that power is exercised through the control of channels of communication (see Chapter 6). Communication processes play at least three important roles in social control. First, information may be severely limited. News of dissent, revolutionary activity, and so forth may be absent from media reports. Particularly in geographically large countries, sections can be isolated by central information control. In addition to the control of information *per se,* channels of information may be controlled similarly to limit demands, or to promulgate policies. The significance of control of communication channels is recognized in developing nations themselves. Among the first priorities of revolutionary governments, following coup d'etats, is gaining control of the electronic media to broadcast success and imposing censorship on print media. In addition, even terrorists frequently communicate information on bombings or kidnappings directly to news media. In all likelihood, two reasons for this exist. First, access to communication channels is assured. Secondly, in developing nations as in developed nations, there is a status conferral function of mass media: to appear is to be a significant actor.

Several scholars have attempted to examine the relationship between communication and development through empirical analysis. Lerner (1959), for example, looks at the modernization of nations as emerging from the interplay of urbanization, literacy, and media exposure ultimately leading to increased participation. The centrality of media lies largely in increasing mobility, opening new vistas through armchair travel, and vicarious wisdom. Media systems, Lerner argues, have different channels, audiences, content, and sources than premedia oral systems. For media systems, the channels are broadcast or mediated, whereas for oral systems they are interpersonal. Audiences are mass and hetero-generous rather than intimate, the content is descriptive (news) rather than prescriptive (rules), and finally, the sources are professionals with skill rather than hierarchically selected individuals based on status. Overall, the differences between media based and oral based systems are so profound that total political upheavals are likely to occur surrounding the replacement of oral-traditional systems by media.

Pye (1963) more or less accepts this view, arguing that communication is really the key to differences between traditional and modern societies. Using more system oriented language, he describes how bifurcated systems can emerge with the introduction of modern communications technologies. Some segments of the system (usually elite, urbanized) rely on new communications whereas others are excluded, remaining traditional. The system fails to integrate; instead it becomes increasingly differentiated, experiencing uneven development. Potentially modern communication offers great promise for expanding, not only the arm of government for policy dissemination, but channel availability for interest and demand articulation. The availability of channels, of course, does not guarantee their proper use (see Chapter 5), but for the politically articulate it greatly enhances opportunities. Finally, the socialization function (Chapter 7) is well served by expanded communication networks. Symbols of unity are easily identified and disseminated, and even beyond the use of the media for explicit political training, their utility lies in presenting the hidden politics of system support in instructional media.

Wilbur Schramm (1964) was probably the most optimistic writer on the powers of mass media to rapidly transform systems by allowing for smooth, even, and painless development. Even then, however, media introduction independent of traditional, interpersonal communication is bound to fail. Basically, Schramm argues for eight functions mass media may serve in developing nations, including focusing attention on problems of development, raising aspirations, enforcing social norms, teaching, confering status, and perhaps even changing attitudes and practices. Some of these may be dysfunctional for system stability, particularly if aspirations are raised beyond the capacity of the system to meet the aspirations or if new norms are created inconsistent with past practices. Still, the areas outlined provide a framework for testing media performance. Interestingly, both Schramm and Lerner (1976) joined to offer an updated conceptualization of political development and its relationship to communication.

Perhaps the most useful perspective on mass media and development appears in the more recent work of Lerner (1974), fifteen years after first considering the communication and development problems. In general, mass communication can only mediate between public policy and social organization. After all, policy emerges from government decision makers and, consistent with Figure 3.3, communications channels help to articulate and diffuse those policies to the governed. Thus, social organization emerges from the institutions established by decision makers and the governed.

Experiences of the past twenty years have shown the communications explosion to fail as a panacea for development. As Rogers (1976a) states, mass communication played only an indirect and contributory, rather than a direct and powerful, role. Certainly audiences have grown, and leaders find it easier to reach their people. Participation, although not automatically increasing, is encouraged. But the conflict between traditional and modern sectors has been somewhat accelerated. Demands have increased at a rate exceeding the capacity of the system to meet demands, leading to frustration and revolutionary action from rising expectations. At some level, suggests Lerner, we need research to systematically explore the communications processes and institutions link to social structures policy and performance in developing nations. Arguably, communication phenomena have created and sustained certain conditions leading to instability. These conditions must be examined closely.

CONFLICT, INTEGRATION, AND DEVELOPMENT

Though treated distinctly by many a political scientist, these three concepts have much in common: they are viewed best from a communication perspective and, moreover, are related. Conflict, as we have shown, builds and sustains relationships, opening channels where none were before, revitalizing dormant groups, creating symbolic identification, and so forth. Perhaps it can be said that there are certain integrative functions of conflict. Integration is really defined by quantitative and qualitative exchanges of messages, common response, and cooperative response to symbols, even those symbols emerging from conflict. At the national level we consider development of political systems as they evolve, become integrated, shift loyalties away from traditional authorities and respond to common cues. But at the same time, potential for conflict is engendered as expectations rise and frequency of communication increases beyond the saturation point until disintegration occurs. The three concepts are related largely through the communication channels central to each concept. Other aspects of communication are central to political participation, the subject of the following chapter.

5
POLITICAL PARTICIPATION

Citizens participate in politics in one form or another. Political participation has been the focus of political philosophy since Plato's time and of empirical inquiry in modern times. Indeed, it has even bridged the gap between political research and communications research more frequently than any other concept. Pioneers in communication research such as Paul Lazarsfeld and his associates chose one form of political participation—electoral behavior—as the focus of their earliest bridging inquiries.

In the context of democratic politics, voting is the most visible form of participatory activity. But all political systems have participation. To be sure, some participants are more active than others, and some systems encourage more activity than others, but even the most passive citizens are found in systems that have overthrown colonial powers or have revolutionary histories in which millions were mobilized. Passivity may result from oppression; it may result from contentment with the status quo. Whichever the case, passivity is a message with meaning to decision makers and fellow citizens.

Even in participatory systems where active contributions to the system are (at least superficially) encouraged, much of the citizenry remains passive. Why, for example do turnout percentages vary around fifty percent of all those eligible to vote, even in highly visible, well publicized U.S. elections? People forget, are too busy, or don't care. Perhaps they are content with the system; perhaps discontented, and feel they don't want to sanction the system with their participation, or, possibly, consider that their participation makes at best a marginal contribution to the operation of the system. In each case there is a political message, ambiguous as it may be. Popular political pundits like to argue that the candidates don't inspire voters, and that non-voting is a symbolic protest against tweedledee, tweedledum candidates. Mass society theorists argue that alienation and personal inefficacy abound and non-voting is only one manifestation of social withdrawal. Still others argue that it is a sign of system vitality when people are sure there is a social consensus as evidenced by their willingness to let others decide. One or all of these views may be accurate in explaining nonparticipation. Yet they all have in common the notion that there is a message communicated, or at least perceived to be communicated, by citizens regardless of their intentions. As long as other political actors such as decision makers react to these messages, whatever their meaning, citizen participation is communication.

PARTICIPATION AS COMMUNICATION

In the systems approach to political communication described in Chapter 3, citizens make demands and offer support for the political regime, as well as receive feedback about system decisional outputs. All of these activities require some degree of participation, some activity through which the citizen interacts with his or her political environment.

Participation, like the other major concepts described in Part II of this book, can be viewed in terms of communication variables, and as a communication phenomenon. At the very least, participation is a means of registering system support. Comparative politics researchers in the early 1960s (Almond & Verba, 1963; Lipset, 1960), using a system framework, found across cultures that citizens viewed participation sometimes as an obligation, but other times as expressive support. How else can citizens express support (or lack of support)? The exit option (Hirschman, 1970) rarely exists in political contexts, so in a sense people have no choice but to participate by either complying passively with governments, or by more active participation.

If all participate, then our concern is not so much with participation *per se*, as it is with the types and degrees of participation. As a language for political expression, participation is precise enough to allow for description and measurement of differences within, as well as across, cultures. Perhaps it is best to view participation on a continuum, where precision of communication increases as we move along.

Several researchers have developed continua, pyramids, or other schematic shapes to indicate different levels of participation. Milbrath and Goel (1977), for example, describe apathetics, spectators, and gladiators, including in each respective level, the inactives with no patriotic input, voters, patriots, and finally, attentives, party activists, protestors, and others who actively engage in politics. Similarly, Rosenau (1974) distinguishes between the attentive public at one end and the mobilized public at the other end. Nimmo (1978) writes of a general public, the attentive public, and the leadership public. In each schema, different specific participatory activities are associated with positions on the scale.

There is another way to view participation in political communication terms. First, participants may be classified by the amount of information they withdraw from the system. Information seeking is a type of political participation, and is a dimension across which individuals manifest substantial differences.

A second way is to consider each method of participatory activity cited by Milbrath and Goel (1977). Each participant—inactives, voters, contact specialists, communicators, party and campaign workers, community activists, protestors— offers a particular message.

All of these modes have in common the fact that they provide information to others in the system about their orientations, supports, and demands. Moreover, decision makers are required to respond to these messages. The extent to which they do, however, may be a function of how legitimate they perceive each channel to be.

MODES OF POLITICAL PARTICIPATION

Citizens participate primarily for three reasons. First, they must communicate their needs to political decision makers, or at the very least to intermediaries such as news organizations, political parties, and so forth. Often these needs are extremely narrow and personal. More system oriented demands are a second reason for participating: to establish system goals. Usually such goals are established directly by public officials, but the selection of public officials in numerous political systems offers citizens the opportunity to choose from among candidates or party platforms professing different system goals. Even in nondemocratic systems, nontraditional modes of participation such as political violence, demonstrations, and especially revolutions (e.g., Iran) offer opportunities to establish goals and set social priorities. Finally, with reference again to Figure 3.3, citizens participate to show their support—or lack of support —for the system and its leaders. Regardless of the mode of participation sanctioned by the system, opportunities to communicate levels of support exist through passive resistance, pro-government rallies, and so forth.

It is difficult, if not impossible for citizens to avoid participating. Improved transportation and communication put everyone within reach of governments. Moreover, the scope of government activities has expanded so much that nearly any activity in which a citizen engages involves at least passive interaction with government. The simple act of taking a pleasure drive through the country on a Saturday afternoon involves much government. The fact that one is not working on Saturday is a partial result of labor legislation. The road was constructed with public funds. Traffic regulations, such as driving on the right hand side of the road, are all government decrees. The right to drive is granted by government license. Similarly, the vehicle, constructed according to specifications for safety and fuel economy issued by government, must also be registered with and licensed by government.

Most, if not all of us passively accept these regulations. Indeed the fact that most of us obey the laws and do follow traffic regulations and secure licenses for ourselves and our cars can be interpreted as a message of system support. The fear of fines or incarceration for failure to obey the law may be a reason to obey for some. But others approve of the regulations, preferring regulation and traffic rules to anarchistic driving where unsafe vehicles driven by untested drivers on the wrong side of the road are life-threatening. These examples point to the most basic mode of citizen participation; general acceptance of government. Those who are hermits perhaps can avoid this form of participation, but in the daily existence of most people, merely going about one's private life implies acceptance of many government actions.

The driving example is by no means trivial, for there are examples indicating that not all regulations are passively accepted, even with respect to automobiles. Dissatisfaction with the 55 mph speed limit is communicated to government daily by the millions of violators who view 60 or 65 mph as an inalienable right. More than almost any other traffic law, the speed limit is disobeyed. Citizens who ordinarily are law abiding, actively and consciously violate the law, and, although not explicitly communicating demands to the government, do communicate nonsupport. Others, of course, such as truck drivers, have engaged in protests and "drive-ins" to more actively express their preferences as demands, in addition to speeding as a message of nonsupport.

Governments occasionally change policies to accommodate noncompliance that undermines support. Rather than face disobedience, officials cease enforcement of certain regulations. It is commonly accepted that motorists violating speed limits by less than five miles per hour will not be ticketed. As a second example, operators of citizen band radios were required to purchase licenses. But when the radios become popular and widely used, the fees for the license were dropped to provide an incentive to secure the license. Finally, when license applications overwhelmed the F.C.C. at a rate of 20,000 per day, they were no longer even read, but routinely approved. And, there is no effort to enforce the licensing law against the millions who have not even bothered to secure a license.

The truckers' protests involve a second form of participation: protests and demonstrations. In some systems, protests are the only form of participation, but more often they are among several options serving as political resources (Lipsky, 1968). A number of researchers have not considered protests and noncompliance as a form of participation, choosing to limit their analysis to legally sanctioned activities. Protests usually reflect both nonsupport for current policy, as well as an extension of demands. When alternative channels are blocked, or when visibility of demands is obscured by gatekeeping actors, protests offer opportunities for expression. To be sure, costs may be high—abuse, arrest, injury, or even death under some circumstances. But for assuring access, particularly when a protest is disruptive—protests guarantee that messages will be heard.

A third mode of participation is citizen-initiated contact with public officials. Citizens write letters to public officials registering their views on issues and making demands. They also personally visit the offices of officials from time to time. Of course, some contacts with public officials may be initiated by officials, as when people are summoned for jury duty or when industrial workers find aspiring political candidates appearing at the factory gates to shake their hands. But such interactions occur without agendas, and are so brief that little substantive communication can occur. Contact specialists' demands rarely reach the systemic agenda, but still, they try to avoid gatekeepers by directly expressing demands. Because they retain little leverage, they rarely succeed in altering decisions, but they can occupy channel space. Many a legislator spends considerable time pursuing requests of constituents for private bills, special favors, or other personal services. This time, of course, limits access to other information or demand channels.

Communicators participate by more regularly interacting with government officials and mass media, writing to them and keeping informed on numerous issues. Alone, they differ little from contact specialists. But collectively they resemble community activists. As members of political or economic organizations, they express demands of decision makers, and indicate the extent to which they can offer support for policies. Internal discussions allow these groups to serve as their own gatekeepers; once a group supports a demand, public officials are notified. Interest-group oriented political scientists argue that participants at this level are most influential in the system.

Traditionally, interest groups or lobbies have been comprised of business, labor, or other organizational interests. In recent years, however, so-called public interest lobbying organizations from Common Cause to Ralph Nader's groups to far more specialized or even single issue lobbies have emerged to offer citizens a collective voice as interest group participants. Interactions between lobbyists and public officials differ from those between private citizens and officials because of the occasional dependency of officials on interest groups and the consequential two way communication.

Some citizens become gladiators. These are the individuals who become actively involved in electoral politics. The degree of activity varies from contributing money to more active roles, such as campaigning or even running for elective office. Only a handful of people, percentage wise, actually hold office, but citizen participation to such an extent allows people to shift roles and become decision makers. Even in nonelectoral systems, participation at lower levels of the bureaucracy or party hierarchy serves as a training ground for ultimate ascension into decision-making roles.

Party and campaign workers, including those who run for office, clearly are working "within the system," and agreeing to abide by the rules, thus communicating reaffirmation of system rules. At the same time, they are in a better position than nonactivists to express their demands—especially if elected or supporting successful candidates.

By far the most common mode of participation in democratic and even many nondemocratic systems, aside from passive support, is voting. Long the focus of inquiry by political and communication researchers, voting has been considered to be the connecting link between citizens and politicians. Of course, only vague messages can be transmitted, and even then the range of possible messages is usually constrained by the number of candidates on the ballot. But many communication institutions have arisen surrounding elections, all of which allow for fresh inquiries into electoral participation.

Voting is often perceived as the communication of preferences, but more generally as an indicator of support. When there are specific policy votes, such as referenda, arguably voting is a form of demand (e.g., Proposition 13 in California as a taxpayer revolt, a modern Boston Tea Party). But even then, voting is on issues already selected by others or for candidates who have met party or other criteria. So voters either vote to place, retain, or expel people from office. But specific demands can only be expressed at the ballot box when there are clear differences in candidate positions—an unusual event to say the least. Overall, then, voting only broadly communicates support for political authorities.

Each of these modes of participation links up with our broad theory of political communication and the major concepts. They offer different patterns of interaction, and consequently different communication patterns with political officials. Different institutions arise to handle the participatory modes. For the major modes, citizen contacts (individual and lobbying), protests, and electoral politics (voting as well as running for office), the following sections offer more detailed discussion.

CITIZEN-INITIATED CONTACTS

Citizen-initiated contacts with decision makers may be either individual or collective. As private citizens, people may contact public officials because they desire some specific political output (such as a private bill) in the case of most instrumental contacts, or because they wish to express an issue preference, or even transmit instructions to elected public officials. Citizens may also communicate with (or rather, send messages to) news gathering organizations in the form letters to the editor or op-ed columns, largely to seek a public forum for the expression of their positions.

Whether the contacts are for the purpose of affecting policy or merely for personal gratification, the procedures are the same. Citizens are able to avoid some gatekeeping organizations and communicate their demands directly. Of course, there are still gatekeepers—editors of letters to the editor columns, staff assistants to public officials, or even receptionists who make decisions on the value of communications—but the usual gatekeepers are bypassed. If there were no costs to this form of private participation, the system would be overloaded. But writing letters to (not even personally visiting) public officials requires time, effort, and if done frequently, considerable expense. Often citizens are content to know the direct lines of communication are there; never feeling the need to use them.

Collective citizen contacts are somewhat different. Groups or individuals with a particular demand may join together into interest groups or lobbies, believing that there is a greater likelihood of success or lower cost of participating. Such groups develop their own organizational hierarchies and internal communication patterns, which, at times, lead such groups to concern themselves more with internal politics than substantive issues with which they are involved. But on the whole, they offer a stronger voice for citizens than they would have individually, as well as opportunities to compete with other organized interest groups in the decisional arenas.

The key elements in citizen-initiated contacts or lobbying are gaining access to decision makers (or intermediary news organizations), and gaining attention once access is secured. In other words, the opportunity to send messages complemented by the receipt of those messages is essential. Citizens are not normally part of the decision makers environment, consequently there is little information about their specific needs. On the one hand, this provides citizens with a chance to provide information without the usual noise. On the other hand, decision makers may decide they can exist without citizen input, and may ignore incoming messages.

In theory, decision makers in democratic systems are supposed to be attentive (if not responsive) to the needs and desires of their constituents. But factors ranging from role perceptions (see Chapter 8) to physical separation from constituents limit the frequency of interaction with constituents. Geographic distance, for example, limits the amount of interpersonal contact. Officials such as legislators may frequently visit their districts, but for most officials these visits are constrained by time and space.

Nevertheless, citizens do find ways to communicate directly with officials. The most frequent method is to write letters. At times, letters are individually written, but often they are inspired (or even written) by organizations to which citizens may or may not belong, but who have an interest in a specific policy outcome. Such inspired or volume mail is easily recognized by officials, and rarely given thoughtful consideration or personal reply. Indeed there is no method of citizen initiated contact that guarantees interaction with public officials.

Studies on congressional mail (Dexter, 1956) have supplied evidence for what officials do with letters. In most cases, mail is read routinely by clerks, particularly mail to senators. It is viewed skeptically by the recipient if for no other reason than it is not viewed as representative of the constituency. Moreover, experience has shown the mail to be less than creative (except where demands are made, in which case they are impossible to meet). Finally, given the effort usually required to learn about pending legislation, the conditions under which most citizens hear about a specific issue or controversy already makes their mail suspect.

Overall, these findings suggest that the most common citizen initiated contact is not effective. But other contacts such as telegrams, phone calls, or even personal visits to offices are similarly less than useful. Some evidence suggests (Brody & Tufte, 1964) that legislators are better off soliciting information in the form of polls than in waiting for citizen contact, for at least return of questionnaires becomes demographically or sociologically biased (i.e., those more likely to respond) rather than issue biased. Collectively, citizens have a greater impact when initiating contacts with public officials than when acting individually. Groups may offer (explicitly or implicitly) electoral support (or threats), collective wisdom, expertise, or other assistance. Even if outcomes are rarely swayed by groups, they have greater access than individuals.

Groups ordinarily represent themselves as trade associations, organizations or other collectivity, or hire specific individuals or lobbyists to represent their interests on a time sharing basis. A variety of methods of gaining access and potential influence with decision makers are used, many of which have been studied by Milbrath (1960) in his work on Congressional lobbyists.

The basis for much lobbying strength lies in the need for information that virtually all decision makers have. Not all necessary data are readily available from the government internal research services. In addition, the haste with which information is needed often causes decision makers to rely on outside organizations that assemble data and expert information. Perhaps the greatest asset of collective participants is their expertise.

The need for information puts the lobbyists in a somewhat difficult position, wherein roles are strained. On the one hand, lobbyists become important sources of information for public officials who come to depend on them. On the other hand, they are responsible for advocating a particular point of view. The lobbyist can, of course, provide distorted information, but only once, because credibility is one of the lobbyist's most important assets. Alternative sources of information do exist—from competing interests also seeking access—therefore, providing unreliable or biased information is hardly a viable alternative. At the same time, organizations frequently attempt to communicate either threats or promises, and they possess power resources (Chapter 6) of interest or use to influential persons.

The techniques available to groups do not differ substantially from those available to individuals. Personal interaction between decision makers and lobbyists is preferred, but there are time constraints, and perceived improprieties that are involved. Interpersonal interaction, of course, allows for the give and take absent in other modes.

A second technique for groups is to provide expert advice or testimony. Occasionally, private citizens may possess this information, but usually decision makers rely on advice provided by lobby.

Third, there are indirect techniques employed, such as using intermediaries to deliver messages to decision makers. Respected friends, colleagues, and sympathizers have more access than known lobbyists (which is why former decision makers are favored as lobbyists in their former organizations), and such friends are less constrained in their interactions by the appearance of improprieties.

Perhaps more than anything else, collective contacts and lobbyists are concerned with opening channels of communication with decision makers. Milbrath (1960) has identified several methods, some of which are legitimate, others less so. Social events such as parties, although perceived as important by lobbyists, rarely open channels because they are viewed as explicit (and amateurish) influence attempts. Second, there is outright bribery, to which no one admits. Third, there are other offers for legislators such as campaign assistance or funding. More often than not these forms of influence buying are eschewed as methods of establishing access.

Overall, it is important to note that not only the lobbyist but the decision maker as well is involved in any communication attempt. Decision makers must be receptive to the kind of information offered and influence sought by the lobbyist, or the private citizen. Decision makers are public servants, and require a certain visibility but complete availability would require losing the information and broader view required in a decision-making role.

PROTESTS AND DEMONSTRATIONS

It was previously noted that several students of citizen participation (Nie, Verba, & Petrocik, 1976) exclude extralegal participation from analysis of participation. To do so when discussing protests and demonstrations in the context of political communications would exclude a significant amount of participation, especially for nonelites. In nondemocratic participatory systems in particular, protests and demonstrations are often the only mode of popular participation and the only method to express either demands or support.

Protests imply dissatisfaction with government policy, although they are subsets of demonstrations, which may be in support of, or in opposition to, policy. Each takes so many forms that it is virtually impossible to enumerate all the dimensions of demonstrations, but they include size, spontaneity, duration, and resolution, among others. The dimensions in many ways parallel the dimensions of power, for in some ways protests and demonstrations are a power tactic used by those otherwise powerless.

The reasons for demonstrations and protest are many, but most important is the fact that they often are the only channels of communication available for demands (or support) to be articulated in totalitarian systems. Citizen demands are not relevant variables in such systems, although leaders inevitably argue that their actions are directed toward citizen demands. When conditions become intolerable, demands erupt in the form of protests, because other channels, such as voting, are nonexistent or meaningless. Examples in recent years abound. Food riots in countries as diverse as Egypt and Poland attest to the power of protest as a form of demand and nonsupport. Not only were price increases in staple foods not passively accepted (i.e., supported), but rollbacks were demanded. In Poland, the regime of Edward Gierick was virtually toppled by foods riots. At no other time in postwar history has an Eastern European leader been ousted because of a lack of popular support.

In systems where alternatives do exist, protests and demonstrations serve different purposes. In particular, protesting provides high visibility for groups otherwise lacking clout in the political arena. Only a handful of protestors can disrupt normal routines, resulting in attention otherwise absent. Pickets sitting in front of bulldozers can halt the building of a road, persons tying themselves to railroad tracks can prevent the movement of troop trains, individuals sitting in at a lunch counter can force a confrontation with authorities over issues ordinarily ignored. By themselves, such protests are symbolic expressions of broader demands. Groups (and occasionally individuals) unrecognized by political decision makers and without access, figuratively present a voice to be heard by forcing confrontations. In other words, protest is a mode of communication to those without access.

In addition to the absence of access, a key to protest is linguistic competence. Mueller (1975) argued that those fluent in the language of politics (negotiating compromise, and familiarity with bargaining and administrative languages) can participate in the division of political spoils. The politically inarticulate—traditionally the lower socioeconomic strata—are excluded from the system. Thus the system perpetuates the inequality, because those outside the system have no access to processes that would balance the system. Protest and demonstrations remain among the few alternatives to offer modes of communication to the politically inarticulate. The language and lexicon is straightfoward and easily understood by the politically articulate as well as the inarticulate: make concessions, or at least hear our pleas and demands, or suffer the consequences. Urban riots in the United States during the 1960s and student protests resulting in burned ROTC buildings, provide plentiful examples. In each case, the message from those ordinarily without channels (or even linguistic competence) was made manifest in threatening activities. To some extent, such tactics expand the power of dissenting groups beyond the power such groups would have in ordinary participatory channels. But fairness according to democratic rules of procedure has limited appeal to those perceiving themselves as unfairly treated victims.

Protest demonstrations offer the participants another advantage over the more traditional modes: greater publicity of demands. News gathering routines (see Chapter 9) have made nontraditional participation newsworthy. Regardless of the reason, (violence is the standard for dramatic programming and much local news) protestors receive disproportionate news coverage, so much so that politicians often refer to the biased coverage of political rallies. Spiro Agnew, for example, questioned why a heckler in a crowd of a thousand and one would be singled out for camera coverage, while a thousand others attentively listening would be ignored. Passivity, indeed most traditional participation, is not conducive to mass media, particularly television coverage. So disproportionately, outliers are covered.

Demonstrations may be supportive as well as nonsupportive. Popular movements in support of political decision, although sometimes staged, present regime support and enhance stability. Sadat's 1977 trip to Israel was followed by a "spontaneous" demonstration of Egyptians in favor of his initiatives upon his return. In the late 1960s in the United States, hardhat "pro-America" rallies were organized to contravene peace rallies of hippies. Despite their occasional use to prop up regimes, support rallies are infrequent, largely because the motivation for participants is lacking. Nevertheless, when incentives are provided, emotional outpourings of the masses to support regimes are recorded.

Other forms of protest behavior and nontraditional participation communicate orientations most directly. Armed insurrections, riots, coup d'etats, and other types of political violence are laden with messages. When traditional or even most nontraditional modes of communicating have been exhausted, political violence emerges, particularly when regimes can be destabilized by violence. No other participatory mode is viewed by authorities as so threatening to a regime, so authorities are forced to act quickly, often overreacting and alienating those who ordinarily would support the regime.

During political violence or even peaceful protests, government officials try to restore order and tranquility. The urban riots of the 1960s in the United States were met with pleas from black politicians and civil rights leaders urging participants to "cool it." These figures for the most part were politically bilingual, able to bargain and to negotiate with the politically articulate and at the same time to address the protestors. Recognition by these leaders of the problems as being largely one of communication, puts leaders in a position to establish and open up new channels of communication with political officials.

One example of this process is offered by Hall and Hewitt (1970) in their analysis of dissent management during the Cambodian situation protests. Political officials can overwhelm a situation, they argue, by redefining the protest or conflict (see Chapter 4) as one of a breakdown in communication rather than as a substantive conflict. The resolution of the conflict, if redefined, becomes simple: establish new channels of communication. In effect, symbolic reassurances of future access are offered in place of substantive concessions to defuse the situation.

In Hall and Hewitt's analysis, the strategy of the President was to describe the reasons for protests as a technical problem. The breakdown in channels of communication (noise? overload?) prevented information about the concerns of dissenters from reaching the President's desk. Disagreement was not the issue, rather it was misunderstanding. Indeed, there was no conflict that could not be resolved with more effective communication.

It becomes very difficult for protestors to disagree with the analysis because the power of a president—or any political leader—is tied to his unique position. His reassurance of concern is magnified by the symbols of office, his status, and the awe and respect for the office. Even for the most bitter dissident, the presence of a high political official can be intimidating in face to face interaction.

Although not the only method for dissenting, protest and demonstrations form an important part of the participation landscape. Citizen initiated contacts offer dissenting opportunities, but with less drama and public awareness. Primarily, protests bring in a wider audience than would otherwise be aware of the controversy, because the protesting voice is amplified by media attention as well as by contagion to others whose activities are disrupted by demonstrations. Clearly, protests are an important channel for demand and support expression and fit well with power and conflict concepts.

VOTING AND ELECTORAL POLITICS

There are two audiences to which electoral participants direct their activities: the self, and the regime. People vote for any number of reasons, but most may be summarized into voting for instrumental or expressive purposes, or in Edelman's (1964) terms, for tangible or symbolic rewards.

Instrumental voting occurs when voters participate because they have a message to communicate concerning some tangible benefit. In other words, demands are expressed through instrumental voting. Policy preferences sometimes are voted on directly, as in referenda, other times they are indicated through candidate choice. For some citizens, participation is limited, so voting provides the one opportunity they can use to communicate with political leaders. Of course, as we noted earlier, often there is little real choice, particularly in two party systems, because candidates cluster around the center of the political spectrum, but as long as the myth of instrumental participation survives, voters view their ballots as important communication devices.

For other citizens, voting is expressive rather than instrumental, symbolic rather than substantive. Those who feel as if their vote will not make a difference and that substantive policy change will not follow, but who still vote to show their support for the system are voting expressively. Similarly, protest votes are often expressive.

Politicians and political scientists both have recognized how symbolic various modes of participation can be. George Wallace, for example, called on voters to "Send them a message." By voting for him, citizens would show the powers in Washington that there was discontent.

Of course it may be argued that all participation is instrumental, and that only the objects of participation change. Expressive participation makes people feel better, providing an outlet for support or nonsupport of the system, but such participation is instrumental for the citizen's self-esteem. In other words, such participation is used as a tool, not for effecting policy change, but for personal satisfaction. Our concern, however, is with participation as a political communication resource, so the expressive/instrumental difference drawn earlier applies.

Inevitably, one or more of Lasswell's questions is posed when one considers a political communication question. *Who* participates? Researchers have collected data and assembled propositional inventories of political participation not only in the United States, but in other Western and Third World countries. Many of these studies are summarized in Milbrath and Goel (1977). For the most part, the literature refers to voting, so there are more accurate profiles of voters than any other participants.

There are many social and demographic characteristics associated with voting: higher education levels, greater occupational status, urban residence, and higher income, although these can be modified somewhat across cultures and specific regions. Certain personal factors also are strongly associated with voting: people with high feelings of efficacy, self-esteem, or subjective competence, the unalienated, and those with obligation or duty to participate. But all these findings, consistent as they are over time, are less interesting from a political communication perspective than the role played by information in participation.

In general, those who vote are the most informed members of a community; persons who receive the most stimuli about politics. Milbrath and Goel report that this proposition holds true in many studies in eight Western and non-Western cultures. Exposure to stimuli from interpersonal communication is particularly likely to enhance propensity to vote, but mass media information is important to voting as well. In other words, individuals with mass media and interpersonal political communication networks are likely to be transmitters of political messages (through participation) as well as receivers. Numerous studies have provided additional information on just who receives information and the type of messages likely to be received during political campaigns. These are discussed more fully in Chapter 10.

LIMITS TO PARTICIPATION

Much of the analysis in this chapter is predicated on the assumption that participatory opportunities are unlimited. Although examples of participatory options in totalitarian systems have been noted, they almost always involve protest and other nonsupport activities. Sometimes these options do not exist. Demonstrators are quickly arrested, or worse, punished as graphic examples of what happens to dissidents.

In nontotalitarian systems, we usually think of participation with broad limits, particularly if it remains within specified legal guidelines. However, there are occasions where limits are placed on participatory rights such as free speech or assembly even in the most open and democratic systems (see Chapter 13). In other nations, elections are suspended, and virtually all modes of communicating with public officials, directly or indirectly, are cut off.

Again borrowing from Mueller (1975), communications in such circumstances are constrained by limiting participation. If all channels are closed, decision makers are isolated. If a handful of channels are left open, they are quickly filled to capacity or overloaded. As long as channel closure is enforceable, the regime remains in power. But historically, it has rarely been possible for regimes to operate without linkages to demands or sensitivity to support Alternative channels arise; underground presses, dissident networks, party or military plotting. Indeed, the resilience of many channels repressed by government always surprises dictators convinced of their longevity.

A FINAL WORD

Participation, like the other major concepts discussed in Part II, is interdependent with power, conflict, and socialization. Participation first of all, is a power resource for citizens in democratic and nondemocratic systems alike. Although not always in command, citizens do have inputs, usually to replace or select decision makers, sometimes to make direct policy decisions. Ultimately, citizens speak out or remain silent, they vote, revolt, or remain quiescent. In a sense, power is in the hands of the people in all systems because of the dependence of regimes on passively communicated support.

Conflicts within the system are both initiated and resolved through participation. Demonstrations and protests point to grievances and differences in graphic ways. Voting itself is a form of conflict resolution. Conflicts depend on participation. At the same time, interpretation and development of systems are measured by social participation. Evidence from several nations (Almond & Verba, 1963) has linked participation to modernization and development.

Finally, political socialization has as its goal, perhaps more than anything else, the training of citizens for system relevant participation and support.

Activities at home, school, or elsewhere are oriented toward future participation—be it as a young Democrat for electoral participation, or a young Viet Cong for revolutionary activity.

As a final word, descriptions in this chapter refer to citizen participants rather than professional participants such as government decision makers or political reporters. Professional participants, although generating much political communication (Nimmo, 1978) do not communicate preferences or supports by their participation (although often these are consequences), but instead communicate through information outputs. Chapters 8 and 9 explicitly cover these political actors.

6
POWER, INFLUENCE, AND AUTHORITY

Historically, political treatises have been preoccupied with power. What it is, how to get it, how to keep it, and how to exercise it, have been questions addressed by political practitioners from princes to presidents. Usually political scientists are at arms length from politicians but when it comes to discussing power, the distance diminishes. Lasswell and Kaplan (1950) wrote during the early years of empirical political science that "political science . . . is the study of the shaping and sharing of power." Some scholars, such as Morgenthau (1960), agreed; others, such as March (1955), were less in agreement. But whether or not power is the defining characteristic of politics or plays a lesser role, it still is a central concept in political relationships.

Despite the role of power in politics and the frequency with which it has been studied, it still remains a vague concept. Nagel (1975) has offered several reasons why this might be the case, calling several approaches to power "dead ends." Much writing on power has been taxonomic; power is defined and assertions are put forth in untestable forms. Other essays have been tautological, substituting terms such as influence or authority for power. Still other studies try at length to develop differences between these terms, but neglect to develop analytical distinctions. None of these approaches have been particularly fruitful.

Two methods of approaching power do have some utility for the political communication researcher. The first is a derivative of the "attribute" view of power. Power theorists taking this perspective suggest power is a tangible asset, one that can be quantified through consideration of skills, resources, or other assets. Although this notion has often been used to compare actors to one another as "more" or "less" powerful, it may also be employed to describe certain characteristics associated with roles in power relationships.

The second perspective, gaining more and more favor with power analysts in recent years, is to view power causally. Taking a page from Thomas Hobbes' early work, power analysts such as Simon (1953) have said that for actor A to have power over actor B, then it must be that A's behavior causes B's behavior. Whether or not it is only behaviors to which power relations apply, of course, is a separate question, but the key to the causal approach is that it depends largely on the relations between A and B. These relations are maintained through communication. Stated another way communication is necessary between A and B for a power relationship even to exist.

Further refinement of the causational approach to power heightens the relationship of communication to power. Nagel (1975), defines a power relation as "an actual or potential causal relationship between the preferences of an actor regarding an outcome and the outcome itself." Beyond replacing the term behavior with the more general "outcomes" (which includes behavior of individuals, dispositions to behave, attitudes, opinions, beliefs, emotions, and nonindividual behavior), this definition introduces preferences (empirical notions of values, desires, wants, purposes). One way or another, these preferences must be made known to the actor at whose outcomes the preferences are directed. Again, communication lies at the core of power.

Beyond the expression of preferences as a communication phenomenon, there exists another view of power relevant to communication. In organizational networks where the need for information (or its possession) is great, it can be argued that power is the ability to control information or communication channels. On one level, this approach does not differ substantially from the previous approach. After all, it posits that communication is rooted in the relationship. However, this information control definition is descriptive of almost all relationships where one actor has information, or more information than other actors. Even simple interchanges ordinarily involve responses to dozens of questions or requests for elaboration. Whereas this second approach is more general in that it suggests power pervades all relationships, it also indicates the importance of social hierarchies and organizations in power relationships.

A variety of power phenomena may be studied from a communication perspective. One hears of community power, or of an individual legislator as being powerful, the symbolic use of terms such as "black power," and other uses in a variety of contexts. Each of these are presented in detail later in the chapter, power is presented in a communication framework, and some of the fundamental dimensions of power are described.

THE CHARACTERISTICS OF POWER

One of the modern analysts of power, Robert Dahl (1970) has described the dimensions on which power analysts must focus to understand power. Each of these dimensions may also be looked at as communication terms.

Dahl (and others) refer primarily to the scope, domain, and distribution of power.

The scope of power is the issues over which a given power relationship exists. Parents, for example, in their relationships with their children, have a very wide scope of power; just about anything the parent wants the child to do must be done. However, a supervisor on the job must ordinarily limit the issue of commands and the expression of preferences to subordinates to job related issues. Commands issued outside the scope of employment are either resented or ignored, largely because they lack legitimacy when the scope of a power relationship is well defined. In the political arena, certain political figures can be viewed as powerful, but ordinarily over a limited scope. During his hayday, for example, Wilbur Mills was considered a powerful member of Congress, but his scope was limited to economic and tax issues.

The domain of power specifies who (or what system) is involved in the relationship. Returning to the preceding examples, the domain of parental power is over children, i.e., the children's behavior theoretically can be controlled by the parents; occasionally parents are controlled by their children. The domain of the supervisor includes those under him or her on the job. Wilbur Mills' power was in the context of a legislative system. Obviously, individuals have a large number of power domains, much as they have numerous roles. Similarly, there may be a wide scope of power when there are a variety of spillovers across roles (e.g., the Dagwood Bumstead employee who is dominated by the employer socially as well as on the job).

The distribution of power ordinarily describes the patterns of power relationships within systems or between individuals. Distribution may be approached on two levels. First, one may specify certain roles through which power relationships are developed. Secondly, one may describe certain attributes of those in roles having their preferred outcomes succeed.

Taken together, knowledge of the scope, domain, and distribution of power in any system or organization yields considerable information concerning the structure of that system, the sociometric networks, and at least the channels of communication. These dimensions, however, only describe power relations, and do not provide clues as to how effective each actor in the relationship is at having successful outcome preferences. Successes in power relations are explained by four additional characteristics: resources, skill, motivation, and the costs of power.

Power resources include both ascribed and achieved status, including such things as wealth, popularity, and physical strength. At the same time, a number of resources are characteristic of social standing, prestige, or access. In other words, important power resources include location, either within a social network at a point through which information must pass, or in occupying a gatekeeping position regulating access.

Skills are another dimension revealing the differences among actors in the ways in which resources are utilized. Given the same resources, one actor is likely to be more (or less) successful in gaining preferred outcomes than another actor as a result of skill differences. Skill may be developed through knowledge, education, or experience in managing power resources, and many roles may be passed from one actor to another.

Because outcomes do not have the same significance to all actors in the relationship, certain differences in power are explained by the motivation of the actors involved. Motivational differences may result from personality, experience, situational variance, or a host of other reasons. Some actors actively seek to dominate relationships, others do not.

The final characteristic is the cost of power. In any relationship, asserting preferences has certain costs. Similarly, there are costs to monitoring outcomes or compliance. Costs may include gathering, exchanging, or processing information, or may be the costs of resources employed to assure desired outcomes. In the analysis of power, costs are important for many actors who compare the benefits of favorable outcomes with the costs of assuring those outcomes either in resources expended or monitoring compliance. The dimensions and characteristics of power taken together lead to what is termed a communications perspective on power.

Over a scope of issues and across a given domain, three goals exist for actors in power relationships. First, assuming they have already established contact and have opened their lines of communication, actors must communicate their preferences or assert their demands. Second, they must make their resources known to one another, whether these resources are greater knowledge and wisdom, or might and weaponry. Third, the costs of noncompliance must be made known, as must the extent to which the parties are motivated or determined to carry out their plans. Finally, there must be sufficiently sophisticated communication technology to monitor the success or failure, compliance or noncompliance of the actors.

Some examples may serve to clarify these relationships and concepts. Take, for instance, an ordinary threat in international relations (see Chapter 4) for conflict between countries A and B. A threatens B and, reciprocating, B threatens A concerning territorial water violations. We know at the outset the domain of the relationship of A and B in this case. The scope is also clearly delineated. It is over territorial waters, and rights and privileges within those waters. Distribution of power is not meaningful in this context because there are only two actors. The resources of each may include military strength and an economic base to support a military effort, but may well equally include the ability to sway world opinion or receive a vote of censure in the United Nations. Skills vary across the actors, as does their motivation, both of which may be based in previous management of similar situations, the need to enhance national respect and credibility, or perhaps motivations by political leaders hoping to draw attention away from domestic problems. Finally, the costs and benefits to each can be calculated and made known to one another.

At each stage of the process—threat, counterthreat, and other responses (appeals to other nations, delivery of ultimatums, reaching a resolution, observing compliance) communications linkages are required between A and B. This seems simple enough for a given event between A and B. But suppose A dominates B, and successfully forces B to observe A's territorial boundaries. This may have an effect on actor C's behavior. As a result of observing A's demands (and resources) C may not venture into A's area, even though A has never threatened C. Thus C's behavior is being modified in a way preferred by A without there ever having been an exchange of messages between A and C. This behavior by C is called anticipated reaction, which, in the absence of direct communication between A and C, A still gets its desired outcomes.

Although there is no direct information exchange between A and C, it can be argued that C is orienting behavior toward A's preferences. A might at some point in the past have communicated preferences to C, which linger in C's memory. Alternatively, C may identify with B, and anticipate A's actions. Whichever the case, at some point information about A's intentions, resources, skills, or possible sanctions or rewards must have reached C.

The problem of anticipated reaction can be linked to the question of whether or not Santa Claus has power. On the surface, Santa wields power in his relationships with children. Around Christmas time each year, they modify their behavior to "not shout . . . cry (or) . . . pout," because Santa Claus is omniscient, and will soon distribute rewards. But, (at the risk of offending some readers) because there is no Santa Claus, how can he have preferred behavioral outcomes? It turns out that rather than Santa Claus, it is of course the parents or other agents who exercise power, both by inculcating the idea of Santa, and by distributing rewards. At the same time, children may not view parents as being powerful because in the child's eye, they have nothing to do with the distribution of presents. If children do not perceive parents as powerful, are the parents in fact powerful? Perhaps only if we think in terms of the parents providing the information-reinforced by department store and sidewalk Santas—upon which children act.

DISTINGUISHING POWER AND INFLUENCE

Much of the literature on power has been devoted to defining power as influence. But certain distinctions can be useful for the communication analysis of power.

Ordinarily, concepts are distinguished from one another if there is some analytic utility in so doing. Rarely are truly fine lines drawn by scholars, most are hazy. But in the case of power analysis, the notion of influence can sharpen the focus.

In common, influence and power are relational; both involve communication, and each has a causal foundation. They differ in terms of what is communicated. Power relationships evolve through communication of coercion, threat, force, sanctions, and rewards, and resources based on the property of things. Influence is rooted in leadership, legitimacy, expertise, authority, or sociological role, or more generally, in social properties. Influence is therefore linked to the sociology of leadership, and joins diverse literatures from community power, social communications, the psychology of groups, and bureaucracy. Unlike power, influence does not imply a conflict of goals possessed by the actors.

In the literature, the characteristics described here are almost randomly given the names influence or power. If such definitions of power as Harsanyi's (1962) including the supply of information on advantages and policies, or "legitimate authority so that there is a disutility to disobeying," power ought to be distinguished from influence. Similarly, Russell's (1938) "influence on opinions through education and propaganda" and Gilman's (1962) "persuasion in terms of accepting other's judgments" require influence and power be distinguished. These definitions are all linked to communications processes and the contexts in which messages are sent and received rather than coercion, force, and so on. What is being communicated is primarily legitimacy—Easton's basic support in system maintenance.

Beyond the legitimacy versus coercion question, the two concepts differ across the other outlined dimensions, particularly costs and motivation. Of course, social systems may employ both power and influence techniques. Indeed, Cartwright (1965) has suggested societies under strain move from influence through authority to power through coercion and force to maintain social order.

Figure 6.1 presents a fourfold table placing power and influence on different axes. In quadrant I, where power and influence are both high, fit political actors are both exhibit the characteristics of a benevolent leader. At one level, such a leader may get subjects to give him his preferred outcomes by simply asking for them. He has legitimacy and authority to be sure, and can even compel people to obey his commands (if preferences are so expressed). But there is no need to use coercion and force because subjects respond on the basis of their love, trust, esteem, or respect for the benevolent leader. One might argue that the most successful political leaders try to cultivate an image of fairness accompanied by strength to ensure compliance with no need to resort to coercion.

In quadrant II are other actors who have little power in terms of coercive resources, but have substantial influence. Family and kinship ties are among the most prominent members of this quadrant. Largely out of love, affection, devotion, role, or duty, people frequently respond to the wishes (i.e., preferred outcomes) expressed by family members. On the one hand, influence often does

POWER

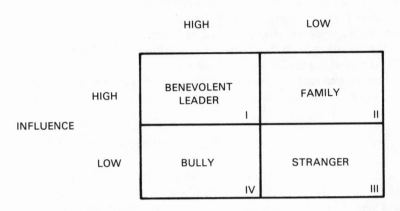

Figure 6.1

diminish over time, partly because of the absence of coercive power as children age (and are no longer spanked or similarly threatened), but may also diminish as children see that parents are not infallible. On the other hand, influence may be viewed as cyclical as children feel guilt concerning the treatment of parents as they age.

Politically, of course, there are counterparts to family. Close allies such as the United States and Britain, for example, have relatively little power over one another, given the strength of their resources. However, the opinions of each nation are weighed heavily in deciding political action in the international arena. In many ways, close alliances between equally strong nations resemble familial power/influence relationships.

The third quadrant is clearly the least interesting from a power perspective. Ordinarily, actors who have little contact with one another are in this category. Strangers who have earned no respect or legitimacy and who offer suggestions rather than coercion or force to earn their preferred outcomes belong here. Internationally, nations with no or significant relationships—such as Paraguay and Afghanistan, to take an extreme example—would have neither power nor influence over one another.

Quadrant IV holds considerably more interest. Relationships sustained essentially through threats, rewards, coercion, and force fit here. Coercive bullies, be they on the street corner or in global politics, usually have their preferences met. Their successes are not due to any legitimacy or respect earned by other actors, but through fear. In these cases, costs of enforcement and compliance monitoring are considerably greater than in the first quadrant.

Whereas Figure 6.1 provides a basis for explaining the differences between power and influence, several analysts have compounded the problem of identifying these differences by describing influence in power terms. French and Raven, (1959) for example, write of expert power (knowledge and respect) and legitimate power (tied to socially prescribed norms or organizational roles), which of course, corresponds to our notion of influence. Similarly, Aiken and Mott (1971) write of role authority and participation in decision-making. Clark (1968) writes of the ability to select the goals of a system, and, perhaps, in the definition that summarizes best the communications aspect of influence, Riker (1959) writes of being in a pivotal position.

POWER, INFLUENCE, AND COMMUNICATION

In control systems theory, Weiner (1955) has stated power requires communication. Those in power relations must have quick and ready access to control objects to issue directions, observe compliance, and preserve system order. In the absence of such information, authorities can be overthrown. Thus, leaders must be in a position to issue, store, and retrieve information.

Arthur Stinchombe (1968) has considered the relationship between power, influence, and communication. The term Stinchcombe employs is power, but according to the definitions previously stated, he is referring to influence. Nonetheless, whichever term is used is related to information processes. In general, within any relationship or formal organization, influence increases as the channels of communication carry more information. It is unimportant to determine whether this information is threat or coercion or merely more opportunity to enhance legitimacy. Applied to administrative systems, Stinchcombe argues, power or influence is increased when messages are highly abstract (i.e., they contain ambiguities, or symbols in general), when there is a high probability that messages are likely to be accurate, and when messages are widely disseminated so that all members of the organization are aware of the sources of the messages. Thus, in Stinchcombe's view, it is largely a matter of publicizing important messages that enhances influence.

However, a number of problems tend to minimize influence. All of these problems are informational. First, too much information transmitted may be irrelevant for the primary purpose of assuring influence. In addition, there are a host of "mechanical" problems that alter the "meaning" of influence messages. At one end, there may be decoding error, wherein the message recipients fail to understand the intended message. With symbolically exercised leadership and symbolic messages, this is often the case.

Not only do there exist encoding and decoding errors, there may also be problems in message transmission at the channel level. Channel distortion may result at this level, or, alternately, there may be too much noise accompanying (and drowning) the influence message. In either case, the impact of A's messages to B will be minimized.

Stinchcombe's information oriented approach to influence has been supplemented by Nagel's (1975). Returning to actors A and B, one can consider occasions for A influencing B's behavior (or outcome). First, A may supply information to B that B would not receive, were it not for A. Alternatively, A may prevent B from receiving information controlled by A. And, of course, related to preventing B from receiving A's messages is the possibility that A will drown out opposing messages from other sources by deluging B with A's information and filling B's channel capacity. Assuming A is in a position to control information flow to B, these all remain possibilities. In other words, if A maintains some strategic organizational or social location, A may exert ecological control in relationships with B by controlling the information environment.

One empirical example of this approach applied cross-culturally has been offered by Wirsing (1973). In the societies he examines, power is maximized in several issue areas where information is centralized in political "teams" or leaders. It is not the quantity of information such leaders have, but the degree to which they control its flow that is the key variable. Other examples in support of Stinchcombe's and Nagel's information oriented approaches can be offered, but the best example is perhaps that of the alleged power or influence of television, both drama and news. Although audiences received news from print media long before the development of electronic media, there is evidence now that most people regard television as their primary source of news and entertainment, and have become television dependent. As a result of this dependence, and the habitual exclusion of alternative information sources, television supplies information that audiences would not ordinarily receive. Moreover, the quality of information—online, both visual and aural—cannot be matched by other sources. Because of the nature of television occupying the two most important senses, television effectively prevents audiences from receiving other messages. Finally, messages from other sources are essentially drowned out by the deluge of televised messages. Both news and drama are available almost all hours of the day, flooding the airwaves with a narrow range of choice, excluding other information from all but the most dedicated information seekers.

The influence of television is compounded by its alleged accuracy (seeing is believing, at least for news) and the fact that it clearly is public. Although the news is not "abstract" in that it is tied to concrete events, the events around which news is built are sufficiently remote from the public to have certain abstract qualities. Who can realistically perceive mingling with kings and presidents, or fully understand the acronyms for SALT, let alone a broad meaning for it? Drama, too, is abstract in that the allegories told and symbols evoked have no uniform meaning for audiences, but taken together provide sufficient latitude for meanings to be widely recognized within a broad social framework.

All these reasons suggest the importance for, and influence of, television beyond the direct effects of the hypodermic theories of the 1950s (Klapper 1960). But at the same time, the problems of assuming unlimited influence of television are raised by the limitations to communication influence posited by Stinchcombe. Much irrelevant information (in terms of important sociopolitical issues) is transmitted and recognized as irrelevant. Often the latent meaning of news and drama is obscured by all the noise of the situation ranging from burial of social and political issues in the bowels of a situation comedy to the presence of superficial graphics in broadcast that simplify the complexity of political disputes. And, of course, decoding errors by audiences often minimize the impact of news or drama with important social meaning.

Nonetheless, the problems found by television in influencing audiences are only a small portion of the problems faced by national politicians, as they must depend, in large part, on mass media to maintain their influence. (Power is another question, because direct use of force or coercion may not require mass media—other than to reduce the costs of threat delivery.) Politicians usually have no direct access to the public, but instead have their activities and positions presented to the public through mass media. Indeed, most of their activity is private, hence politicians are not as visible as those who summarize their activity (i.e., Walter Cronkite). In any case, the problems of politicians exerting maximum influence are engendered because their activities are reported on the news, accompanied by much irrelevant information. Aside from the problems of political bias in the news with which the networks have been charged, there are other encoding biases introduced by the demands of electronic journalism, including selective encoding, requirements of visually stimulating activity, or other institutionally imposed demands. There is much noise in the system from competing messages to extraneous materials irrelevant to message substance. And, of course, there is the audience decoding problem. Overall, these problems may serve to minimize the influence of politicians but maximize the influence of television news departments where decisions of access, editing, and so forth are made.

It can be argued, however, that the existence of television may enhance the influence of a given political figure by providing a large audience, more access, and a more multidimensional presence than would otherwise be the case. All this may be true, evidenced perhaps, by the ascendency of the executive in many political systems. Nevertheless, an important question is how much greater this influence might be were there no intervening influential actor such as television.

POWER AND AGENDAS

Controlling the flow of information by engaging in gatekeeping behavior is only one aspect of information control. Often, certain actors, institutions, or roles lend themselves to modifying information flow. There exists, however, another type of control over the type and range of issue brought up for discussion. More than influence or power, in terms of successfully securing favorable outcomes on controversial issues or policies, this type of power is applicable over the very issues raised for public discussion.

Several political scientists have addressed these questions in power terms. Recently they have been joined by communication scholars with a shared viewpoint. Indeed, one of the fundamental cleavages in democratic theory—the division between proponents of elite and pluralist theories—occurs here. Believers in elitist theories, ranging from Bachrach and Baratz, to Lowi, to Mills, all argue that many issues are omitted from the civic agenda by influential individuals or groups, effectively precluding the dissemination of information on these issues. Bachrach and Baratz (1970) argue that there are "non-issues" in society. These topics never arise for public discussion and scrutiny because powerful groups in society keep them off the agenda. These issues might include, as Lowi (1963) argues, the redistributive issues—class-based, fundamental economic and social issues. In Mills' (1956) discussion of the power elite, he argues that elite interests on crucial issues, such as the nature of society, coincide, and hence elites (including mass media institutions) suppress tangible politics.

In many ways, these arguments are consistent with the discussion of symbolic politics. Rewards for the nonelites are largely symbolic or, if tangible, inconsequential. Symbolic issues divert attention from the more important social problems, solutions of which require structural change. The key to elite success, in other words, is an ability to keep items off the political agenda.

From a communications perspective, agendas and the related concept of agenda-setting are more narrow in meaning. Derived from the work of Bernard Cohen (1963) and pursued by Shaw and McCombs (1977) and their associates, agenda-setting theory basically argues that the "mass media are not so successful in telling us what to think, but are notoriously successful in telling us what to think about." In other words, mass media may define the agenda of items about which we think and for which policies are made.

Research on agenda-setting has looked to the electronic and print media as primary agents. Mass media selectively attend to certain issues, artificially heightening their significance. The public, as a result of repeated exposure to these items, develops beliefs and attitudes toward these issues and, moreover, considers them to be the social issues worthy of attention. Thus, certain issues emerge publicly (and may be resolved) as a result of media attention. But other issues—and again these may be the more consequential, system oriented, nonsymbolic issues—may be neglected. Like political nonissues, media nonissues serve to stabilize the system and narrowly focus public concerns.

Cobb and Elder (1972) have drawn one further agenda distinction—the difference between the systemic agenda and the institutional agenda. The systemic agenda ordinarily defines the parameters of what is relevant to be decided (i.e., what is the scope of the agenda), whereas the institutional agenda refers to what actually is decided or what topics are considered by social decision-making bodies. These agenda notions are relevant from a communications perspective because the flow of information and demands from citizens to decision makers is shaped largely by the items on the agenda for social decisions. The difference between the systemic agenda and the institutional agenda, of course, reflects the extent to which some topics are kept off the institutional agenda in the form of nondecisions and nonissues.

Most communications research on agenda-setting has been in the context of political campaigns. Ordinarily, this research suggested that citizens are in a limited information environment, constrained in their range of thoughts by dependence on mass media to raise issues. Without necessarily engaging in mind control, mass media are argued to be influential in shaping the agenda over which outcomes result (without necessarily having a preferred outcome). In a sense, people are not the masters of their own destiny to the extent they think they are.

Communications media can be influential—if that is possible without expressing preferred outcomes—in other ways besides raising issues for public discussion. Mass media may create a reality surrounding events or personalities that may heighten the power or influence of specific actors. In other words, access to mass media can serve as a power resource for some actors. At the same time, even without the use of mass media by specific actors, certain images or events brought into the public eye can have their own effects on audiences. Mass media thus highlight the significance of some actors or activity and minimize the significance of others.

Mass media bear a large responsibility for the creation of certain images of society. Mass media present a face of society upon which individuals or groups depend for their notions of social and political reality. Images may be created of other cultures (as weak or strong, moral or immoral, aggressive or nonaggressive) to provide a framework for action within a culture. In many ways, these images help to structure and bring order to the social and political environment. Political candidates in particular depend on images projected through mass media; images of honesty, strength, or competence created largely through news or advertising. Effective manipulation of image in mass media becomes an important resource, assuring at least a minimal level of influence.

Mass media may create a second reality through the status conferral function. In general, mass media's central role in the information processes—including the ability to withhold information—is to legitimize (or delegitimize) political contenders. Time on television or space in print media are scarce resources; by their very nature, mass media must be selective. Popular recognition of this scarcity combined with the rise of the glamour mythology in the information processing industries (such as television journalism) suggest that appearance in mass media implies a symbolic legitimacy. People on television are those to whom audiences must at least attend, if not adhere. For politicians, media access in the presence of scarcity is crucial in establishing legitimacy, and building up power resources. Who, after all, become spokespersons for social groups and movements? Is it the leadership, or the most colorful (in a media sense) characters? As some politicians have asked, "who elected Walter Cronkite" to be the most trusted man in America, more influential than many politicians? The question may be meaningless if elections are irrelevant, because there is another method by which one gains legitimacy.

Other characters have had their legitimacy enhanced by mass media. Jimmy the Greek, for example, is now indirectly responsible for establishing betting odds, having achieved mythical status as the Las Vegas odds maker. During the 1968 demonstrations at Columbia University, Mark Rudd became spokesman not only for the SDS group of which he was a member (although not its leader), but symbolically represented all youth. Similarly, when he turned himself in to police officials in 1977, he did so by calling media attention to his action in the form of a press conference. Again, symbolically, as he surrendered, the 1960s were declared by journalists to be over.

The third aspect of media influence is through the creation of the media event. Given the scarcity of media time or space recognized by event participants, mass media are permitted to transform events. The pseudoevent (or media happening) occurs at two levels. First, certain events are created by the very presence of mass media, which signals the significance of an event by a decision to allocate resources to its coverage. Second, some events are transformed by the presence of mass media. Each of these occurrences is related to the status conferred by mass media. Politicians do not merely make announcements, instead they convene press conferences. Many demonstrations and riots, important fare for 1960s television, were transformed by the presence of television and further provided a context for future events to be modeled after what was seen on television. Although done with some regularity in actuality, the Hollywood film *The Taking of Pelham 1-2-3* provides an unusually lucid and explicit example of this. In the film, New York City is compelled to deliver a ransom to save the lives of passengers aboard a hijacked subway train. The money is assembled with only moments to spare, but the police are instructed not to deliver the ransom, despite the approaching deadline, until the mayor arrives. He arrives grooming himself for the television cameras before stepping from his limousine, because he needs media coverage as a hero, on the scene of a crime during an election year.

Similarly events occur in real political life. In 1976, the mayor of Philadelphia broke his leg at the scene of an oil refinery fire, desperate to be on hand for film crews. On several occasions it has been argued that urban riots have been transformed by media coverage. In other words, behaviors of riot participants were altered by calling attention to the occurrence of the riot, and even indicating to riot participants where the primary police activity was so they could either avoid the police or go where there was action.

Often there is little correspondence between media-presented reality and actual events. In one of the earliest documented examples of this phenomenon,

Lang and Lang (1968) demonstrate how individuals attending General McArthur's homecoming parade witnessed a very different event than those observing the parade on television. Similarly, they demonstrated that perceptions of the 1952 political party conventions varied not only among those attending and those observing on television, but among those watching different networks as well.

Overall, these and other examples demonstrate that on some level, mass media are influential. In other words, outcomes and behavioral paths of actors are altered by the presence (or absence) of information in mass media. From a political perspective, keeping items off the agenda, as well as putting them on, is an indicator of influence or power in relationships. However, one question exists if we are to consider mass media in power relationships. Earlier in this chapter it was noted that preference is a key dimension in power analysis. Mass media, however, it can be argued, do not express preferences, particularly news media with strong conventions of neutrality. How then can media have influence? We are certain that behavioral paths are altered, but in the absence of specific preferences. Nevertheless, one can consider the overall preference of mass media institutions and organizations to inform, teach, educate, pursuade, entertain, or otherwise convey information. When this is done, and as a result behaviors or outcomes are altered from what they would have been in the absence of mass media, it can be concluded that the media are, in the true sense of the word, influential.

COMMUNICATION AND PERSUASION

If power is the ability to gain successful outcomes, it is also the ability to persuade. The elements of such persuasion may range from making offers that cannot be refused, to possession of data and logical reasoning capabilities for intellectually convincing others to change behavioral paths. Regardless of which approach is used, something must be effectively communicated within the power relationships.

In the case of influence, persuasive success may rest in authority or organizational role capacities. In meritocracies, persumably supervisory personnel have earned their positions through achievement, intellectual prowess, or substantive expertise. Subordinates assume they have much to learn from superordinates. Therefore, it is with little difficulty that supervisors resolve problems and reason with fellow workers. Moreover, there are always power resources available: employees can be disciplined or dismissed for failing to follow orders.

Thus, under ordinary circumstances, with governments, bureaucracies, families, and industrial organizations persuasive communications are rarely interesting to study. However, in situations where there is less formal (or informal) legitimacy, persuasive communications are more noteworthy. A great deal of empirical work on persuasive communications has been done ranging from studies of wartime propaganda of military enemies to information campaigns (see Chapter 14). Experiments by social psychologists (Hovland, Janis, & Kelly, 1953) in particular have led to conventionally accepted research findings that have guided our understanding of persuasive communications. And, although these findings have occasionally been questioned, they have at least underscored those aspects of communicatory relationships worth pursuing in the study of persuasive communication.

Persuasive communications characteristics have generally been divided into those of the source, the audience, and the message itself. Experimental and other research has identified personal attributes and social status of sources of messages, for example, to be important variables for successfully persuading audiences. Indeed, whole lists of these attributes have been developed: sources are mostly likely to be successful in their persuasion if they are credible, trustworthy, attractive, or perceived of as expert. In short, source esteem is an important variable if influence resources such as popularity, skills, or socioeconomic status are considered.

In addition to these personal characteristics, however, the influence of a source is also a function of the "referant power" of the source. The prestige of a source may lead audiences to identify with it and comply. Or, the source can be a member of a group with whom audiences identify, or with which audiences would like to be compared. Group related influence may also take a very different form, such as through behavioral contagion. Individuals may find that any reference group member takes on influence as a source. All of these phenomena are group related but still enhance the influence potential of any individual with appropriate group affiliations.

A number of audience or target characteristics have also been cited as crucial in the influence process. In general, these characteristics may be divided into four categories: motivations, cognitions, resistance forces, and socialization. Influencing attempts and the success of persuasive communications depend upon these characteristics.

In terms of motivation, targets or audiences seeking acceptance or conformity are most easily persuaded. The desire not to be different is a strong one. Where there is enforcement of group standards in particular, motivations to conform are often important as well. Individuals may have psychological needs to conform, or may be differentially suggestible. Persuasibility of a given individual may depend on the extent to which beliefs are dogmatically held, as well as needs for consistency with other cognitions, stages in need hierarchies, or many other psychological variables.

Many of these personality questions spill over to the domain of cognitions. Capacities (cognitively) of targets to adhere to the demands or requests imposed by persuasive communications vary. Similarly, the extent to which any source tactic (such as appeal to identification) is successful depends on the levels of aspiration maintained by the target. To avoid problems of cognitive consistency targets may avoid certain messages completely and selectively expose themselves to only consonant messages.

Resistance forces may also constrain the effectiveness of persuasive communications. Target audiences may resist for some of the personality related reasons cited above. But perhaps most important are the group oriented resistance factors. Because messages, be they persuasive or not, are often received in a group of social context, it is essential to take this context into consideration as a resistance force. Individuals may be members of several groups, thus a persuasive message appealing to one group may have no effect on an individual belonging to several groups. In such a situation, there may be cross-pressures as group loyalties cut across message effectiveness. In general, the group context shapes attitudes and opinions; with respect to persuasive communications it shapes effectiveness and influence. The more salient the group, the greater its effect on persuasive communication influences. Messages are ordinarily sent to audiences that are not mass in the strict sense of the word, but instead are parts of groups in which messages are ordinarily heard.

Finally, the socialization of targets bears on the effectiveness of persuasive messages. The rules of the game, so to speak, are defined through acculturation. Similarly, the respect accorded sources, their legitimacy and authority, are rooted in the socialization processes as well.

Several scholars have isolated certain message characteristics important in influence attempts. Because so much of power and influence analysis is rooted in the transmission of threats, rewards, or legitimacy and authority, message types vary considerably. Messages may be implicit or explicit, but again certain principles are relatively fixed. Research, again by social psychologists, has suggested that variables such as fear appeal, recognition of salient group norms, order of presentation of arguments, presentation of one or two-sided messages, amount of change advocated, or the use of summary conclusions are important for determining the success of persuasive messages. Whatever the case, in conjunction with source and target characteristics, the effectiveness of persuasive messages and propaganda are constructed with these variables in mind.

Regardless of its success, propaganda has been considered an integral part of political communication. But the failure of isolated propaganda (in contrast to fundamental propaganda that envelopes the whole culture [Ellul, 1965]) to be proven useful, does not minimize its worth as one more power resource. At the very least, as indicated earlier, it can play a major role in the assertion of legitimacy in situations where legitimacy must be established.

COMMUNITY ANALYSIS

Power and influence in communities has intrigued both sociologists and political scientists. Machiavelli wrote normatively of how to govern a larger community such as a kingdom; popular psychologists write of how to wield influence or power in small organizations. Moderately sized communities are, perhaps, best studied by communication researchers and other social scientists, because what occurs in communities is largely a function of communication patterns within the community.

Hawley and Wirt (1968), and Jennings (1964) write of five modes of community analysis. Each of these has implications for the political communication scholar concerned with power and influence. The first mode is the study of traditional decision-making politics. Local cultures and institutions are noted, channels of communication and access described, and so forth. Second, there have been a variety of studies of interpersonal influence, in which particular cases are explored. For the most part, these studies have demonstrated an instability of influence across issue areas. Issue studies themselves have been a third major avenue of inquiry. Specific decisions made within communities are researched in terms of who made the decisions, what interaction patterns characterized the decision, and so on. Fourth, power structures within communities have been examined. Specifically, the roles and processes through which influence operates are identified. Finally, communities have been analyzed from the sociological tradition. Social norms, subgroup interaction or even the formation of groups, and other identifiable characteristics of communities have been identified.

Each mode of community analysis has several research examples. The decision-making process across three issue areas was studied by Dahl (1961), who found each issue to have a single leadership. At the same time, he noted a certain reciprocal, circulating leadership across issues. In communication terms, access was the key; information ordinarily was circulated only among small networks, suggesting ultimately that his community (New Haven) was characterized by oligopolistic politics rather than democratic or elitist politics.

Other research cuts across the distinctions previously noted. The Lynds (1929) for example, in their study of Middletown, found a business elite to dominate politics. The power structure itself, and decision-making analysis both led to the same conclusion. Hunter's original (1953) study of Atlanta employed sociometric measurement techniques to reveal the flow of power in the community and the importance of group affiliations. In particular, he noted the resources of the powerful economic sanctions potentially imposed and the ability to establish the agenda. Although research by Jennings (1964), a decade later, suggested that attributed influentials had no impact empirically, actual influentials were still characterized by extensive interactions.

The community study most intimately linked to communication processes and behavior was Merton's study of Rovere (1949). In his attempt to identify the influentials in Rovere, Merton found that peers more often than economic or political elites were considered influential. Largely as a result of continuous interaction and interpersonal communication on certain matters, there were local influentials who differed from cosmopolitan influentials with broader concerns and influence areas. Interestingly, both local and cosmopolitan influentials used mass media more than average persons in the community. Merton's work, although in the tradition of community analysis, was different because it positively focused on communication variables to identify influentials. Moreover, it led to a line of research—opinion leadership—that has been at center of communication research for two decades.

OPINION LEADERSHIP

Opinion leadership as a concept derived from the work at the Bureau of Applied Social Research at Columbia University, particularly from the work of Lazarsfeld and Merton (1948). In many ways, this concept has endured more than almost any other in communications, and, it might be argued, has been misapplied or misunderstood more than any other term.

In Lazarsfeld, Berelson and Gaudet's (1948) classic election study they found that, among other things, that late deciders in the political campaign were influenced by interpersonal relations. They argued that there was a "two-step flow" of influence originating from mass media, which generated ideas adhered to by certain individuals. These individuals in turn then discussed what they heard with inattentive or nonexposed individuals. In general, they found that the former group served as "opinion leaders" for the latter group, the followers, and also as a bridge between mass media and the politically undecided.

Several plausible explanations were offered to analyze these findings. Interpersonal contact, because it is viewed as nonpurposive, can be particularly influential because resistance by the listener is low. There is no selectivity of reception, and, in general, barriers to the flow of information are not constructed. Second, interpersonal communications are flexible, tailored to the needs and desires of persons involved in the interchanges, to meet objectives and adopt to the situation. Third, there are certain implicit rewards to the follower (and to the leader), such as approval or enhanced prestige. Fourth, of course, there is greater trust and confidence in intimate sources. And finally, friendship often serves to motivate compliance. Although this may mean that persuasion occurs without any real conviction on the part of the follower, the net result is a change.

Follow up studies to *The People's Choice* reinforced the credibility of the two-step flow. Work by Merton (1949); Katz and Lazarsfeld (1955); and Lipset, Trow, and Coleman (1956) supported the concept. Generalizations about who were opinion leaders emerged. Opinion leaders were found to be monomorphic rather than polymorphic and, in general, opinion leaders differed from followers in information sources, status, cosmopolitanism, innovativeness, or technical expertise. Nevertheless, the implication that opinion leaders were identifiable by attributes did injustice to the concept: opinion leadership was developed originally as a sociological concept, but emerged later as an individual (or role) characteristic.

In any event, before the confusion over the nature of opinion leadership emerged, there were certain implications to opinion leader findings. Mass media were viewed as having only a limited role in the formation of beliefs and attitudes. Indeed, whatever "influence" mass media had was through strategically located individuals availing themselves of the media. Still, in a variety of cultural contexts, this research continued. School teachers, priests in rural Greek villages, were placed into the framework (Stycos, 1952) as were political and religious leaders in Turkey (Stycos, 1965), agricultural innovators in India (Ruhadkar, 1958), and village leaders in Egyptian rural communities (Harik, 1971).

Despite continuing opinion leadership research, there have now been several research projects resulting in "revisionist" notions concerning opinion leadership. First, some rural sociology studies (Rogers & Shoemaker, 1972) showed different types of leaders evolved for different situations. There were stimulators, who argued for the necessity of innovation in communities, but there were also legitimizers, trend setters influential in sanctioning new ideas, and implementors who were early users of innovation. Each actor was a leader with a different constituency and had roots of authority in different stages of innovation.

The most recent research has suggested that the concept of opinion leadership was really an artifact of mass media use patterns at the time it was first articulated. Indeed, researchers began to break down the concept into a learning component and an evaluation component. For learning, it was argued (Troldhal, 1966), that there is a one-step flow, directly from media. In an era of high literacy, pervasive media use, easy access to information from various sources, the notion of only some people attending to mass media seemed limited. The second component, evaluation, may be linked to a two-step flow, or at least follow from interpersonal discussion of relevant information. Opinion leadership was viewed in several research projects, including diffusion studies (Ostlund, 1973; Robinson, 1976, Troldhal & Van Dam, 1965), no longer to be an information concept, but literally a source of opinion. A new, multistep flow of communications emerged, with a variety of permutations and combinations.

Information flows to leaders through the mass media. At the same time, it flows from the media to the less attentive. It also flows from the leaders to the less attentive, and vice versa. And, of course, within groups it flows from leader to leader and from the less attentive to others who are equally inattentive. Thus, there are a variety of possible information and opinion sources, and the two-step flow no longer universally applies. As we have seen, when divided into its learning and evaluation components, the two-step concept takes on different meanings.

If there is opinion leadership, it is modified considerably from its original conceptualization. One must consider the pervasiveness of media use. But even more important is the social interaction that gives certain individuals more clout within a community. No longer is it merely access to information that enables some individuals to become more influential. It is also the other characteristics— those ordinarily associated with membership in social and political elites, particularly strategic location in groups—that underlie influential status.

LEADERSHIP IN GROUPS

Consistent with the notion that power is based largely on access to information, is the idea that leadership is information based as well. Leaders may emerge in groups for a variety of reasons. Proponents of trait approaches argue that individual qualities result in leadership, whereas others have noted situational variables to be crucial (Hollander, 1968). Regardless of how one comes to occupy such a position, leaders must be perceived as such by group members. In the absence of such perceptions, potential influence over other individuals is minimized.

Janda (1960) has defined a group leader, in communications terms, as one who has the right to issue certain stimuli, which are considered as such by others in the group. Thus, leaders are responsible for goal setting. Methods used by leaders vary, of course, with the size and composition of the group. For example, small groups rely much more on face-to-face interaction and are likely to be characterized by less formal communications than larger, more bureaucratic groups. Independent of group size, however, commands will be issued.

Regardless of the leadership of the groups, groups themselves may wield power within a political system or large organization largely as a result of communications phenomena. Ordinarily, as Collins and Guetzkow (1964) point out, groups consolidate and centralize information from their task specialization. The most authoritative groups gather information from a variety of sources, such as direct personal investigation, and observation of the investigations of others. As indicated in Figure 3.3 groups wield power because of their ability to consolidate as well as filter demands and decisional outputs. Although a fuller discussion of groups in the political system would reveal the depth of their influence in the political system; more complete analyses by group theorists address the subtleties far better than can be done here.

CONCLUSION

Throughout this chapter, diverse literatures and theoretical approaches to power and influence have been consolidated to yield a communication view of political power. Fundamentally, there are two crucial elements to the approach: first, power and authority can exist only where there is information exchange. Second, strategic location in relationships in which an actor is in a position to control the flow of information is essential to understanding power and authority. Perhaps, with these two communication based notions, political scientists and communication researchers can better explain processes ranging from community power, to agenda-setting, opinion leadership, and to the persuasibility of audiences.

7
INFORMATION
AND POLITICAL SOCIALIZATION

For some students of politics, the range and scope of political participation help define a political system. Differences engendered across individuals in terms of the type, quality, and degree of participation have, when aggregated, significant implications for the system. Underlying the propensities for individuals to participate, however, lies their political socialization. Thus, a question political scientists must face is explaining those factors in the political socialization process that result in differential participatory orientation.

Research on this question requires the integration of both micro and macropolitical analysis. Political socialization has been a part of the political scientist's active vocabulary for only two decades (Hyman, 1959), but in that short time period it has come to be recognized as a concept of major significance (Renshon, 1977). In part, this rapid recognition of political socialization stems from its strategic location at the interface between micro and macropolitical analysis. But its relative youth as a legitimate field of political inquiry has limited the integration of the micro and macro perspectives. Furthermore, only recently have theories been offered to explain the empirical findings political scientists were quick to gather.

In this chapter only one communication approach to the concept of socialization is offered: message exposure during critical periods is argued to assure the significance of information in explaining orientations and understanding of the political world. Alternative communications based explanations can exist including consideration of political socialization as the intergenerational transfer of information, and approaching political socialization through information exchange and transfer theories. But because one purpose of this book is to illustrate how political concepts may be viewed as communications phenomena, the perspective of this chapter serves equally well as an information exchange theory to conceptualize and explain research findings in political socialization.

PREVIOUS APPROACHES
TO POLITICAL SOCIALIZATION

The research questions upon which political socialization researchers have focused are many. Lasswell's question, so often asked by communication scholars, has been adopted by political socialization researchers and reformulated as "*who* learns *what* from *whom* under *what circumstances* and with what effect." Dennis (1968), for example, has outlined ten distinct dimensions to political socialization research, including the system relevance, cross cultural, elite, and subcultural aspects of political socialization; generational and life-cycle socialization analysis; as well as the learning process, content, effects, and agents of socialization. However, Dennis' enumeration tells of the subject of socialization research, not of contending approaches. Sears' (1975) review of the literature enabled him to claim that researchers explore only three broad categories despite the number of subjects Dennis could identify: (1) attachment to the political system; (2) partisan attitudes; and (3) political participation. This limited number of variables of interest to political scientists has in part been responsible for leading micro level researchers into analysis of the content and timing of political socialization, rather than an understanding of its processes. Concentrating micro level research on content and timing to the exclusion of an explication of the process through which individuals acquire attitudes, drives a wedge between the research approaches of macro level political theorists and political psychologists. As Sears notes:

> ... theories of political socialization take two forms. Psychological theories treat individual predispositions (e.g., the child's political attitudes or level of involvement) as the primary output variables whereas "political" theories treat them as way stations to the key output variables which involve some aspect of the political system (e.g., its persistence) or political policy. [95].

On the one hand, macro-oriented political scientists study political socialization because presumably early attitudes have consequences for the political system. Political psychologists, on the other hand, are more interested in the process of development itself. The issues and systemically important findings, which interest some political scientists are, therefore, of little concern to psychologists; whereas psychological theories directed at exploration of the socialization process, but without specific empirical political referents, are of little concern to system oriented scholars. As a result, political scientists have failed to employ many potentially useful psychological theories, and have avoided research inquiries directed at the process of socialization itself. Again, Sears calls attention to this problem, arguing that instead of limiting political socialization inquiries to the study of conformity and maintenance of the status quo, political scientists should look at personal growth and development processes that enable individuals to express themselves, meet needs and values, and attain unique political identities.

As a micro or individual level concept political socialization can be defined as the process by which individuals come to learn about the political norms, beliefs, values, and institutions of the society of which they are members. From this perspective, the concern of political socialization researchers has been with the content of individual beliefs, individual attachment to political systems, knowledge about the system, the dynamics of political learning, and so forth. Although this individual level approach can in itself contribute to understanding *homo politicus,* it largely ignores the systemic import of aggregation of politically socialized citizens.

Macro level theorists concentrate on the consequences or functions of political socialization. From this perspective, a working definition of political socialization would identify it as a field of inquiry concerning the transmission of those political values resulting in political orientations of consequence to the political system. This approach emphasizes the political system as the dependent variable, and concentrates on the continuity (or discontinuity) of political regimes or the development of participatory behavior resulting from the political socialization processes.

As was suggested earlier, neither of these two approaches is by itself fully satisfactory. Macro theorists are concerned with the core problems political scientists grapple with—how political systems operate—but gloss over the processes by which the political socialization of individuals and resulting idiosyncratic differences leads to different political cultures. On the other hand, micro level analysts fail to discuss the political import of the individual differences they isolate. What is called for, then, is the linkage of these two analytic approaches by developing explanations of the political socialization processes that explore the genesis of differences in individual political orientations and a description of the systemic consequences of the aggregation of those individual differences.

Between these two views lies the approach taken by communication researchers. With the possible exception of participation, socialization has been the most widely researched major political concept by communication scholars. Long concerned with demonstrating a linkage between exposure to information and specific effects, communication researchers have in particular tried to isolate the effects of various media. Moreover, many of these scholars have focused on children under the implicit assumption that socialization is a finite process, the end product of which is carried through life. Communications scientists have not been alone. Anthropologists (Benedict, 1934; Mead, 1929), sociologists (Cooley,

1902; Mead, 1934), psychologists (Whiting & Child, 1953), as well as political scientists (Renshon, 1977; Sears, 1975), all have explored the socialization process from the perspectives of their own disciplines. In each case, the assumptions of the analysis vary as much as the phenomena to be explained, making the development of a comprehensive theory of the socialization process difficult. Although general theories of social phenomena are always sought, factors which tend to minimize the comparability of phenomena or differences in available data have in the past required that explanations of the socialization process within each social science discipline be more or less unique.

CHILDREN AND POLITICAL SOCIALIZATION

Expressly political socialization has long been of concern to political theorists and politicians alike. In ancient Greece, Plato noted the need to develop a civic awareness of the *polis* among young citizens. In modern political systems politicians have created the Hitler Youth, the Komosomol, and the young Democrats, which, to a varying degree, all have as their goals the training of young citizens and the development of loyalties to a particular system.

Although Plato referred to citizenship training and thought it an important part of the school curricula, more modern political scientists have recognized a variety of "agents" as having an impact on young citizen's orientations. Through the more active vocabulary of the socialization process, modern scholars have also attempted to avoid the implied passivity of "citizenship training." The concept of political socialization has become recognized as an ongoing process rather than one which terminates with the completion of formal education, although the major emphasis of political socialization research has been, and continues to be, on the developing political awareness of children.

Although rarely made explicit, there are several reasons why children have been at the core of political socialization research. First it can be argued that under specified circumstances, early learning is enduring. This primacy principle suggests whatever is learned first by the maturing child is permanently etched on a *tabula rasa*. Secondly, even if this early learning is displaced, vestiges may linger structuring later socialization through early learning. A third, empirical justification for emphasizing children has been offered. Children, as naive informants of the adult culture, can offer insights into the process of political thought.

The assumptions of the validity of the primacy principle and research on children almost exclusively has been called into question from several quarters. Critiques by Renshon (1977); Schonfield (1971); and Searing, Schwartz, and Lind (1973) have been particularly attentive to the failure of proponents of the primacy principle to link children's political orientations to adult orientations more theoretically. Proponents of recency theory offer opposing hypotheses to the primacy theorists, arguing that learning occurring closest to adulthood is of greater influence and political relevance than childhood learning.

Despite the intensity of the debate, neither proponents of the primacy principle nor of the recency theory can claim the ability to explain fully the processes of political socialization. Synthetic models, such as that of Weissberg (1974), offer the most promise. These synthetic models draw on early learning for political attachments, identifications, and general ideological preferences, linking specific issue orientations and behaviors to adult learning.

Although these first efforts to create synthetic models offer hope that the primacy-recency dichotomy will become less polarized over time, the key issues in the debate still require further clarification. By rephrasing the critical questions of the primacy-recency controversy, rather than dismissing the arguments generated by proponents of one or both, this clarification can be made, and the possible linkages between children's and adults' political behavior be made more explicit.

AGENTS OF POLITICAL SOCIALIZATION

Empirical research from a decade ago (Easton & Dennis, 1969; Greenstein, 1965; Hess & Torney, 1967) demonstrated that children have some degree of familiarity with the political system. Early studies concentrating on the content of children's political cognitions and hinting at the sources of these cognitions led to the development of the traditional "agent" approach to political socialization whereby the family (Davies, 1965, 1977; Jennings & Langton, 1969; Jennings and Niemi, 1968, 1971, 1974; and Langton, 1969), school (Levin, 1961; Merelman, 1971; Patrick, 1977), peers (Dawson, Prewitt, & Dawson, 1977; Silberger, 1977), and mass media (Byrne, 1969; Chaffee, Jackson-Beeck, Durall, & Wilson, 1977; Chaffee, Ward, & Tipton, 1970; Conway, Stevens, & Smith, 1975; Hollander, 1971; Roberts, Hawkins, & Pingree, 1975) were identified as primary socialization agents. Although empirical studies concentrating on agents of political socialization frequently showed correlations between children's political orientations and the orientations of the various agents, the explanations of the causes of these correlations have frequently been deficient. Among other things, it is argued by Hess and Torney, for example, that the school is the most important socializing agent because classroom politics provides a structural model for politics. Moreover, schools are crucial because teachers spend as much time with children as parents do, and children recognize their teacher as an omniscient expert, whose wisdom includes what can be called political wisdom. Similarly, Jennings and his associates argue that parents may directly preach their political views, provide role models (which includes political role modeling) for the children to imitate, or create an atmosphere conducive to feelings of efficacy or a trust generalized to politics. Those arguing for the importance of the mass media often assume there is a "hypodermic effect," wherein messages transmitted through the media impact directly on individuals without any other mediation.

All these approaches continue to divide and compartmentalize our understanding of the political socialization process and tend to obscure those variables common to the many possible agents. In addition, this segmented approach is usually limited to explaining limited findings of specific political attitudes or beliefs held by children.

COMMUNICATION AND POLITICAL SOCIALIZATION

The contributions of communication researchers to an understanding of political socialization have been limited to a continuing controversy over the presence or absence of indirect or direct effects of mass media exposure on political behavior. In their recent review of the political socialization literature, Kraus and Davis (1976) have been particularly critical of the failure of researchers to entertain specific media variables in their conceptualization. Kraus and Davis argue that mass media, pervasive as they are from early childhood through adulthood, must have direct effects on political behaviors.

Although the direct effects notion has considerable common sense appeal (after all, why would candidates spend money on political advertising or the U.S.I.C.A. on radio broadcasts or propaganda campaigns?), its popularity nowadays is in marked contrast to the conventional wisdom of two decades ago. At that time, Klapper (1960) suggested that mass media's role in politics was limited, largely because people expose themselves to messages consistent with their pre-existing beliefs.

Though such limited effects findings no longer apply in an era of pervasive and indiscriminant media use, we still need evidence to support a direct effects notion. Mass media messages are received in a social context, in families or with groups or at the workplace; these contexts provide an ever changing background for interpreting messages. As a result, whereas evidence is mounting that mass media provide information (particularly for young people) (Conway et al., 1975; Dominick, 1974; Hollander, 1971; Johnson, 1973), evidence on what implications this information has for behavior is not yet conclusive.

Whether or not mass media have limited or direct effects on political behavior, they are only one aspect of communication. Previously, we defined communication as a relational concept, involving more than simply mass media. Communication scholars are as much at fault in this regard as are other social scientists, for they fail to conceptualize the entire political socialization process as a communications process, consisting of a variety of agents (senders) with numerous messages for the emerging citizen (audience).

Because the focus of the agent research approach was on specific actors (parents and teachers) or institutions (the family or school) transmitting political information rather than the message itself or the receiver of that information, there is little understanding of how people (particularly children) come to learn about the political world.

A communications oriented theory would approach the notion of an agent somewhat differently. Taking a cue from early social psychologists (Hovland, Janis, & Kelly, 1953), for example, would lead to the recognition of certain communication characteristics capable of explaining the persistent (yet not particularly strong) relationship between parent and child political orientation. Parents are communicators who have demonstrated their expertise, knowledge, and judgment to the child in numerable nonpolitical contexts that a child may generalize to the political world. Parents are held in great esteem, and in general, exhibit many of the traits associated with effective communicators. Another aspect of parental significance in the socialization process is that during early years, parents are the only source of political information. But the most important aspect of parents (and the family) as socializing actors is that they provide a context and framework for the receipt of messages from other sources.

The findings of political socialization researchers with respect to the role of the family can be explained through this communications notion. Parents, unlike other information sources such as teachers or much mass media, have no constraints on partisanship. Hence children exhibit the same party identification as their parents (Butler & Stokes, 1969; Jennings & Niemi, 1968) but maintain few other orientations consistent with their parents, largely because political affairs are rarely discussed, or because by the time the child (audience) can understand politics (if discussed), there are already alternative sources of information competing for the loyalties of the child. Indeed, even within a single home, sources (mothers and fathers, siblings) may be providing mixed messages. For example, Jennings and Niemi (1974) suggest that when both parents espouse similar political orientations, children are more likely to have parent-linked political values then when there are parents holding different viewpoints. In other words, equally credible, trusted, and loved sources are in a standoff when they present opposing messages. But when parents do disagree, children, spending more time with mothers are more likely (Jennings & Niemi, 1971) to agree with mothers than fathers.

For providing a communications environment, parents and families are even more significant. They provide a context and framework for the receipt of political messages from other information sources, and to some extent shape the degree to which children might desire political information. The findings of Chaffee, Ward, and Tipton (1970), for example, support the notion that varying family environments directly encourage or discourage conflict and conflict avoidance, and indirectly develop political interest and information seeking. In addition, families provide structural and role models in the home environment. The ways in which authority is used in the home, the development of strategies for bargaining within the family, all are part of the home political environment. This information need only be generalized to the external world for the family's role to be enhanced. Overall, both in terms of the explicit political information provided and in structuring the environment for access to and receipt of other information, the family plays a role in the political socialization process.

Schools house a variety of sources of information. Teachers, textbooks, and classroom media provide formal information, whereas certain activities such as student government and class elections are less formal structural models for the political world. Findings underscoring the significance of teachers in the political socialization process reflect perceptions of teachers as knowledgeable sources, with whom school-age children spend a considerable proportion of their time. Although teachers may not be loved to the extent that parents are, they may be more respected as expert informants. Hess and Torney's (1967) research, which presents a case for the influence of schools (teachers), however, is the only one of its kind supporting teacher impact. In part, the norms against presenting partisan viewpoints in the classroom are quite strong, thus minimizing teacher discussion of politics.

Although teachers themselves may not be important communicators, they do use texts and do provide information in specialized curricula. From only limited evidence (Litt, 1963) students are exposed to materials supportive of the status quo, providing views of culture and history consistent with prevailing values. Most significant, however, is the fact that when exploring differences between students exposed to civics courses (and texts) with those not taking such courses, differences in political orientations are negligible (Langton & Jennings, 1968; Merelman, 1971). The only exceptions are nonwhite students who apparently learn from civics courses and texts, and strengthen their levels of political tolerance. For all others, the absence of significant findings may be explained by considering civics course information redundant; everything presented has simply been heard elsewhere.

Supplemental classroom media, such as the *Weekly Reader,* also have been shown to be less important sources of information when alternative sources exist. Content analysis (Meadow, 1977) of the *Weekly Reader,* for example, showed it provided broad cultural news rather than explicitly political information, so its role as a political informant is minimized. Nevertheless, the symbolic aspects of classroom media ought not be overlooked. Week after week, school children are provided with a newspaper or news magazine format not unlike their adult weekly news magazine counterparts. And, although the messages themselves may have little relevance to politics, the fact that the adult world is emulated underscores the potential significance of schools in an information oriented socialization process.

What is significant about schools in the political socialization process is that so many levels of communication are involved through relationships with teachers and peers. Interpersonal communication is a part of experiential learning of political roles. Mass communication through texts and supplemental classroom materials is employed as well. In short, although there may be little empirical evidence attributing a significant role to schools, the lesson to be learned is almost McLuhanesque: the variety of sources through which political values can be learned is the message of schoolhouse socialization.

Families and schools have been the information sources most frequently considered by political socialization researchers, because they are the sources to which children—the usual focus of political socialization research—have traditionally been exposed. Indeed, according to Beck (1977), they occupy 100 percent of the waking hours of children.

But this division of the child's time is inaccurate. Since 1961, when Schramm, Lyle, and Parker first presented their data on children's television use, evidence has been mounting that children spend more time watching television (about 18,000 hours up through age 18—four to six hours per day) than almost any other activity besides sleeping. And, if the conceptualization of political socialization is expanded beyond children and considered as a lifelong process, other sources of political information, social peers and coworkers, join mass media as sources of political information.

Looking first at peers, there is relatively little empirical evidence available to which our information based conceptualization of politics can be mapped. Longitudinal studies by Newcombe (1943, 1967) have shown peer groups to play important roles in shaping lifelong political orientations. At a theoretical level, however, sociologists such as Coleman (1961) and others have argued for the significance of peer groups. Later in life, as other sources of information (except the family of procreation and mass media) no longer occupy adult life space, peers and coworkers are the only interpersonal information sources. Moreover, they become sources as most people begin participating politically on a regular basis. Finally, politics—at least certain social and economic issues—becomes more salient just as interaction with peers peaks.

On a day-to-day basis, coworkers share experiences and insights. Adults with secondary association memberships find additional people with whom to share their views. Sociometric and interpersonal influence studies (see Chapter 6) suggest how important other adults become as sources of information and opinion. Of course, a modified version of a limited effects model could be argued: people only join those groups or associate with people sharing political viewpoints. But as likely as not, there is little choice involved in selecting one's workmates, and politics rarely plays a significant role in most social affiliations.

Peer groups thus play a role, both as sources of information and in providing a context for the reception of messages. Peer group political interaction may occur in subtle ways in nonpolitical settings. Removed from the home environment where people live with spouses usually sharing viewpoints (Finifter, 1974; Newcombe, 1967), social support for opinions often is absent. In a mobil economic and social system, individuals from a variety of backgrounds may share the workplace. All in all, new information (or any information for nonmedia users) is part of the daily experience. Undoubtedly, some may counter one set of peers by socially interacting with those of backgrounds or viewpoints similar to long held values. But for those who don't, peer interactions are an important source of information.

TELEVISION AND SOCIALIZATION

For both children and adults, interactions with (or rather exposure to) mass media exceed interactions (quantitatively) with people. Yet, as noted earlier, studies of mass media's role in the political socialization process have been bogged down with arguments emanting from "bullet" or "hypodermic" effects paradigms, where mass media as stimuli are likened to Pavlov's bell, and audiences, like the dogs, salivate or otherwise behave as directed (Figure 7.1).

More sophisticated treatments of mass media as political socialization agents have recognized that effects are not direct and consistent, but instead vary by context or across individuals. Political (or other) behaviors do not follow automatically from stimuli, but are filtered first through perceptions, and then through individual habits, values, personality attributes, and social contexts (Figure 7.2).

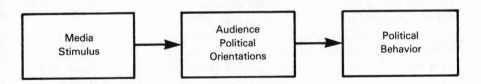

Figure 7.1 Simple Stimulus Response

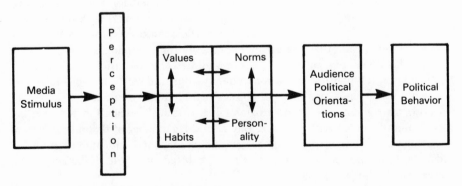

Figure 7.2 Filtered Stimulus Response

Even the most sophisticated notions of major intervention between mass media and political behavior fail to adequately conceptualize the political dimensions of mass media. Research studies focus primarily on explicit sources of political information: newspapers, television news, news magazines. But so limiting mass media's role in the political socialization process to the overtly political is to oversimplify their role considerably for both children and adults.

Explicitly, political mass media (using political to signify dealing with government activities) without doubt contribute to political cognitions of adults and children. Political events and personalities change frequently, and new issues emerge or old ones evolve and are reported in news media. Ample evidence collected over the past twenty years has demonstrated the importance of news (Chaffee, Ward & Tipton, 1970; Conway et al., 1975; Dominick, 1972; Johnson, 1973; Roberts, Hawkins, & Pingree, 1975). For young children, television news glimpsed while parents watch is the most important source of political information. The appeal of television as a source of political information is readily identifiable. It is attractive to two senses, and thus is more vivid than other mass media. In particular, because it is graphic and appeals to the eye, viewers perceive it to have a high fidelity to actual events. Seeing is believing; hence, television is credible. Unlike print media, it requires little attention, and can be employed as background noise or "viewed" while engaged in other activities. Few skills are needed to watch television, it has no marginal cost to view, and can be viewed at home, in a congenial setting, with little or no effort. But perhaps the biggest factor enhancing the audience's high affect for television is that it is the medium that brings them their daily entertainment.

Without doubt, other media serve entertainment functions. Berelson's (1949) classic study on newspaper use revealed people use newspapers to provide entertainment through sports pages, comic strips, and fashion sections. Indeed, even the most prestigious of newspapers, the New York *Times,* has added entertainment feature sections to all of its workday editions. But the number of hours spent with newspapers, or the number of households even purchasing a newspaper, is paled by the hours households view television daily. Radio, too, may provide news, but its pattern of use reveals consumers seek immediately relevant news such as weather reports or traffic conditions rather than political news on radio, and otherwise use radio primarily for entertainment.

The popularity of television news underscores television's potential for contributing to political cognitions directly. But, indirectly as well, television contributes to understanding the political world (some would argue shapes the world) through entertainment programming. Although research in this area has been almost nonexistent (Kraus & Davis, 1976), a number of theoretical reasons for television's importance can be cited, and anecdotal and limited empirical data already are being gathered (Frank & Meadow, 1974; Katzman, 1972; Meadow, 1973b; Merelman, 1968).

Much of the study of television's role in the social and cultural systems has sprung from research on violence in television. Work by the President's Commission on Crime and Violence (1967), later work on television and aggression (Feshbach & Singer, 1971), and continuing message analysis of many dimensions of entertainment programming (Gerbner et al., 1978) have outlined the basic arguments for television's portrayal of society, its dilemmas and actors. However, these studies have failed to consider the political implications of entertainment programming at the individual level of analysis, although on occasion, systemic implications are drawn. At times we are narcotized; our attention is drawn away from the real issues of the day by our access to instant entertainment. Our capacity for reasoning and critical thinking is in many ways dulled by dependence on formula comedy and drama. Social lessons are also made clear. The good guys always win, crime does not pay, violence in the presence of justice is no vice, and a host of other television cliches are presented.

For individuals, television's political socialization role is less clear. Entertainment programming at one level provides a context for the individual's viewing of news. In many ways, television news is entertainment, sometimes it is presented as a soap opera unfolding daily, at other times (e.g., the Watergate hearings, Army-McCarthy hearings) like a suspense show. Daily lives are so pervaded by drama through television, it can be argued that citizens come to expect the real world of politics to be shaped as a drama, lest it be unexciting. Of course, at a second level, television entertainment programming provides information about the political world and political personalities at both cognitive and affective levels through portrayals of politicians and politics (see Chapter 12).

This description of the political socialization aspects of entertainment programming is not without empirical referents. Studies are beginning to emerge linking political knowledge and values to entertainment. Dominick (1974), for example, demonstrated that viewing crime shows was correlated with the belief that criminals usually get caught. Moreover, such viewers have higher levels of knowledge concerning the rights of arrested people than nonviewers.

Political content is not limited to entertainment programming on television. Other fictional mass media, such as novels, commercial motion pictures, and even popular music or comic books contain political dimensions as well. Each of these media have their unique characteristics in terms of the viewing, reading, or listening context, audience size credibility, immediacy, or range of phenomena discussed. On the whole, although the effectiveness of media may differ from television, the principle is the same and political content abounds. Studies of films (Butler, 1974; Isenberg, 1975; Jarvie, 1970; Shain, 1974), popular music (Denisoff, 1969, 1970; Denisoff & Peterson, 1972; Fox & Williams, 1974; Sinclair & Levin, 1971), or novels (Blotner, 1967; MacDonald, 1974; Sanders, 1969); all reveal manifest or latent political content. And their impact as sources of information in the political socialization process has been studied as well. For example, Lovibond (1967) demonstrated that young children exposed to comic books accepted the ideology of comics of the strong dominating the weak, and those exposed to television believed more in the use of force in resolving disputes (see Chapter 12).

On the whole, the evidence, although not plentiful, suggests fictional media content may have important consequences for political values held by individuals. In the context of the Easton model of politics presented in Chapter 3, support for the system (or lack of support) is (or is not) developed partially through mass media as one of several sources of political information.

All of the agents cited by political socialization researchers can be viewed as sources of information. Indeed, all the findings in political socialization are adequately explained by reference to information emanating from various sources, with varying degrees of intensity, frequency, and accuracy at various points in the life cycles. Such a reconceptualization of agents, however, is not without its limitations or complexities. Specifically, individual differences in political cognitions or beliefs can be argued to be the result of exposure to different messages and information sources. Yet in mass society, where individuals are said to be fragmented and isolated, there are common experiences through exposure to national media. School systems provide roughly similar courses, texts, and social mobility to broaden the range of interpersonal contacts. So what then accounts for differences across individuals? In some cases it might be different levels of information exposure. But more generally it may be in the capacity of individuals to process and package the information to which they are exposed. In fact, it is the processing aspect of the information based theory of political socialization that offers improvements over the agents-through-the-life-cycle approach.

THE PROCESS OF POLITICAL LEARNING

Knowledge of the political orientations of children is in itself a goal of some political socialization research, but more often children are studied because of the linkages that children's political orientations presumably have to adult political behaviors. It has already been argued in this chapter that there is a need for theoretical underpinnings to political socialization research. Theories that purport to clarify when children have matured sufficiently to have the capability to think and act politically as adults and process political information, can thus bridge the gap between childhood and adult orientations.

A search for theoretical explanations of the political socialization process has recently been initiated. In particular, several scholars from both political science (Adelson & O'Neill, 1966; Bennet, 1975; Best, 1973; Meadow, 1976a; Merelman, 1969; Merelman & McCabe, 1974; Mladenka & Hill, 1975; Patterson,

1979; Riccards, 1973) and mass communication (Becker, McCombs, & McLeod, 1975) have considered a variety of cognitive and psychological development theories as fertile fields from which explanations of the processes through which children come of age politically can be gleaned. These researchers have argued that increments in the quantity and quality of political understanding are linked to progress along one or several psychological developmental continua. In other words, advances made by the child in terms of reaching an age at which political information from a variety of sources can be understood depends on developing cognitive skills, moral reasoning capability, personality, and ego strength.

Processing political information requires at the very least, possession of cognitive skills. As Merelman points out (1969, 1971, 1973), children must have the ability to think causally, to see interrelationships of events and ideas, and to arrange the world into meaningful order. In addition, the world must be viewed as malleable, so that there are incentives to take political action, and there must be communication skills so that ideologies can be shared. At the same time, Best (1973), and Sniderman (1975) have suggested how important personality and self-esteem are to developing (at least in the U.S.) participatory orientations. And finally, from Plato's time to the present (Fishkin, Kenniston, & MacKinnan, 1973; Patterson, 1979), politics has been viewed as having a strong moral component. Notions of good and bad, or right and wrong suffuse political decisions, the creation of laws, and the governing of society. Hence moral development and the capacity for making moral judgments can be seen as a third essential for political understanding.

Each of these developmental dimensions has been studied extensively. Most of the work of Piaget (1952, 1954, 1965, 1969) has been devoted almost exclusively to cognitive processes in children. Similarly Kohlberg (1968, 1969) has had a focus on the stages of developing moral reasoning capacity. Personality development is not as readily identifiable with a single psychologist, but among political scientists (Sniderman, 1975) self-esteem emerged as one of the crucial components of personality relevant for politics.

These developmental dimensions are cited for one main reason: they are independent dimensions along which humans develop, and are dimensions upon which the importance of information sources in the political socialization process depend for their impact.

Alone, each of the developmental variables can explain only a portion of political attitudes and awareness. Cognitive development is associated with political knowledge and a comprehension of the complexities of political institutions, thus accounting for the finding that older children are more informed and understand more about politics than younger children (Mladenka & Hill, 1975). But cognitive development alone cannot account for affective orientation, or behavioral disposition. Taken together, however, the development variables can offer explanations for a wide range of pre-adult orientations. The dynamic interaction of moral judgments moderating political cognitions, which give rise to particular attitudes and behavioral dispositions through a sense of self-esteem can lead to a fundamental understanding of political attitudes. Once the precise levels of development and the nature of the interactions and intervening factors are specified, predictions of individual capacity to comprehend the political system—and one's role in it—can be made. This capacity for comprehension (political maturity) may be viewed as a three dimensional space in which individuals are located at any point in their development.

The characteristics of children at various points in the development space are discussed in detail elsewhere (Meadow, 1976b), as are the measurement techniques for assessing individual location. Suffice it to say that development along the three dimensions varies across individuals, and each dimension is essential for increasing political maturity. When the three developmental dimensions reach specified levels, children (or young adults) are said to be "politically mature" and are as capable of responding to political cues as adults.

This capability, by itself, does not assure adult political sophistication. Required, in addition, is exposure to information about the political world, which is where our concern for an alternative to the agent approach is rooted. Therefore, explanations of the acquisition of adult political sophistication is the result of a two-stage process. First, the child must be developed along the three dimensions. Second, the child must be exposed to political information. This information will only be understood and applied if there is sufficient political maturation to enable the child to process the incoming information and meaningfully apply it. In other words, political information can only be digested if the child is "ready."

CRITICAL PERIODS AND READINESS

William James argued that organisms have an enhanced susceptibility to a given experience at certain stages of development. He referred to transitoriness of instincts, but in folk wisdom the expression, "strike while the iron is hot," is used more frequently to express the notion of the diminution of malleability over time. Recent research suggests that there are periods of malleability, known as critical or sensitive periods, during which important psychological processes are developing most rapidly. Intervention during these critical periods affects these processes in important ways. Whereas this notion has profound implications for the indoctrination of political values in youth or resocialization and brainwashing in adulthood, it also suggests that there may be a very limited period of time when adult or enduring political orientations develop during the political maturation process.

For children, the effectiveness of various sources of political information depends on whether or not these sources interact with the child when he or she has reached a high level of development across all three development dimensions.

During this time frame, known as the critical period, the child begins to understand political ideas and evaluate them. The idea of the existence of critical periods during childhood speaks to the issues of why children are at the core of political socialization research. As Dennis (1968) notes, once the period of the most rapid changes of political concepts and values has been located, scholars can focus more germanely on the proximate factors that serve to bring about these transformations.

Were it not for the notion of readiness or critical periods in the maturational sequence, political maturation during the pre-adult years would be of limited utility. Beyond the question of determining what forces are relevant to the child (and thereby influential) during the critical periods, knowledge of the time frame during which the most rapid changes occur speaks to the primacy problem raised earlier in this chapter. The value of the political maturation concept is that it provides a defining point for when the developing child is most susceptible to both political ideas (i.e., during the critical period of readiness) and fundamental political orientations, which are hypothesized to remain relatively enduring throughout the life cycle.

A number of political scientists have argued that crises during the critical period shape political values throughout the life span. Although longitudinal research designs best speak to that question, limited findings suggest critical periods may be at the core of generational political differences. In the absence of crises, so-called normal socialization and political orientations become implanted during the critical period.

The fundamental reason children fail to comprehend, or have naive perceptions of the political system until they have attained high stages of cognitive, moral, and personality development (i.e., reach high levels of political maturity) is because they simply have not reached readiness. The principle of readiness suggests that attained capacity limits and influences an individual's ability to profit from current experience or practice. In terms of the political maturation process, the critical period on the political maturation continuum occurs when the child has progressed sufficiently along the developmental dimensions to acquire sophisticated cognitions about politics, morally evaluate those politics, and have sufficient ego strength to feel capable of meeting the demands of politics. Readiness influences the efficiency of the learning process, and determines if particular skills can be learned at particular times. Knowledge of when readiness occurs offers advantages to those charged with political instruction, for postponement beyond the age of readiness wastes valuable learning opportunities and reduces the complexities that can be taught.

Although maturational change usually is accompanied by a readiness for the appearance of certain patterns of behavior, it is important to note that readiness is not coterminous with maturation, because it depends on both maturation (internal processes) and prior learning (external processes). Thus, having knowledge about an individual's level of political maturity does not necessarily enable one to predict political behaviors, for the notion of readiness suggests there must be information or prior experience in conjunction with maturation. Consequently, access to, and possession of, information, which serves as a basis for learning, can play a key role in determining readiness for adult political behavior. Because political maturity has been defined as the *capability* to maintain an accurate view of the political system, an individual with a high level of political maturity may exhibit low levels of political information or have no desire to seek information about the political world and may not engage in adult or sophisticated political thinking.

INFORMATION, MATURATION, AND POLITICAL SOCIALIZATION

The discussion of readiness and critical periods allows us, at last, to draw the linkage between information and maturation in the political socialization process. Alone, political maturity is unable to assure adult political thinking in children, for political sophistication—unlike physical growth or even abstract reasoning skills—is not innate. Both maturity *and* information are essential to political learning. In general, the information sources to which an individual is exposed during the critical period will be the source with the greatest effect on the individual. In other words, there is in fact a critical period during the child's development when a child is most susceptible to political communications. At some point nearly every one has a period of maximum susceptibility to political information; these can be identified either by individual or, more generally, by age.

For all practical purposes, children who have high levels of political maturity are capable of perceiving information as adults. However, they need adult information. A failure to provide information during the critical period wastes learning capacity and may have enduring effects. If, during the critical period of political readiness, adult political information is absent in some ways, the child's political orientations are trapped at a pre-adult level. Thus, the entrapment at lower cognitive levels about which Merelman (1969) writes can be the direct result of failure to provide access to political information during the critical period rather than a failure to develop cognitively.

As implied in this discussion, the linkage between childhood and adult political orientations and behavior lies at the political maturity threshold, and the information incoming to the child during the critical period is determinative of later political orientations. Indirectly, this notion questions the utility of explaining political socialization phenomena through primacy or recency theory.

As other scholars have shown, affective orientations toward the system or political leaders are learned early and maintained into adulthood. However, this may only be operative under the condition that no dissonant information about the systems or its leaders is received later, particularly during the period of political readiness when susceptibility to political information is at its peak. If the critical period is passed without information likely to result in discontinuities, early images are retained. However, if inconsistent information is made available during the critical period when political orientations are about to gel, this information can be used as the basis for reevaluating early learning. Thus, implied in this maturation approach is a greater influence for various sources of political information at various stages in the life cycle, when susceptibility to new information—for whatever psychological reason—is high.

In a sense, this suggests a new primacy principle. This new primacy is not of the absolutely first perception, but of the early perceptions during the period (or periods) of political readiness.

Political scientists analyzing generational differences in political attitudes (Cutler, 1975, 1977; Inglehart, 1971) have suggested that particular events or crises which occur during what they term the "formative" years have lasting effects on political perspectives. It can be suggested that a redefinition of perceptions to be considered the primary politically relevant or potentially enduring ones may be valuable. Specifically, those images formulated during the critical periods of political readiness are the enduring ones if there are discontinuities between early learning and critical period learning.

It is important to note that much of this discussion focused on the first critical period (occurring in early adolescence empirically). Experiences may rekindle cognitive learning. Self-esteem and ego strength may fluctuate across time. So too may moral thinking. Overall, throughout the life cycle, several critical periods may surface. Implied in this multiple critical period notion is a greater strength for a variety of political information sources. Early critical periods are marked by high levels of interaction at home or at school or with children's media. Later periods may occur when peer interaction and media use are high. Thus, throughout the life cycle there are many information sources from which political orientations may be learned, but the extent to which each source is used depends on individual psychological states.

CONCLUSION

It has been suggested that where there is information—from any source—during the period of political readiness, orientations toward the political system can be shaped at varying levels of sophistication. Individuals are always faced with competing sources of information, so the key element to explore in political socialization is the information to which one has access during periods of political readiness.

In part, the search for this element has been conducted unwillingly (or atheoretically) by students of political socialization subscribing to the agent approach. Agent theorists argue that parents are most influential in the political socialization process. Why they are most influential, however, is not because they are imitated or loved or omnipresent or omnipotent, but because they are often providers of political information, meeting the criteria for effective communicators—esteemed, valued, trusted, and so forth—providing a political environment, encouraging outside information seeking during the critical period. When there are no competing information (or opinion) sources during the critical period, parents achieve preeminence. Parents who fail to seek information themselves are unlikely to encourage their children to do so. Parents thus remain the sole or most important source of political information. A more appropriate way of viewing the role of parents than as agents of political socialization is as providers of an environment for the reception of political information. The sources of this information are parents as well as the other so-called agents—peers, media, school, experiences, and so forth. But rather than weighing the importance of each agent, the quality and timing of the information from these various sources is the crucial factor in the informational approach to political socialization developed in this chapter.

To some extent, the systemic consequences of the reception of information from one of the competing sources of political information, or the failure to provide political information during the critical period, are only hypothetical when children are the subject of inquiry. Much can intervene before a child is called upon to act politically, including new development and critical periods. But the real consequences of this conceptualization occur when access to children (or adults) during critical periods directs them towards specific political behavior.

III
COMMUNICATION IN POLITICAL INSTITUTIONS

8
DECISION MAKERS IN
U.S. POLITICAL INSTITUTIONS

In the systems approach to political communication outlined in Chapter 3, it is argued that demands are made of political decision makers who in turn generate policy outputs. Involved in these decision processes are three major actors: citizens, mass media, and decision makers, each with complex and multidimensional communication activities. In this chapter, the discussion focuses on decision makers only; Chapters 9 and 10 consider mass media and citizens as the other actors.

Although limited to decision maker communication only, this chapter considers three levels of communicatory activity. At the first level is the question of how decision makers receive policy demands. Recalling that there are both politically articulate and inarticulate individuals, and different languages for expressing demands, capacity for attending to political demands is a major focus. Second, decision makers do not operate alone as individuals, but instead operate in organizations or institutions. Such organizations have their own communication dynamics that shape both inputs and decisional outputs. Thus, the second focus is on the internal communication in decision-making political institutions.

Third, and especially relevant, but not unique to political institutions in the United States, are the multiple centers of decisions. The three major branches of government at the federal level (not considering other governmental bodies at the state and local level) have some unique responsibilities, but there are other powers that are shared, or for which "checks and balances" apply. In addition, there are decisions that require interaction among the branches, or intragovernmental communication.

At each level of communication involving decision makers, there are a variety of symbols employed and languages used. There exist also institutional factors enhancing or confining the flow of information for decision makers. To explore this communication flow in government, we look across political institutions, branch by branch, focusing primarily on the executive and legislative branches, but with some discussion of the judiciary and the bureaucracy.

Across all the institutions runs one common property: authority. Decision-making by definition involves authority and/or power in a political environment. Thus, prior to addressing the unique attributes and characteristics of each branch of government, authority and power in decision-making contexts are discussed.

DECISION-MAKING AND INFORMATION

At the core of democratic theory there are a number of assumptions about the role of information in decision-making. In representative democratic republics citizens select their representatives and decision makers, presumably on the basis of information about these decision makers. For their part, elected representatives must have access to information to weigh the competing needs of constituents or others. In the United States, the overlapping jurisdictions fostered by the system of checks and balances further imposes a knowledge requirement on public officials, for they must be aware of the actions of other decision makers. Ultimately, the relationship of information needs of some political actors within a given system often come into conflict with the needs of other actors. As a result, a number of policy problems in political communication (see Chapter 13) have arisen in areas such as the public's right to know, conflicts between government secrecy and information needs, free speech versus rights to privacy, and so forth.

Communication and information are the essentials of government. Earlier, it was noted that social communication is central to political development and nation building. Even in developed systems, the goals of those seeking access to decision makers include having information in hand and eliminating the flow of contrary or competing information. And, among those already in positions of political authority, maintaining authority and its accompanying influence and power requires careful control of the nature, quality, and quantity of information available to oneself and competing power centers.

As Deutsch (1963) points out, one of the most important functions of government decision makers is to manage information. This is essential for the stability of the system, its power, and efficiency. Continuous surveillance of the environment and ongoing intelligence serve to preserve systems (or individuals) from internal as well as external threats, but requires extensive information gathering. Decision makers thus face the problem of acquiring as much information as possible, but at the same time they must avoid information overload and reduce incoming information to a manageable amount. Inherent in information reduction is another problem: those responsible for information reduction have more information than those requiring information for decisions. Decision makers are therefore at the mercy of information gathering and information storing underlings, unless there are methods for monitoring information monitors.

To avoid this problem, subordinates charged with information gathering and reduction are specialized, so no branch of an organization has all the pieces of the puzzle. It can only be assembled by the decision maker, using strategic location to gather necessary (but greatly reduced) information. Among executives, this practice is particularly important, as the next section on the presidency demonstrates.

PRESIDENTIAL INFORMATION

The presidency, or for that matter chief executive roles in many large organizations, have several characteristics that define information needs. The first of these characteristics was stated most bluntly by Harry Truman, and has been restated by Jimmy Carter: "The buck stops here." Ultimately, the president is held responsible for decisions. This responsibility and accountability is an artifact of a second characteristic: the president is most clearly in the public eye. Third, the president's need for information reflects the multiplicity of roles a president is expected to play. Finally, the president is at the head of a large executive organization and responsible for interrelationships with other branches of government. Each of these characteristics is described in more detail.

Because of the final accountability and responsibility of the president, the stakes in presidential decisions are greater than for those of other government officials. In theory, the president requires more information than any other official, because the range of phenomena over which decisions must be made is greater than that of other officials. Nevertheless, the sheer quantity of information required necessitates modes for reducing information to manageable dimensions. Accompanying this data reduction, however, is a loss of information.

More than any other example of what is involved in data reduction, the president's daily news summary shows the extent to which only a small portion of information is made available. Daily, 1700 newspapers are published throughout the United States, and many more abroad. By early morning every day, many of these are sorted by various subordinates. The highlights of major national and international stories, editorials, and columns are made available to be read in approximately one half hour. Clearly, only a fragment of the national press, let alone the world press, is viewed in these summaries. The same limitations apply to diplomatic cables, reports, and other government memoranda.

To prevent information overload, or drowning in a sea of paperwork, presidents rely on staff to reduce the load. By necessity, this increases the power of certain staff members. In the Nixon White House, for example, H. R. Haldeman reputedly not only prevented access to the President for interpersonal communications by cabinet and other high level officials, but also spent considerable effort boiling down lengthy complex policy memoranda to a paragraph or even a simple sentence (Rather & Gates, 1974).

Information loss through summaries may in itself be severe, but combined with isolation from interpersonal interaction with other officials, it weakens the executive, and strengthens his aides. Access to the president has long held symbolic importance among his staff. Indeed, the pecking order is established through such access. Chiefs of staffs, or even appointment secretaries, gain significant power through access control, and gain this power out of the president's field of vision.

The visibility of the president is undoubtedly greater than that of any other public official. At times this visibility heightens executive power, but at other times weakens it. Regardless of which is the case, the president can do little to avoid public scrutiny. The reasons for executive visibility are many, but the simplest explanation is that the president is the focus of mass media. Symbolically, both at home and abroad, the president is the United States. Presidential behavior, personality, and often decisions, symbolically represent those of all Americans.

Domestically, political socialization researchers have shown the president to be the focus of early political cognitions and affect. Empirically, mass media have been shown to focus considerably more attention on executive action than on legislative or judicial action, so much so that observers of news would be hard-pressed to consider the branches of government to be co-equals. For the mass public it is well documented that presidents are praised or blamed for most government action, largely because presidents are so visible. The president is only one person to follow (despite a White House Staff larger than Congress) instead of 535. Presidential presence in mass media, from news to speeches, makes the president the focus. Overall, presidential activities are carefully scrutinized by mass media, from gossip magazines to political telecasts, that make the public constantly aware of presidential actions.

The multiplicity of roles in which a president is incumbent is greater than almost any individual can fill. Political scientists refer to many presidential hats— as head of government, chief of state, party leader, and so forth. What is crucial about these multiple roles is that although requiring the president to divide presidential time into small fractions of the amount needed to adequately fulfill the responsibilities of each role, the president has access to information from many sources. There is, in a sense, an inherent contradiction or dialectic process. Many roles require the president to divide personal time and in fact increase personal dependence on digested material even as the number of possible channels for receiving information increases. As examples, in executive capacity the president may order specialized information in the form of presidential commissions; or, the president can rely on the role as leader of the presidential political party for access to congressional information. Overall, a variety of sources are opened up. On the negative side however, are the role conflicts engendered by multiple demands. For one, time becomes limited. But more important is that presidential roles create uncomfortable role strains. As a party leader, for example, there may be a strong interest in political patronage. As chief executive, needs may be for merit selection of assistants. At times these demands are difficult to reconcile.

Finally, as the chief executive of a large organization, the president has a unique vantage point. Although the notion of a strategic location underlies Johnson's (1971) use of the term "vantage point" in his presidential memoirs, the most complete description of the presidency in these terms has come from Neustadt (1976). He argues that the president's power to persuade, or even to govern depends on his ability to get various bureaus to compete and report to the executive. A strong president, Neustadt argues, must push and constantly survey subordinates to assure that a president receives all the information necessary to govern. A president can use the presidential vantage point to bargain. But more important, a reputation as a perceptive leader can be enhanced by "anticipating" the needs and demands of subordinates, which the president is able to do because needs have been determined through inter-action with others. In a sense, the vantage point at the top of the organization allows the president to manipulate subordinates, isolate them from one another, and further their loyalty—all because of presidential control of information.

RESTRUCTURING THE PRESIDENCY

A number of proposals to restructure the presidency have been offered over the years, some serious, others less so. These proposals take into account the massive information problems inherent in the office as presently structured. Among the proposals have been those centering on dividing the responsibilities of the chief executive. At one extreme have been ideas basically dividing the roles of head of state and head of government. The head of state would be a ceremonial position, not unlike monarchs or presidents in many parliamentary systems in which there is a Prime Minister to head the govern-ment. A head of state would essentially be a protocol president, freeing the head of government for more substantive and less symbolic concerns.

A second proposal, more radical perhaps, would be to specialize the presidency, perhaps with a president for foreign policy, a president for economic affairs, and a president for social policy. Without doubt, such a scheme would encourage the development of substantive expertise in a number of areas and at the same time increase the accessibility of technical information to political leaders.

Obviously, these are not without severe limitations. The very power of the president is rooted in the number of roles he occupies. To replace a decision maker with an essentially symbolic leader (perhaps dressed as Uncle Sam?) weakens one source of decision maker strength. A troika of presidents, each with a substantive area and separate responsibilities has its weaknesses too. Separate channels of communication to each minimizes policy coordination within government. Cohesive policy making requires as much time spent with interaction among the presidents as with separate concerns. Beyond these massive coordination problems lie the symbolic issues. Who really is in charge, who is more powerful? Much of a president's ability to get things done is due to the weight of his office as a symbolic unit. This element clearly dissipates with the diffusion of presidential power.

Of course, these proposals are attempts to correct some of the limitations of the presidency. Demands of the office are high, perhaps overwhelming, both in terms of quantity and technical sophistication. As a result, much presidential authority is delegated, and the president becomes more of a manager than a decision maker, a manager at the mercy of gatekeeping subordinates. Watergate and corallary events offer one testimony to this phenomenon. At the same time, the Watergate tapes do reveal many of the limitations on the president, and provide unusual insights into the information demands of the office. The president is shown at times to be unconcerned and uniformed about many issues in private, although he publicly appears informed on these same issues in press conferences or other public forums. He is shown to be dependent on his subordinates for information, subordinates who later reveal themselves to have sheltered the president. Of course, these are just examples, but they underscore the problems and the isolation of presidents hidden behind a dam holding back a flood of information.

LIMITS OF EXECUTIVE POWER

Proclamations by presidents do not always result in action by subordinates. Nicholas I of Russia was quoted once as saying "Whoever thinks that I control Russia is mistaken. Russia is ruled by ten thousand government clerks." No doubt every head of state has expressed similar feelings about political impotency in the frustration of working with a large bureaucracy. Still, it is difficult to imagine how the will of a leader can be neutralized by replaceable functionaries.

Simply stated, the will of the leader is executed by the bureaucracy. Execution of executive orders, moreover, is not automatic, but depends on the interpretation of several lower bureaucrats, each of whom may have a particular interest in a certain type of outcome. Professional (i.e., nonpolitical) civil service employees are operating under a different set of constraints than political appointees. Career employees ordinarily manifest a certain rigidity and inflexibility, relying heavily on tradition as a justification for many procedures. Demands imposed on the bureaucracy (and they may well be viewed as impositions) often require much adaptation and innovation, behavior in which bureaucracies do not excell.

Most likely, unwillingness to adapt has two causes. First, are the lines of communication within bureaucracy. Often an order must pass through several levels in the hierarchy, and, much as in the children's game of telephone, something is lost at each level because of the perspectives, needs, and wishes of mid-level officials. Second, much bureaucratic activity, especially at the lowest levels, is routine. Changes in policy or procedure are considered disruptive of routine and may be seen not as policy change, but as impositions by supervisory personnel. Lower level bureaucrats, particularly clerks, fail to respond to political motives of higher level authorities even if the reason for changes is made clear.

At the clerk level, the average citizen experiences bureaucracy in action (inaction?), and this has led to the development of stereotypes and images of government employees. Ordinarily, and in the short run, frustrations are the result, and grumbled complaints about government inefficiency are expressed. In the long run, system support may be undermined by continuous exposure to the least innovative or even responsive face of government. The bureaucracy becomes symbolic of the waste of government, its inefficiency and mismanagement. And responsibility for this management is shouldered, real or imagined, by the chief executive; the visible representative of government.

At higher levels in the bureaucracy, the problems differ. Bureaus are much like interest groups with an interest in having their own goals served. Expertise in bureaus makes the president dependent upon information. Combined with the authority to implement decisions, the power of the bureaucracy waxes as executive power wanes. Occasionally, bureaus become constituencies of even the legislature, particularly if bureaucratic policy implementation affects a congressional district. Nevertheless, a strong executive using his vantage point effectively, can isolate varying bureaucracies, and at the policy level can weaken their impact. At the implementation level, of course, solutions are far more difficult.

CONGRESS

Empirically, Congress is the most widely researched branch of government. Studies of congressional voting patterns, interaction with lobbyists, and perceptions of constituents abound, but the analysis is often political, whereas the variables examined are largely communication variables. As a result, political analysts have much to say about how legislators are elected or what coalitions develop in Congress, but they have little to say about how these coalitions are maintained or how constituents develop the perceptions they do about their officials.

The nature of Congress as an institution defines its communication needs and practices as an institution, and of its members. Congress is characterized by an extremely diverse membership, particularly in the House of Representatives. Although many members may share backgrounds in terms of occupation (lawyer), income level (high) or educational background (Ivy League) (Domhoff [1967]), many variables separate them. Different political party affiliations, urban and rural residency, regional perspectives, and substantive interests are as important as the similarities in socio-economic status. The diversity is more apparent in the House, whose members more nearly reflect the ethnic, religious, educational, and occupational (but not gender) categories in the country.

The importance of this diversity in information and communication terms is reflected in the information needs of the members. Attorneys have different views (and information requirements) than nonlawyers. Experts in one substantive area may require highly detailed technical information before rendering a legislative decision, others may require a nontechnical summary. Some members of Congress arrive with expertise, others cultivate it through experiences on the job. In each case, the needs for outside assistance, staff dependence, and so forth, follows.

Perhaps more than the diversity of Congress, role perceptions for members of Congress are responsible for their information needs. Eulau, Wahlke, Buchanan, & Ferguson (1959) describe three roles in which legislators might fit; trustees, delegates, or politicos. Trustees are members who view themselves as entrusted with the responsibility of making the proper decision, they are sent to Washington not with any specific set of instructions from their constituents, but rather as one member of a large legislative body. A trustee is charged with using his or her judgment for the good of the country. Trustees are distinguished from a second set of members; delegates. Delegates view themselves as representatives of constituencies, and have the welfare of constituents as the top priority, rather than the good of the nation as a whole. The sovereignty of the constituency, so to speak, is embodied in the delegate, who summarizes and weighs the competing interests (or the consensus) of the constituency as the basis for action. Finally, there are the politicos, who essentially follow the most politically expedient course. Sometimes they act as trustees, at other times they are responsive to party hierarchies, colleagues, or others. Although politicos are not necessarily any less representative of constituencies or the national interest than trustees or delegates, they are far less predictable.

Each of these roles is described in some detail, because, like the background of the membership, they shape information requirements of the legislature. As a simple hypothesis, one can predict, for example, that trustees are likely to be far more demanding of technical information and expertise than politicos or delegates. They are likely to use professional committee staff to supplement their own staffs. They are likely to require Congressional documents and be more attentive to expert witnesses and testimony before committees than others. They are also likely to seek out a variety of information sources, particularly on controversial and multifaceted issues when "the national interest" is most difficult to determine.

Delegates require a very different type of information. They are most likely to use those sources of information that keep them in touch with their constituents to congressional offices, and the mail is more significant than technical advice. Members with this perspective rely on the judgments of their own staffs and seek out information supporting the viewpoints of their constituencies. Without doubt, surveying the political environment at home dominates the information-seeking behavior of the delegate.

The politico is in a complicated position, for in many ways his information needs are greatest. On the one hand, there must be accurate information concerning the wishes of the constituents. On the other hand, there must be technical information available if the issue is not salient to the constituency but to other groups in the nation. There is a third hand needed by politicos, however, because they must be aware of the demands of party leaders, lobbyists, and others who might have an interest in a particular outcome. Thus fellow legislators become important sources of information for politicos more often than for others.

All legislators, regardless of their role perceptions rely on other legislators on occasion. Respect, trust, expertise, or any number of factors may be involved in legislative cueing. In fact, the third characteristic of Congress is responsible for this practice. Although there are constitutional parameters, there are very few practical limits on areas subject to Congressional involvement. The range of phenomena subject to legislation requires some degree of specialization. With specialization comes expertise, so a number of legislators increase their power (see Chapter 6) through the possession of information needed by other legislators. Nonexperts may take their cues from experts, who in turn may take cues from those who have other expertise.

Cueing is only one method of reducing information overload in the legislature. There is the equally simple method of vote trading wherein legislators agree with one another to support each other's proposals or programs; "if you vote for my bill, I'll vote for yours." Often this occurs on bills of extreme importance to one member of the dyad, but of marginal importance to the other. This is a frequent occurrence, so there are considerable implications for information needs. Legislators often need only one bit of information: how the trading partner stands on an issue or what his or her vote is. Of course, trades may be interrupted by additional information such as special constituent needs, party demands, or other factors, but trades are usually successful and drastically reduce information needs.

The organization of the legislature is another factor influencing information processes. Congress is a formal organization (although the Senate less so than the House) with rules, hierarchies, and norms, all of which play roles in the information processes. Legislators may come to the Congress as individuals, but quickly are submerged (again more so in the House than in the Senate) into the organization. Political parties divide the legislature, they too are organized. Party caucuses provide partisan information, and an occasion where assignments are made. Rigid floor rules (again in the House) require much work to take place in committees rather than on the floor. Indeed the size of the House has made it limit floor debate. If each member exercised an option to speak on a bill for even three minutes, it would take over twenty hours to hear from the House. The result, of course, is much work off the floor, and more specialization. In the Senate there is a tradition of unlimited debate, and fewer formal rules. But legislative schedules rarely permit the luxury of leisurely debate, so committees and subcommittees bear much of the information-gathering burden. Committee assignments in each house are party and seniority based, so newer members on committee find themselves struggling to develop expertise to match that of senior members. Little time is left for wider learning. As a result, legislators become more and more specialized. In fact, to supplement both the committee and party systems, there are specialized groups, clubs, or caucuses that provide a forum for specific concerns of certain members. Such groups include those from oil-producing states, or black members, representatives from urban areas, conservatives, southerners, and so forth. In each case the groups discuss problems unique to their interests, and have opportunities for strategic planning.

The structure of Congress, its committee specialization, and its diversity have complicated information needs. To some extent, Congress has recognized the need for timely and accurate information. The Library of Congress was one early development recognizing this need. More recently, committees have been staffed with professionals, and research capacity through such channels as the Congressional Research Service has been expanded to make information quickly available.

Several studies of Congress have taken close looks at the communication patterns of legislators, and the sources of information they employ. Hattery and Hofheimer (1954) in one early study queried fourteen Senators and thirteen Representatives concerning how useful they found these sources to be. In each body, committee hearings, staff, and personal reading and consultation were the most important information sources, whereas the political party and legislative counsel's office were the least useful. Overall, there was little reported use of executive agencies, and floor debate was considered important on occasions when little information concerning committee hearing results was available.

The study focused only on expert information and therefore is more limited in scope than others focused on *all* communications interactions by legislators.

One such study was by Kovenock (1973), wherein all interactions and information exposure for each legislator in the study was noted. Kovenock was concerned primarily with influence from frequency of interaction. Using a communications audit, six representatives were observed for seven full days over a three month period. All interactions were observed and recorded as they occurred or immediately afterward. In general, influence through communication was minimal, for the Representatives ordinarily had their minds made up before the interaction. The one exception was the case of negative influence. Some communications resulted in the opposite effect from the attempt of the communicator. Although there is a norm of openmindedness, empirically this seemed not to be the case. On those occasions where influence attempts succeeded, usually the communicators were staff or Senators (not fellow Representatives) rather than lobbyists or media. Still excluded from the analysis were home, social, and other interpersonal communication—but most Representatives agreed these occupied relatively little time.

Kovenock's work excludes interaction with constituents as a source of information. There are many possible channels of constituent communication including letters, editorials from hometown newspapers, polls commissioned within the district, face to face contact with constituents, or lobbyists, or even campaigning. Most of these channels have been explicitly analyzed. Studies of congressional polls (Brody & Tufte, 1964), and constituent mail (Dexter, 1956), for example, reveal a similarity of viewpoints between constituents and congressmen, but show a very limited input. Dexter's study indicated that attention paid to the mail was a function more of the importance of the letter writer than almost anything else. Its utility was further limited by often arriving after an issue is decided, or because its content is simply too vague to be useful.

All of these studies, when taken together, reflect the difficulties inherent in determining specifically what sources of information are important to legislatures. In part, role perceptions shape information needs. So too, do legislative structures and organizations and groups. Within the legislature are a number of information processes. Demands from constituents—whether attended to or not —are transmitted in a straight-foward manner. But the support for the legislature is not so easily established. Undoubtedly, some support is rooted in learning and political socialization concerning whole political regimes. But further support (or lack thereof) follows from knowledge of the activities of Congress. In other words, public information about Congress, from mass media or elsewhere, serves as a source of support for the institutions. In light of this, recent action by the House of Representatives to broadcast its proceedings becomes important. From the perspective of the representative, as well as from the viewpoint of a citizen, the proposal has several implications.

The proposal as implemented allows for broadcast of sessions from the floor of the House. Aside from procedural issues of who would actually staff the camera and direct the program (resolved in favor of House staffers), are issues of how Congress as an institution would be affected and how public knowledge of, or respect for, the institution might be altered. These are discussed at length in Chapter 14, but to summarize, much of the work of Congress occurs off the floor, in committees, cloakrooms, or smoke-filled rooms. The question then becomes: will televising or broadcasting proceedings from the floor of the House accurately reflect the workings of the House? In all likelihood, the answer is no, if only floor proceedings are shown. Including committee hearings and other open meetings might accomplish this goal, but even then (unless many channels are made available to broadcast "Your Congress of the Air") only a small portion of available activity would be shown, and decisions must be made as to what is shown.

More important are the changes that may occur in the institution as a result of increased visibility. If floor proceedings are shown, the locus of activity may well shift from the hearing room to the floor. Given that members of Congress report committee work to be far more important than floor work, net information loss will occur. Moreover, different characteristics of members will be emphasized, including oratorical skills or even photogenic appearance, rather than substantive and analytic capability. These are, of course, only speculations, but their significance warrants careful attention to the effects on other legislatures (Colin-Ure, 1974) of broadcasting.

For audiences, the problems of broadcasting are different. Although proceedings were always open in theory, only those in Washington could take advantage and then only on a very limited basis. Whereas the concept of an open Congress may meet with wide public approval, broadcasting sessions can demystify the institution. Part of the strength of Congress—however little it has —is from diffuse support within the system. The symbol of the dome of the Capitol is widely acknowledged as the strength of the system and the ultimate sovereignty of the people—but few know what goes on inside. Presumably, elected officials are hardworking people, debating the issues of the day in the tradition of Henry Clay or John Calhoun before an attentive chamber. Instead, we find a nearly empty chamber, with those few members present chatting, reading reports and newspapers, or even dozing. On television, it would all be as plain as day, but without broadcasts the myths can be perpetuated and the strength of the institution maintained.

Obviously, there is much to consider in a decision to broadcast or not to broadcast the sessions of Congress. Successful broadcasts of committee hearings during intense periods of national concern (McCarthy Hearings, Ervin Committee Hearings, Nixon Impeachment Hearings) may not be the appropriate models from which public commitment to watching government at work should be drawn. On a day to day basis, the work of Congress is not terribly exciting (visually), and the costs in terms of demystification may be too high a price to pay. After all, why is it that the focus of much television news has been on the executive rather than the legislative or judicial branches? Largely because the legislative process is slow and diffuse and at times confusing in contrast to the highly visible president. In all likelihood, this won't change with broadcasting, but soon there will be the evidence for empirical judgments.

THE JUDICIARY

If one branch of government conscientiously adheres to the perpetuation of rites and symbols, it is the judiciary. From the scales of justice (held by a blindfolded woman) to the architecture of the courtroom, to the black robes of the judge, the message from the judiciary is clear: the system is equitable and fair. When addressing questions of political communication with reference to the judiciary, our concern is not so much with information gathering as it is with the other branches. Instead, the focus is on the symbolic aspects of legal activity.

There are several ways to approach the communicatory aspects of the judiciary. On one level, legal proceedings are designed to maximize one type of information—truth. In jury trials, or before the judge, advocates for the prosecution, or plaintiff, or the defendant seek to present their side of the story or resolve conflicting stories. Ordinarily, the items over which there is a controversy are not political as we have defined the term elsewhere in this volume. Underlying the controversies are, of course, political decisions ranging from what behavior is antisocial and punishable to how resources are allocated. But these decisions are usually legislative, and the courts serve to interpret them.

At a second level, however, the judiciary is important in political communication. The authority of the political system itself is embodied in the courtroom. And, although law enforcement is technically an executive responsibility, popular perceptions of "the law" link the administration and implementation of law and law enforcement to the courts.

Finally, the judicial system may serve as a forum for political participation and enfranchise, so to speak, groups that feel otherwise excluded from political processes. Often the very act of litigation brings issues into the public arena. Demands are thus presented in the courts. In much the same way, support (or lack of support) for varying government activities can also be made manifest in the courts: disobedience, swelling caseloads in criminal courts, and other indicators serve as a warning system that authority is breaking down.

On the first level, the proceedings are, as noted, designed to determine the truth. However, the methods for searching for the truth involve many rites and rituals, all of which apply the symbolic or second-level aspects of judicial political communication. Legal proceedings, first of all, take place before a judge. Constitutional limitations on honorific titles notwithstanding, judges are referred to as "Your Honor." Wearing a religious type of black robe, he or she sits on a podium behind a high bench. Literally, as well as figuratively, the judge is above it all, presiding over the courtroom from above. The judge, as God, reigns supreme. The judge is tended by several aides (footmen?), and functionaries who take messages, swear in witnesses, or observe the proceedings. In any case, they form a small army—not unlike those attending a feudal lord—to assist the judge.

Next to the judge's bench is a witness stand, often constructed as part of the bench, but at a lower level. It is usually enclosed, physically isolating its occupant from others in the courtroom. The stand is constructed in such a way that literally and figuratively again, the witness is required to swear before God that the truth will be told. Next to the witness is the jury box. Jurors too are isolated from others in the courtroom, but not from each other. Unlike the judge or witness, they are not alone, but part of a group that must emerge with a collective judgment.

Before the judge and jury are the prosecutor (or plaintiff) and the defendant, each at a separate table. Defendants sit with their attorneys, always in the eye of the jury, witness, and judge. Indeed, the major actors in the court are all within view of the judge and jury under the assumption that nonverbal clues, especially eye contact, offer much information about truth, nervousness, fear, and so forth. All the actors are separated from the spectators and witnesses not testifying. Others in the courtroom may include ushers, bailiffs, secretaries, clerks, and stenographers.

Overall, the architecture of the courtroom is a symbolic political message. Although not every courtroom has the appearance of a television stage-set courtroom (wood-paneled, attentive jurors, and articulate lawyers), the broad outlines are similar; majestic settings, flags, robes, gavel, bailiffs, and so on. The strength and authority of government is on the line in the courtroom; proceedings are open to the public, so every effort is made to underscore the fairness and impartiality of the event. The setting is so important, the visible symbols of government powers omnipresent, the message is clear: the government is fair but strong. All efforts are made to seek out the truth. Social order is extremely important. And, of course deviance is punished.

Murray Edleman (1964) has noted that legal language, a uniquely confusing language to nonspeakers, is an essential symbolic element in judicial and other government proceedings. On the one hand, legal language constructs a verbal barrier—not unlike the physical barrier separating spectators from gladiators in the courtroom—between lawyer and layman. Only experts versed in the language of law may participate, only experts can interpret the law. On the other hand, legal language is symbolic in its implications of fairness, neutrality, and objectivity.

The symbolic aspects of legal language are similar to the symbolic use of legal participation. Vose (1961), for example, has suggested that getting on the legal agenda is a crucial aspect of political participation. In his words, litigation may be used as a form of political pressure. In the model in Chapter 3, much effort is spent describing how demands are aggregated, one method of which is litigation. This method is particularly important to those groups which are politically inarticulate, or for whom other channels of access are closed.

Litigation, particularly in the past two decades, has been used by a variety of groups to issue or highlight social and political demands. Civil rights groups, such as the NAACP and the ACLU, have spent millions of dollars forcing confrontations within the courtroom. Social and political activists from Martin Luther King Jr., to Muhammed Ali and Jerry Rubin have sought to violate the law to force the courts to address, if not redress their grievances. Although not always successful in changing laws, or even avoiding punishment or prison sentences, legal proceedings involving these individuals have attracted wide publicity, and called attention to the problems.

The reasons why the inarticulate or the disenfranchised use the legal system are fairly simple. In theory, all are equal before the law. Unlike legislatures or executive branches, where access is limited to those elected or appointed, or where testimony is invited, courts must deal with those who violate the law or bring suits. Moreover, whereas the tools of the trade are specialized and familiar only to those who participate, any group or individual may engage a lawyer to argue on their behalf. Thus, for the inarticulate, demands are expressed through the articulate. Of course, it can be argued that the disenfranchised or inarticulate may hire lobbyists or others to speak on their behalf before legislatures. However, legislators must be convinced of the merits to even sponsor legislation. Then a variety of institutional constraints may limit a bill ever being discussed or developed. Overall, lobbying becomes institutionalized, and only the most hearty interest groups can sustain the effort. For individuals or ad hoc groups, litigation remains the best way to assure judicial, if not general attention to a problem.

Although the public has access to most aspects of judicial proceedings (except those occurring in chambers or appellate judicial conferences) as open events, there has been almost no broadcasting of courtroom proceedings. There are, of course, newspaper reporters, and even professional artists who sketch during judicial proceedings so that television news will have visuals to accompany reports, but electronic coverage has been severely limited until recently. The prohibition of broadcasting or even photographing proceedings was through a ban under the cannons of the American Bar Association's Code of Judicial Conduct.

Several states are now reconsidering the ban. In the first televised case in Florida, 1977, the trial of a teenager charged with murder was televised gavel to gavel. Ironically, the defense argued that the boy was under the influence of television violence at the time, and that an episode of Kojak triggered the murder. This and later cases were widely reported. The arguments for televising are simple: the public has a right to know what really goes on in the courtroom. Moreover, jurists argue that people will become familiar with their rights and procedures if coverage is televised, and that confidence in the system and in the law will be restored. In other words, direct exposure to judicial proceedings informs the viewer, perhaps even corrects the misinformation of fictional courtroom drama (see Chapter 14).

There is, of course, one element missing from such reasoning: that the symbolic aspects of judicial proceedings are as important as the nonsymbolic. Undoubtedly, the myth of the courtroom is developed through fictionalized representations of judicial activity. Proceedings are orderly, jurors attentive, attorneys articulate, and, most important, the guilty are caught and the innocent freed. This myth is one that jurists would like to see survive. People may well learn from Hollywood versions of the courtroom, but what they are likely to learn is far more system supportive than what they view in real trials. In fictional events, often the events themselves are seen by the audience. They *know* what happened and just wait for justice to be done. The facts are not so clear in reality, nor are the methods for searching out the truth so effective. Besides, sometimes the guilty go free and the innocent are convicted.

Always there exist the changes brought on by publicity. Attorneys play for the cameras. Jurors fear recognition and public or private reprisal for their decisions. Witnesses lose their relative anonymity. And too, there are questions of public taste and morality, and editorial decisions of what is to be shown as the "trial of the day," and what is not. Overall, there are a host of questions that must be dealt with before the benefits of televising can be said to outweigh the problems and difficulties of publicity.

A FINAL WORD

All decision-making takes place in a social and political environment. Pressures come from constituents, interests, and fellow decision makers. More often than not, decision makers are pulled in opposing directions by groups with inconsistent or contradictory demands. There is always the risk of the loss of support. And, there is always the judgment of peers.

Students of decision-making of all political actors have noted all of these pressures and consider them to be the most important factors in the failure of decision makers to innovate. Whether called satisficing (March & Simon, 1958), incrementalism (Lindbloom, 1957), or group thinking (Janis, 1972), the constraints are there. Decision makers act only to the extent necessary to remove demand pressures (satisficing). Often decision makers are incapacitated by a lack of information, or an unwillingness to take bold initiatives (incrementalism). Finally, within groups of decision makers, there is a strain toward consensus. None want to be isolated and as a result of dynamic processes within decision-making bodies, consensus is formed at the expense of innovation (group think).

The extent to which these decisional phenomena can be eliminated or minimized is a function of group coherence, personality, information access, and other factors. But the potential of these factors to disrupt decisions and channel them away from a social optimum requires that they be investigated further.

9
NEWS GATHERING
AND DISSEMINATING

Although news has always been with us, the methods through which news is gathered and disseminated have changed. A century ago, before widespread global literacy, news—and rumor—was transmitted interpersonally, from eyewitnesses of an event to others, or from literate opinion leaders with access to newspapers and magazines to the illiterate. Nowadays, news is transmitted primarily, if not exclusively through mass media. There are, of course, times when interpersonal communication serves as a source of news information, but such occasions are rare and easily documented.

With the growth of mass media as providers of news, politics itself has been transformed. Public officials come to rely on news media to disseminate official positions. At the same time, the public relies in part on mass media to provide forums for airing views and calling their concerns to the attention of public officials. In the model in Chapter 3 the role of mass media—including both fictional and non-fictional—in Figure 3.3 is central; virtually no information exchange occurs without news media. Indeed if there is a power of the press, it may be more in the strategic, central location at the interface between the public and government decision makers than in the ability to persuade or otherwise exhibit direct effects on behavior. Recalling the argument in Chapter 6 that power can be defined through location in an organization or a system, news media ought to be considered powerful.

To write of news gatherers and news disseminators is to write of both people and organizations. On one level, there are individual reporters and editors charged with collecting information from the environment. At another level, there are organizations involved; large bureaucracies directing all but the most

144

liberated freelancer to seek information in particular environments or to widen, deepen, or abandon news coverage. In a sense, news gatherers and disseminators can be viewed as political communicators at two levels as well. First, they function at the interface between decision makers and the polity, transmitting demands or decisions between political actors. In other words, they carry political information. Second, they operate in their own political environment, in an institutional framework marked by bureaucratic politics, infighting, and conflict.

There are a number of overall perspectives from which the news can be viewed, all of which are interconnected. Rivers, Miller, and Gandy (1975) for example, offer four broad areas of inquiry: the setting in which news media operate, how news media function, the characteristics of journalists, and the nature of news content. These are some of the most widely researched areas, and deserve summary in this chapter. Ultimately, however, these concerns must be connected to the broader question of how the nature of news and the collecting of individuals and organizations link up with the model in Chapter 3. News after all, serves functions for both public officials and mass audiences, as well as for the journalists.

DEFINING NEWS

News is many things. Definitions of news are as numerous as definitions of "political" or "communication." Notions range from edicts from the editor ("News is what I say it is"), to the amateur etymologist (news is merely an acronym for *N*orth, *E*ast, *W*est and *S*outh, the points on the compass from which information flows) to the practical journalist ("when a dog bites a man, that's not news, when a man bites a dog, it's news!"). It does not matter which nonoperational definition one accepts, for our empirical concern is with operationally defined news. News items are those reports which ultimately are perceived of as news by their appearance in the news media.

Fundamentally, news comes about in one of two ways. First, there may be an unusual event which a news gatherer attends. It may be political, catastrophic, meteorological, and so forth. Reporters witness the event, record information collected at the scene, return the story to an editor who decides to go or not go with the story. It is edited, appears in print or over the air, and is made available to audiences. Second, there may be officially generated news in scheduled news events. Decisions may be made by officials, who then rely on public information officers to disseminate the news to reporters, and from there the news proceeds as in the first case.

At each stage in the flow of news, questions of importance arise. What kinds of events are unusual? What is the likelihood of a reporter being present at an unusual event? Even if he or she is there, what does the reporter's training, ideology, or perspective bring to bear on the event? What factors are involved in the editor's decision about using the story? What accounts for the audience size? What will the audience do with the information? For official events, more questions can be raised. Why is the information being released? How much reliability is there in official pronouncements? All of these questions can be looked at separately or as a whole, but they far exceed the goals of this chapter. Instead, we focus on the factors influencing the collection and dissemination of news as they relate to linking the public with decision makers.

JOURNALISTS

Journalism, like many other occupations has specialized training, sometimes formal and academic, other times on the job (although fewer and fewer journalists rise from copy boy or copy girl to reporter and editor). Regardless of whether the training is formal or not, certain values, norms, and procedures are followed.

The uniformity of the norms and procedures is somewhat surprising given the diversity of individuals in the profession. In a major study of over one thousand journalists, Johnstone, Slawski, and Bowman (1972) found a wide range of educational and sociological backgrounds, although among younger journalists training and background were more uniform. Nevertheless, despite these differences of origin, journalists arrive at a professional consensus on what constitutes good journalism. To be sure, reporters exhibit wide ranging political beliefs, but normally these are suppressed in light of other norms.

One can consider six variables as important determinants of what or how news is covered by a journalist: personal values, peer values, job pressures, professional socialization, aesthetic norms, and professional experience. Personal values, as with political values, are often suppressed. Of course the journalist does not give up his or her identity, but presumably, it is minimized in favor of impersonal, detached reporting and analysis. The primary indicator of the minimization of personal values is the overwhelming concern for objectivity. Tuchman (1971) has lucidly outlined many of the techniques of objective reporting, but more important, has indicated the rationale for it: organizational constraints. The ritualization of objectivity, as she states, protects the individual reporter from everything ranging from libel lawsuits to discipline by editors. This is not to argue that journalists are ideological eunuchs, but that as they exercise their trade, they limit the introduction of personal values to the inclusion of skeptical wording or searching out viewpoints to cover all sides of an issue.

Peer values operate on two levels. First, there is a considerable amount of peer evaluation. Each day's output is available to one's colleagues, making evaluation a daily phenomenon. Peer review in the form of awards such as

Pulitzer Prizes similarly reflect the importance of peer values. More important, however, are peer values concerning what is news. Crouse (1973) documents this well in his discussion of "rat-pack" journalism on the campaign trail. Journalists follow each other closely, scoops by one reporter are followed up by other reporters. In large part, definitions of news are collective as all reporters converge on the same events.

The hierarchical structure of the newsroom and the constant deadlines create job pressures on the journalist, placing parameters on his or her view of news. Events covered are linked to the command structure of the news organization. As in any occupation, journalists seek promotions and other recognition, hence avoid rocking the boat. The nature of a newspaper or news broadcast is such that deadlines are constant. Reports must be filed by a certain time in many cases, limiting the extent to which a journalist can dig and investigate. Sigal (1973) lists numerous job constraints in the news, among them the beat system. Reporters are assigned regular locales or departments from which to collect news, ritualizing news collection. In addition, the deadlines serve to help define news: if it hasn't happened by the time a newspaper is put to bed, it isn't news.

Aesthetic norms play a major role for the news gatherer. Standards for what is good news coverage or fine photography, or what makes good electronic journalism, often dictate what becomes news. Aesthetic considerations frequently lead to manipulated news and staged events.

Finally, professional socialization and experience dictate what appears as news. News gatherers learn what constitutes good journalism, and ritualize their news collecting accordingly. As in all professions, journalists learn the extent to which they can use sources or rely on peers. Similarly, their experiences shape the news they seek and the stories they write. Past history of getting stories through the editor's desk and into the paper or over the air provides a framework for news collection in the future, assuming criteria for successful articles remain the same.

All in all, journalists are pushed in many directions during the news gathering process. Selectivity is exercised, not because journalists want to be gatekeepers, but because they want to pursue stories that appear in print, and are favorably looked on by editors and peers. The result is that content of news is severely constrained by journalists.

NEWS ORGANIZATIONS

News is not gathered by journalists working in isolation, but is collected by members of large organizations. For the most part, news organizations are (or are designed to be) profit-making enterprises, sometimes owned individually, other times as part of chains and syndicates, and still other times as part of large conglomerates. News organizations are businesses; economic considerations remain important in circumscribing the day to day operations. At the same time, news organizations are large bureaucracies, hierarchically structured, with managerial and supervisory personnel directing the frontline journalist. Finally, news organizations operate in an unusual legal and regulatory environment, given the first amendment rights and privileges, as well as constraints for electronic news media. All of these factors help shape the face of news and its implications for political actors.

The economic variables in news organizations bear directly on news gathering and dissemination, despite ritualistic protests from the editorial staff. Perhaps the most severe constraint imposed by financial considerations is that of available space (print media) or time (electronic media) in the news hole. Simply stated, the amount of news cannot, with rare exceptions, exceed the number of pages planned based on advertising sales. Similarly, broadcast news is limited to news that fits the time slot, (with subtraction of commercial time sold).

Related to the news hole limits are deadlines, which again, based on economic factors, limit the news. Aside from the function deadlines serve to encourage reporters and editors to complete their assignments on a timely basis; they are also important for the economics of the organization. Deadlines assure a uniform publication time (or broadcast time), which is essential for distribution of the final product. Despite popular notions to the contrary, the "stop the presses" phenomenon is very unusual, because it means disrupting the distribution schedule in addition to imposing costs ranging from overtime salaries for press operators to resetting the presses. The presence of deadlines, though economically mandated, has effects that spill over the editorial side: after a certain time, events face considerably more difficulty becoming widely disseminated as news. Evidence for this was clear even in the early "Mr. Gates" gatekeeping study (White, 1950), where the editor marked several rejected pieces as coming over the wire "too late" or "would have used if earlier." This suggests that as they are approached, deadlines severely tighten the definition of what is news.

The reluctance of publishers to stretch deadlines makes for a limited news day, and imposes limits not only on those who gather and disseminate news, but upon those who make the news as well. Whenever possible, political events are held at times best suited for evening news coverage and morning newspaper coverage. At times, political events, announcements, or similar phenomena are released prematurely, simply to maximize potential publicity. Thus, economic limits on news organizations indirectly shape aspects of politics, particularly when news media serve as the vehicles for intragovernmental information transmission.

Costs of gathering news further shape the nature of news. Reporting is ordinarily a very labor-intensive operation, particularly certain types of investigative reporting. Quests for news often fail to turn up anything useful, and reporter time is wasted. Consequently, there is a tendency towards routinization of news gathering. Reporters are assigned to familiar beats where news is likely to be generated and where they are not likely to come up empty handed. The system clearly is a self-perpetuating one, for news making itself becomes centralized, and political officials tend to release information where it is most likely to reach reporters. At the same time, reporters from different news organizations cluster in the same beats and in-breed the news (Crouse, 1973).

Competition is another important economic factor. Although fewer and fewer cities have large numbers of daily newspapers, there still is intense competition where there are choices, largely because advertising revenues depend on circulation figures. The same is true of electronic news, particularly at the local level where revenues generated from local news advertising generate a substantial portion of local station budgets. The results of intense competition often are reflected in the quality of news. Increased attention to entertainment, sports, fashions, and other speciality sections in daily newspapers are said to come out of the news hole, reducing total space available. At tne New York *Times,* for example, all five weekday editions have special supplements for sport, science, food, home furnishing, and weekend entertainment that have been added over the past three years. (Cynics on the *Time's* staff have argued that the best way to get a news story published now is to include a recipe! Others, more optimistically, think the remaining weekday issue will have a supplement called "News.")

Although these examples may be extreme, recent events in television news programming have underscored the importance of competition and how it shapes news. Local stations now rely exclusively on "action" news or "happytalk" news, which includes substantial banter among correspondents. New technology such as the mini-cam have been used to promote news freshness; in some localities stations have made efforts to update their late news (such as "The 'Hot' News"—what is cold news?) from the early evening broadcast, even when few or no significant events have occurred. Even network news executives have experimented with alternative formats in response to competitive pressures (e.g., the Western Edition of the CBS Evening News). Overall, for print and electronics, one might argue that news organizations have increasingly emphasized the entertainment function at the expense of information function and have "cheapened" the news because of competition imposed by economic necessities. Although such an assertion is difficult to prove, it warrants further examination.

News gathering organizations have not only the characteristics (and needs) of economic enterprises, but of large bureaucracies as well. As organizations, they exhibit many of the sociological attributes cited by organizational analysts. In addition, sociologists focusing specifically on the newsroom, cite many problems in news organizations that are of bureaucratic origin.

The primary question that must be asked when looking at news organizations from a sociological perspective is whether there is anything unique to the newsroom that lends itself to news organizations being different from other organizations. News organizations have a special legitimacy in the system, particularly in countries with a tradition of free or independent press. To an extent, democratic theory requires lively press debate, service as a watchdog, or that the press be a fourth estate. The burden of independence of the mass media provides a unique environment for journalists, in that they perceive of themselves as independent, outspoken, truth-seeking individuals. Such is not the case for both economic and noneconomic reasons. Journalists hardly have the autonomy one might imagine. Assignments are routinized, severely limiting creative enterprising journalism. Daily needs for copy essentially require output quotas. Even high level editors are caught in the bureaucratic maze. Prestige within the organization is a valuable commodity; desk chiefs seek to maximize prestige, i.e., front page or prominent news displays. Consequently, there is much posturing and bargaining over the allocation of space or time.

The hierarchical command structure of most news gathering organizations is linked very closely to what becomes news. Choice assignments are those likely to yield important news or even potential for professional recognition. Only in the rarest of circumstances do untried journalists have the opportunity (or the initiative) to make stories bigger (Bernstein & Woodward, 1974). More often they choose the safe route to avoid scolding or to enhance prospects for promotion. Still other aspects of the centrality of organizational and bureaucratic notions to newsgathering are cited in studies of the newsrooms of newspapers (Sigal, 1973; Tuchman, 1971), and television news (Althiede, 1975).

Perhaps the most difficulty facing news organizations is generated by the role strain imposed by the strategic location of news organizations at the interface between the public at large and government officials. News organizations, in reality, are gathering, and (especially) disseminating news for three audiences. Besides officials and citizens, there is the news industry, where reputation among peers is important.

As Sigal (1973), Nimmo (1970), and others have pointed out so well, officials and journalists are in a mutually exploitive relationship. Reporters try to cultivate relationships with officials to gain the inside track on new policies or events. At the same time, officials seek to use their relations with reporters to their own bureaucratic advantage by covering themselves, launching trial balloons, or transmitting messages to other agencies through unofficial channels. Yet both reporters and officials have to maintain a certain distance from one another because of their obligations to the second audience, the citizen. Cozy relations between reporters and their sources lead audiences to view reports with a certain skepticism. To some extent, the same is true of journalist peers. Loyalty to the source official can result in uncritical reporting where personal relationships are involved, or where there is a fear of being denied access at a future date. The public official has an obligation to a broader constituency than that provided by a single reporter, hence must widely disperse information. Finally, journalists are very judgmental of one another and, unlike members of other professions, constantly have their product available to be evaluated by peers. This judgment provides a third audience and increases role strain, for the product must please professional colleagues as well.

The recent expansion of investigative journalism, at least since Watergate, has minimized the cultivation of press-official friendships and on several occasions has resulted in adversarial relationships. Although one result has been the expansion of the so-called credibility gap as politicians and press lost faith in one another, there has also been an increase in respect for the press as an institution.

The final problems faced by news organizations are those imposed by the legal and/or regulatory environment in which news media operate. Print media face legal limitations on what can be printed, although given First Amendment rights in the U.S., these are relatively few. Nevertheless, possible lawsuits for libel (both costs of defense and possible monetary judgment), or even for printing certain documents such as the Pentagon Papers, suggests that there are economic consequences for unrestrained print news organizations. Electronic news organizations face the same constraints, plus the problems of fines or loss of broadcast license for failure to cover news, provide equal time for candidates or editorial reply, or for similar violations of F.C.C. law. The regulatory threat, although rarely exercised, is strong enough to give broadcasters considerably less leeway in news presentation than print media face. The costs of violations simply are too high. The results, of course, are apparent in the news: less dynamic reporting, conservative (i.e., status quo) bias, lack of innovation, and tendency to avoid conflict areas.

NEWS AVAILABILITY

Given the strategic location of the news media between officials and the public, the potential power of the press is awesome (see Chapter 6). Ordinarily, journalists have viewed the press power to be linked to its arousal and persuasive effects, but arguably its greatest strength lies in its ability to control the flow of information through gatekeeping, agenda-setting, and biasing the news. Without doubt, the power of the press is limited by news availability and policy decisions by the government, as well as the receptivity of the audience, but on the whole the potential of the press is overwhelming.

In the original Easton model (Easton, 1964), note is taken of gatekeepers in the political system. They limit the flow of demands to decision makers, preventing system overload. According to Chaffee (1975), such gatekeepers are extremely functional to the system. However, in their view, gatekeeping operates only between demands and decision, not between decision makers and constituents. In other words, they fail to consider that information about decision maker response is an important dimension of gatekeeping, particularly where mass news dissemination is involved. Thus, citizens may be unaware of government action addressing demands or even new policy initiatives.

The dimensions of gatekeeping are not fully known. Given the economic imposition of space and time, clearly not all information can be presented. We know only a small percentage of wire copy makes it into print, and there are estimates of the percentage of total news available that appear for a few newspapers. But this only hints at the extent of gatekeeping, for we have no data on primary level gatekeeping by front-line journalists who fail to pursue stories or simply choose to ignore them. Nor have we qualitative information, with few exceptions, on just what types of reports are likely to be kept, and the reasons for it. The notable exception again is White's (1950) study of "Mr. Gates," which reveals personal priorities of an editor to be as important a factor as institutional constraints.

Whereas journalists acknowledge that there is more material available to be printed or broadcast than there is space or time, they argue that the selection process is made simple by presenting the information about which people want to know, or about which they should know. What's more, they add, as long as information is presented fairly and there are multiple sources of information, gatekeeping has little significance for political action.

Whether news disseminators present what people want or should know, raises the question of agenda-setting, one of the more important concepts to emerge in mass media research from the past decade. McCombs and Shaw (1972; Shaw and McCombs, 1977), drawing from Cohen (1963), derive their notion from the fact that mass media do not tell us what to think so much as what to think about. In other words, only those topics laid before the public are the issues of concern to the public. In the absence of data on topics about which people want to hear, journalists provide them with what they *should* think about; "All the news that's fit to print," for example. To be sure, publishers do make some assumptions about what people do want to hear (i.e., the plethora of crime and fire or disaster news), but these rarely extend to political controversies.

Kraus and Davis (1976) have written that media agenda-setting creates a type of reality, presenting an image of society, issues, or the culture upon which citizens depend. The agreement across information sources as to what is significant further reinforces this image. Indeed, if there are effects attributable to mass media, they are fundamentally linked to image creation.

All the time the media set the agenda of important events and issues, they confer a certain status upon both issues and individuals. Although this status conferral function is nothing new (Wright, 1975), it perpetuates the list of those capable of making news. Individuals who are news makers gain a certain credibility. Given that the media are somewhat selective because of gatekeeping, the very fact that one appears as a spokesperson guarantees some authority.

Research findings on agenda-setting outside the context of election campaigns are quite limited. During elections, McCombs and Shaw (1972) report agenda-setting effects to be greatest for the undecided voter. Tipton, Haney, and Basehart (1975) suggest that newspapers play some agenda-setting role during local elections, although there is some doubt as to the patterns of causality. Finally, McLeod, Becker, and Byrnes (1974) show no blanket effects, and when there are agenda-setting findings, they are limited by many contingent variables. Obviously, the relationship of agenda-setting to observed effects is complicated, and requires further investigation. Despite the absence of strong empirical data, there are some theoretical reasons for when the agenda presented in mass media is likely to be important. For most audiences, there is little or no direct access to news sources, so citizens must rely on news disseminators. In some circumstances, there is direct access to the source, at which time it is possible to explore the degree of agenda-setting. One such example is during presidential debates. Candidates have direct access to the public viewing the debates. At the same time, the extent of media fidelity to what was said in debate (i.e., the agenda of the debaters) can be determined by comparing media reports to actual content. Moreover, public opinion measures synchronically taken can reveal if news reports reflect the wishes of the public, the candidate statements, or if they reflect editorial agenda-setting. Evidence from recent research (Jackson-Beeck & Meadow, 1979b; Meadow & Jackson-Beeck, 1978) suggests that, indeed, there are several agendas operating at any time.

The extent to which agendas are established through the press is one result of gatekeeping decisions. A second result is the introduction of bias into the news. More than any other value, journalists consistently and uniformly seek to present the issues and controversies under discussion fairly. Thus journalists actively avoid conscious insertion of prejudicial terms, or otherwise seek to ritualize their objectivity (Tuchman, 1971). Nevertheless, even in the absence of nonobjective reporting, there is bias in the news that flows from gatekeeping.

This is visible on several levels. First, there is selectivity involved in assigning reporters. In a sense, news can't be made, with rare exception, if there is no one to collect it. After all, the tree falling in the forest does not make news if no one hears it. Next, there is the gatekeeping selection on the part of the newsmaker, who decides what is revealed to reporters. To some degree, news released is usually good news, otherwise it isn't made so readily available. Third, there is the selection by the reporter as to what he or she feels is news. And finally, there are the bureaucratic, economic, political, or even aesthetic factors that are behind some gatekeeping, which lead to shifting story emphasis or even exclusion of the story altogether.

All told, there is a bias in the news from selective encoding (Frank, 1973) of the full range of environmental phenomena. However, selective encoding is not the only form of bias said to exist in the news. In particular, television news came under attack from leading politicians for being biased. A flurry of studies followed, including major ones conducted by Efron (1971), Frank (1973), and Hofstetter (1976).

Efron chose to look for bias in television news by exploring audio tapes and written transcripts of network newscasts during the 1968 Presidential campaign. Her findings, based on statements taken to be either "for" opinion or "against" opinion on the issues she isolated, revealed the networks to be biased along several dimensions, including against Richard Nixon, the Silent Majority, and other causes or actors. Of course, her analysis failed to consider the visual dimensions of television, but nevertheless provided a framework for others to investigate the problem of bias.

Frank's (1973) study, based on the early efforts of Cutler, Tedesco, and Frank (1972) grappled with the theoretical issues of bias, finally isolating two kinds of news. The first is the presentation of favorable (or unfavorable) news (i.e., news which presents optimism, desirable means or ends, or successes), and the second is the (un)favorable presentation of news (i.e., news, whether representing optimism or pessimism, good or bad, success or failure, treated in a [non] supportive fashion). Only the latter news may be said to be biased in the common meaning of the term, in that it explicitly reveals ideological preferences. The former news in itself may be fairly reported; the only issue involved is whether news organizations consistently present favorable news. Then, of course, there is selective encoding bias introduced. In Frank's analysis, relatively little explicit bias was found, as several facets of issues were given air time. However not all issues ever make it to the air to be portrayed equitably, so there is always the selective encoding phenomenon, (i.e., some issues never make it to the agenda).

Hofstetter's (1976) analysis offers several definitions and typologies of bias. First, bias may be outright lying by journalists. This, he argues, hardly ever occurs. Next is bias as distortion, which can occur as the significance of an event is overdramatized, or emphasis is established through location within the newspaper or in the broadcast. Third, there is bias as value assertion, in which explicit judgments about the event are made in line with the journalist's value priorities. Joining these three forms of bias are four other dimensions: fairness and balance, scope of attention, accuracy and truthfulness, and breadth and depth of analysis. Fairness and balance is akin to the explicit bias (favorable presentation of news) discussed by Frank. Scope of attention, of course, is a gatekeeping dimension referring to the range of issues explored in the news. Third is accuracy and truthfulness. Although journalists strive for accuracy and truthfulness and sometimes go through elaborate procedures to attain these ideals, inevitably there are inaccuracies in news reports. Breadth and depth of analysis are partially in the hands of the journalist, but also depend on the cooperation of news sources and institutional variables as well.

Overall, these biases can be divided into those which are political, i.e., rooted in ideological preferences of journalists or news institutions, and those which are structural, based on institutional constraints, time, budget, and news availability. Hofstetter's close analysis of television network news coverage of the 1972 campaign reveals a remarkable uniformity of reporting across the networks, and moreover demonstrates that whatever biases are present result from structural rather than political factors. This structural bias includes more film sequences because of more active campaigning, the presence of more spokespersons, or simply the attraction that a disorganized fledging campaign had as news (McGovern's) compared to an efficient noncampaign (Nixon's).

Taken together, all these studies suggest that bias is a very complicated concept, referring to ideological and nonideological aspects of news presentation. The most methodologically rigorous studies (Frank's and Hofstetter's) failed to show ideological bias in their analysis of electronic news during a campaign period, but they both agree that nonideological, institutional factors limit the amount of news available, and, through selective encoding, "bias" the news.

Undoubtedly there are relationships between news and public policy for politicians and citizens alike that make news gathering and disseminating organizations so important in political communication. First, news organizations serve to organize public opinion in several ways. Individuals can observe what their fellow citizens are reading, if not thinking. In addition, support for positions through editorials and columnists can be found. Third, news disseminators, particularly newspapers, offer a forum (op-ed page, letters to the editor) for the exchange of ideas. And finally, through political advertising and poll reporting, citizens can further surveille the political environment. More important, however, is the fact that news gathering organizations are in themselves important political participants, for their presence at an event can be crucial in shaping that event. In the following section, this phenomenon is explored more fully.

NEWS ORGANIZATIONS AND CRITICAL EVENTS

News organizations, and particularly electronic news organizations, have often been accused of staging news events. Whereas governments themselves are not strangers to this practice of organizing allegedly spontaneous events, the trust in visual media by citizens makes the accusation more serious. Staging events usually arises for aesthetic reasons: asking an interviewee the same question twice because the sound level was insufficient, having a police officer re-enact his or her actions, asking a picket to cross the street to where the lighting is better. The significance of the interaction of the news gatherer with the news maker is limited in these circumstances.

On other occasions, the presence of mass media on the scene has a significant effect. The very presence of news gatherers in those circumstances, changes the event, not only for the viewer, but for the event participant. Again, electronic news gathering teams bear more responsibility for this. Print journalists may arrive on the scene and inconspicuously observe and take notes. Electronic journalists arrive with an entourage of camera operators, sound teams, and well marked equipment vans, creating a circus wherever they go. At the same time, news makers, becoming actors, enliven their performances for the camera. News makers play to the camera as individuals or as members of organizations seeking publicity and, through the status conferral function of mass media, legitimacy.

Perhaps the foremost example of the role of news gatherer in events was reported by Singer (1972). In his study of prisoners arrested during the Detroit riots in 1967 (referred to in Chapter 4) he found that a significant number of riot participants were quite attentive to mass media during the disturbances. Not only did some individuals first find out about the riots through electronic news media, but they also used the electronic media to find out where the riot activity was centered and more specifically where the police were concentrating their efforts. Subsequently they would begin their activity elsewhere, hoping for a successful looting episode before police knew of their whereabouts.

Of course, not all effects of news organizations on the course of events are so direct. More often, the significance of news media is in establishing a framework through which events can be viewed and ordering their significance. To a limited extent, this notion has been raised in discussions of "critical events" (Kraus, Davis, Lang, & Lang, 1975), defined as those events producing full explanations of social change, and characterized by producing an informed citizenry which is stimulated to social action. In other words, in their view, a critical event has significance in and of itself; the role of mass media is confined to bringing the event into public view.

This implies an important role for the media, at least in bringing the event to wide audiences. In some instances, even the mass media play a less important role, for information about some events is transmitted interpersonally. Indeed, the most important events of a lifetime, even in recent periods of high media use, are still transmitted interpersonally. Examples such as the assassination of John F. Kennedy (Hill & Bonjean, 1964) reveal extensive interpersonal communication, lesser events such as Trudeau's marriage (Fathi, 1973), and the papal enclyclical on birth control (Adams, Mullen, & Wilson, 1969) reveal the usual dependence on mass media for the diffusion of information. Because most events are not of the type in which interpersonal communication plays a major role, mass media are important in calling attention to the news.

News display and other modes of emphasized presentation present priorities for the news. And frequently, the context in which news is reported, establishes the way it is viewed by audiences. Recent research (Ducat, 1978) on particular events, such as the power failure in New York, provide support for this notion. The failure in 1965 provided a filter for looking at the 1977 blackout. To what extent were people cooperative? Why was there looting in 1977, compared with the absence of violence in 1965? Similarly, Holz (1978) looked at reporting of the so-called Legionnaire's disease, at times finding scientific conspiratorial or mysterious explanations appearing in news media with inevitable comparisons to similar, unexplained deaths.

Perhaps the most recent example drawn from the political arena is the coverage of the presidential debates. As we know, much media coverage at the time of the 1960 debates was devoted to the staging of the debates and physical appearance of the candidates (Meadow & Jackson-Beeck, 1978). This coverage resulted in both mythology and tyranny for the 1976 debaters, who, as a direct consequence of the factors most emphasized in 1960, spent hours practicing delivery, shaving carefully, selecting the proper clothing (Ford wore vested suits because they were "presidential") and otherwise having their action dictated by expected news coverage in 1976, based on the 1960 experience of Kennedy and Nixon.

In events, mass media coverage has implications for the political variables raised in Part II of this volume. One could pose, as always, the Lasswellian questions: What is demonstrated by an event? For whom? With what effect? But more important for explaining what occurs, both in an event and in looking for its social consequences, are other factors. In terms of power, event coverage in mass media establishes the legitimacy of the participants. Status is indeed conferred on political actors by appearance in mass media. At the same time, social control is encouraged by reaffirmation of authority as active, particularly in time of crises. Power relationships within society are defined in many ways by the communication networks, especially for those who have access.

Also, the existence of conflict is called to the attention of audiences by play in mass media. If there is competition over values or over the distribution of scarce resources, how, in a mass society, are individuals to know without mass media? Conflict expansion thrives on mass media and depends on those who join the conflict following its appearance on the agenda. Decision-making, too, depends on mass media in critical events situations, by forcing government authorities to react to the "level of criticalness" assigned to an event by mass media. Moreover, constant reminders of how others in similar situations respond may direct decision makers more than one might consider to be socially optimal.

All of this suggests that there are many levels of events in which news media play a role, and further suggests a number of research areas. First, there are individual level questions, considering citizens as participants in events, observers of events, and as information recipients. How do individuals respond to mass mediated information about events? Are there differences in expectations, or even behaviors, between the exposed and the unexposed?

At the organizational and group level further questions are raised. How do groups arise? Does the presence of mass media account for group memberships? The dynamics of group communication are altered by news dissemination: news media may provide a free publicity service for group members. At a very simple level, the size of cohesiveness of anti-war forces during the latter stages of the Vietnam War was said by Vice-President Agnew to be a direct result of the publicity and media coverage given demonstrators and protestors. Similarly, the Detroit rioters owed some of their success to media coverage.

Finally, there always are the systemic questions that deal with the broadest implications for the political culture as a whole. Are there events critical for a historical period that lead to fundamental reevaluations of the political world? If there are, the way in which those events are brought into the cognitions of political actors have extreme importance. How are system members to know when an event matters unless they are told? Perhaps this brings us full circle, for again it leads us to reconsider the role of news gatherers and disseminators in the political process, in telling us what is an event and ultimately what is news.

THE NEWS: A FINAL WORD

Given the discussion in the previous section, we must reconsider what constitutes an event. Clearly it is something out of the ordinary for news gatherers, participants, and audiences. But more than that, critical events have a significance enduring beyond the moment, such that future, similar events are looked at in light of the first event. In addition, critical events create a new public through developing a common interest in an event.

Because of this creation process, critical events differ from ordinary news in which the processes for gathering and disseminating are routine. Despite what journalists would claim—that news is event based—the organizational dynamics of the newsroom combined with infrequency of critical events prevents creative news gathering. Journalists, like other professionals, see in events what they are trained to see. As Lippman (1922) says, often only the stereotyped phase of news is reported. Moreover, unconventional news is not good newspaper economics.

This structure of news clearly works to the advantage of those in power, and to the detriment of aspiring political actors. Reporting, again according to Lippman, is system maintaining, because events are more likely to be reported than are the reasons behind those events. As a result, those without access to events are likely to be excluded from the news. Interestingly, out-groups have begun to recognize the importance of event creation to publicize substantive issue demands. The civil rights movement of the 1960s relied on massive demonstrations, sit-ins, marches, and similar activities. Later, urban riots underscored racial tensions and the depths of frustration and animosity toward traditional solutions. The protestors of the Vietnam War also relied on the demonstration as a means of gaining access to wider audiences. And, of course, governments are not immune from creating the big event, whether it is a prime time telecast of a presidential speech, or continuous coverage of a moon landing.

It is not surprising that the frequency of demonstration as a form of social grievance has increased in recent decades, given the growth of visual news media. Traditional modes of registering protests, such as the petition or meeting, simply do not survive in visually oriented news. When searching for the effects of news on the polity, one can turn away from individually based explanations and look towards whole new ways of participating as a major effect.

Perhaps the best statement on news and its role in the political process comes from an early work by Robert Park (1940) in his explanations of news through the sociology of knowledge. News, he argues, is not systemic knowledge, but is concerned primarily with events. Moreover, it is news only until it reaches the audience for whom it has news interest and until something else comes along to replace it. Once news directs the audience to the environment, it makes political action possible, for it has an authenticity not attached to rumor and gossip that compels people to act. Therein lies the basis for objective news collection and dissemination, because the only grounds for the authenticity of news is the reliability of previous news reports.

News, in a nutshell, is really events; those events that bring about a sudden change, a decisive change from the previous situation, or status quo. But, because events are so transient, at least for Park, they do not live. Instead they endure as symbols, comparative yardsticks by which to measure future events or to set standards for action. News, therefore, has at the same time, a transience and a permanence. For day to day political action and response to the action, what appears as news is not consequential. Over the long run, however, the news is cumulative, establishing how the system is viewed, providing landmarks for action, identifying actors and appropriate modes of action, and setting an agenda for citizen concerns.

10

ELECTORAL POLITICS

More than anything else, political communication researchers have focused on electoral politics. The role of communication in general and mass media in particular during election campaigns has been studied from many perspectives. As a result, we know more about the relationship between communications and electoral behavior than any other political behavior. In addition, a number of communication institutions and practices have arisen during election campaigns, all of which make elections unique among political communication phenomena. No other area, with the possible exception of violence, has been studied with a view toward "direct effects" of exposure to media. Indirect and long-term enduring effects have also made elections a focus of inquiry.

In reality, there are four aspects of the media's role in electoral politics that are worth pursuing. First, there is the impact, direct or indirect, on campaigns and campaign strategy. Second, there are effects on voters. Third, there is the analysis of the problems of campaign reporting. And fourth, are the problems of democratic theory generated by the presence of mass media in election campaigns. Each of these aspects is reviewed in detail later in this chapter.

In electoral politics, all political communicators mentioned throughout this volume play important roles. Decision makers holding (or seeking) elective office, news reporters covering the election campaign, and citizen participants all play special roles in electoral politics. In particular, for ordinary citizens, elections provide an opportunity to express support (and perhaps demands) for political regimes (see Chapter 4). Consistent with the other institutions and processes explored thus far, elections fit neatly with major concepts: they resolve policy conflicts, they provide legitimacy for authorities, they are a vehicle for popular participation, and they are the focus of much political socialization research.

The centrality of elections in most political communication research is both for historical and theoretical reasons, although in some ways the earliest empirical research guided the development of theory. So many facets of electoral political communication research have been explored that inventories of the dimensions of electoral politics have been recorded. O'Keefe (1975), for example, outlined thirteen areas of political and electoral research including: the nature of poliical influence, voter use of media during campaigns, campaign media content, cognitive effects of campaign communications, interpersonal communication in political campaigns, and others. Similarly, Nimmo (1978) has enumerated the important actors in electoral communication. Whether we focus on processes or actors, the depth of electoral political communication research is considerable.

EFFECTS OF COMMUNICATION ON VOTERS

The reason for focusing on the effects of campaign communications on voters is quite simple: the view of popular political pundits and social scientists alike was that voters responded to campaign messages automatically. Directly in response to political messages, it was assumed, individuals would decide how to cast their votes. This notion applied to all voters. The most independent, rational, issue oriented voter would carefully attend to information from mass or interpersonal sources, weigh the merits of each candidate, and cast a vote. The most image oriented voters, too, would attend to political messages to develop their understanding of candidates. The effects on partisan voters was less certain, but it was argued, particularly with the growth of electronic media, that partisan voting might diminish because issue information would be so readily available.

The evidence gathered thus far presents a different view. Attributing electoral communication information seeking to media variables rather than voter variables leaves some question as to the causal agent. Over time, between the first studies of the 1940s and the most recent work of the 1970s, our understanding of mass media's role certainly has changed.

In *The People's Choice*, Lazarsfeld, Berelson, and Gaudet (1948) undertook a major study on all aspects of voting behavior but focused specifically on the role of mass media in the campaign. Not surprisingly, their content analysis of the press revealed a pro-Republican bias, with the focus more on the campaign itself or the candidates' past records than anything else (a finding which has been corroborated since). As far as the relationship of mass media and interpersonal communication to voters goes, they found the same people exposed to a variety of sources, but, more important, interest in the campaign heightened exposure considerably. In terms of changing the intentions of voters, the mass media were shown to have little influence. Generally, the undecideds were less interested and less exposed. Perhaps most important was the fact that interpersonal communication had such an important role in influencing the undecided.

A few years later, a similar study by Berelson, Lazarsfeld, and McPhee (1954) again found little relationship between media exposure and candidate choice, the effect with which researchers have been most concerned. Instead, they found a more subtle influence: interest and intensity of concern for the election could be modified by high exposure, as could level of information about the candidates.

This research from Columbia University, supplemented by further work at the University of Michigan fundamentally argued that external forces independent of the specific election had the major role in shaping electoral behavior. Communication variables were relevant in only the broadest sense: intergenerational transmission of party identification or social status shaped voting more than specific information about issues or candidates. The conclusion baldly stated by Klapper in 1960 summarized this research: mass media have little effect beyond reinforcement during election campaigns.

This position was somewhat embarrassing for political communication researchers, because conventional wisdom had it (and we all felt) that there had to be more direct effects than reinforcement alone. Only recently has it become clear that it was not so much the nature of mass media that failed to show direct effects, nor even faulty research designs. Instead it was the voter himself. Voters of the 1950s and 1940s were more partisan, issues mattered less, and information about issues was less relevant than in the 1960s and 1970s. Over the past decade, more and more evidence has been accumulating to suggest that voters are not fools (Key, 1966; Nie, Verba, & Petrocik, 1976) and that issues are indeed important.

Part of the problem with the reliance on past data and findings to guide our understanding of the present, was that much of the research took place before the widespread use of television for explicit political information. Moreover, the visual dimensions of television, its graphic and redundant opportunities for campaign coverage from the conventions through debates to election night, increased the visibility (if not the sophistication) of campaigners. Now, of course, it is much easier to find data supporting the importance of mass communication to voters.

In their study of British elections, for example, Blumler and McQuail (1969) found how important television was as a source of information about the issues and candidates. Again, the effects are less direct in terms of the S/R paradigm, but within an issue oriented campaign the information role is critical. In the United States, evidence on the most independent voters, the ticket splitters (DeVries & Torrance, 1972), shows them to rely heavily on mass media for issue information.

The most recent approach to electoral political communication arguing for direct effects is that of the agenda-setting theorists. Shaw and McCombs (1977) summarizing much of this work, have attributed direct effects to mass media in election campaigns: the issues of the campaign are those emphasized in the mass media. Again, we have no direct effect on the vote decision—too many factors are important to isolate just one—but on the context in which the vote occurs. The framework established for viewing candidates is one established by mass media.

The lessons from all these studies are clear. Effects of political messages on voters in terms of changing vote intention, or even crystalizing votes in the short run, are very difficult to isolate, if they exist at all. Instead, what mass media do is more subtle, and occurs over a much longer period of time than one election campaign. People isolate issues into this larger mold shaped by mass media. People rely on mass media to inform them of issue positions, but not necessarily to sway them.

The nature of media messages today is an important factor in this information function. Striving to present a fair and nonpartisan perspective on the news within the context of a two-party system, television, the most widely used medium, fails to decide for the voter. Options are presented, but no more, for conclusions are not drawn. Television has simplified the process of voters acquiring information, but it is still up to the voter to put the information to use. This suggests that political communication researchers may well have been looking at the wrong variables when searching for "effects," for they are only long run as mass media information enters as a single variable to interact with attitudes, predespositions, and socialization phenomena.

What remains, of course, is to look at the information available to citizens during, and, perhaps, between election campaigns. During this periods, voters are provided with the raw material to forge into meaningful decision inputs. If effects are located in the preservation of issues and the formation of candidate image information, mass media are significant for what they emphasize over the course of a campaign. Election news, therefore, combined with special campaign phenomena such as debates or political advertising can be the focus of political communication research rather than the voter.

CAMPAIGNING AND MASS MEDIA

In the United States there have been mass media for as long as there have been elections, so identifying the unique impact of mass media on election campaigning and campaign strategy is difficult. However, prior to the nineteen thirties, print media were the only news media to cover campaigns (although, of course, there were other media for political campaigning: handbills, campaign buttons, rallies). Candidates would campaign personally, or have surrogates campaigning on their behalf according to campaign strategies designed to maximize electoral success (e.g., a Northern strategy, an urban strategy, etc.). Transportation was slow, so during the course of a campaign, only a handful of voters could see or hear a candidate for national office. Thus, most voters would have to rely on secondary reports of candidate statements and positions, either through print media or interpersonal communication.

In the 1930s, with the growth of radio, many more voters had the opportunity to hear, if not see, candidates, and to hear them directly address issues without depending on media accounts or gatekeepers for information on what was said. Political conventions were broadcast, and it was said that more people were included in the political processes than ever before. Again, with the introduction of national television coverage of the 1952 political conventions (Lang & Lang, 1968), popular participation was said to be unbounded. Of course, with electronic media coverage of campaigns, there was still much gatekeeping: news broadcasters had limited time slots between entertainment shows to present news, technical facilities also prohibited complete coverage of political campaigns, and news judgment was still an important criterion for determining about which portion of a candidate's day the voter would hear.

Although electronic media may have provided voters with more information about political candidates than they had in the past—even if only marginally relevant to the hypothetical "informed" voter (e.g., the quality of candidate voice or physical appearance)—they played an even more important role in candidate strategies. In the era of print media, coverage was essentially local. Certainly there were national magazines, but they had relatively small circulations. Only a few newspapers had reporters wiring in stories from whistle stop rallies. With electronic coverage, and particularly television coverage, exposure every day was national. Candidates could reach voters without physically being present, freeing candidate time for more selective campaigning. At the same time, with a new national audience, it became more difficult to segment voters: the audience was heterogeneous as well as omnipresent, so it became impossible to say different things and make different promises to different audiences. To do so would lead to accusations of "waffling."

Despite the relative fidelity of electronic media to "reality," there are still severe limitations to them as noted in the previous section. For the political conventions, voters have a relatively unlimited access to proceedings (although not to smoke-filled rooms), and see much of what delegates see, if not more. But for the campaign itself, voters must depend on the news for information about candidates' stands on issues, or even for their images. There are, however, two exceptions to this: the first occurs when there have been political debates, the second occurs through political advertising.

PRESIDENTIAL DEBATES

In the United States there were two elections promising voters escape from the typical pattern of media dependency. In the 1960 and 1976 elections, televised debates were held between the presidential candidates. In these elections, voters had the opportunity to see and hear the candidates present themselves and their issue positions in direct response to questions posed by journalists. Tens of millions of voters in 1960 and 1976 saw the debates, and as a result, had raw material from which to assess similarities and differences between Kennedy and Nixon, and Carter and Ford.

Each debate series was both "historical" and unique in its own way. In 1955, Stevenson challenged Eisenhower to debate (Lang & Lang, 1968), but Ike rejected the idea as not presidential. In 1960, candidates of the major parties saw advantages to debating, and efforts were made to minimize technical and legal obstacles. For his part, Nixon felt he could win the debates. His effectiveness on television was underscored by a successful "Checkers" speech in 1952, his reputation as a debater enhanced by the famous "kitchen debate" with Nikita Khrushchev. Kennedy was the lesser known candidate, in need of national exposure. At the same time he was anxious to dispel rumors of his greater allegience to the Catholic Church and the Pope than to the U.S., and was anxious to disprove notions that he was not old enough for the job (he was four years younger than Nixon).

In 1960, Congress temporarily suspended section 315 of the Communications Act of 1934 so that the sponsoring networks and presenting stations would not have to provide opportunities for minor party candidates making claims for equal time. Four debates were scheduled, one limited to domestic affairs, one to international topics, and two general debates. They were to last sixty minutes, allocated between opening and closing remarks, questions, answers, and rebuttals. Questions were posed by a rotating panel of questioners, all journalists by profession.

The representatives of both candidates were concerned about the visual dimensions of the debates. Careful preparations went into originally constructed set designs. For the split screen debate where Kennedy and Nixon were at opposite ends of the country, duplicate sets were built. Despite all these preparations, popular mythology surrounding the 1960 debates suggests that Nixon "lost" the first debate because the make-up cosmetician failed to disguise his five o'clock shadow, and he looked tired and haggard. In addition, the studio lights made the room quite hot, causing Nixon to perspire heavily and look nervous, while Kennedy remained relatively cool.

The 1960 debates were studied in great detail (Kraus, 1962) by researchers from several disciplines. By far the greatest emphasis in these studies (Katz & Feldman, 1962), was on who won or lost the debates. However, presidential

165

debates as political communication events are more than just contests to be won or lost. Images are developed, supporters cultivated, and undecideds wooed.

Conventional wisdom has it that Kennedy won the debates and, causally, the election. For 1976, when the second series of presidential debates was arranged, this myth grew in stature. Neither candidate wanted to lose, for losing would cost the election. Again both candidates saw advantages in debate. Ford, despite his incumbency, was behind in the trial-heat polls. Carter sought to diminish his image as a "waffler" on the issues, and wanted to meet the President on equal grounds. Congress, however, did not see fit to suspend section 315 again, so the debates were arranged under the auspices of the League of Women Voters Education Fund (see Alexander & Margolies, 1978).

Considerable effort went into preparing for the debates. For Carter, briefing books were prepared. Ford had a duplicate of the debate studio reproduced in the White House Auditorium and practiced answers to questions to fit them into the alloted time frame. Most important, both candidates sought to avoid any of the difficulties encountered by Nixon and Kennedy: neckties were properly adjusted, make-up carefully applied. Indeed, even the lecterns were cut to different heights so that the same proportion of body and head would appear for Carter and the taller Ford.

In 1976, the debates were similar in format to the 1960 events, with few exceptions. There were no opening remarks, the debates were ninety minutes rather than sixty, but there were three presidential debates and one vice-presidential instead of four and none. One presidential debate was for domestic issues, one for international issues, and the third on all topics. All questions were posed by a panel of journalists selected by the League of Women Voters.

This description of the debates only scratches the surface of the importance they held in political communication processes. Besides the opportunities they offer voters for direct access to candidate remarks, they offer researchers a chance to explore many dimensions of political communication. Research compiled by (Bishop, Meadow, & Jackson-Beeck, 1978; and Kraus, 1962; 1979) touches on many of these dimensions.

Perhaps the most important question that can be posed concerning the debates is what contribution they make to the candidates and voters. Under the assumptions of a need for information by the electorate, debates presumably are worthwhile events. But does the information voters receive, or are at least exposed to, meet what they seek? There is little evidence to suggest that this is the case. Given the debate format as presently constituted,, there are actually three agendas; the public's, the journalist's, and the candidates' (Jackson-Beeck & Meadow, 1979b). Candidates can determine the agenda by failing to respond to questions, and instead change subjects to suit their needs and strong points. Journalists provide rough parameters for candidate answers, but there is no guarantee that their interests match those of the public. To some extent there is a complicated coorientation problem (McLeod & Chaffee, 1972), where each party in the debate is concerned with different issues and engages in what would seem to be a tirialogue.

Even if voters don't hear about the issues concerning them, surely they do learn something. Evidence from both 1960 (Kraus, 1962) and 1976 (Bishop, Meadow, and Jackson-Beeck, 1978; Kraus, 1979) suggests that cognitive learning is enhanced by debates, so at least one function is observed. Arguably, legitimacy of the candidates is enhanced as well. Why, then, would debates not be institutionalized as requirements during campaigns?

First, for minor party candidates, two-candidate debates diminish any hope of legitimacy. Indeed, efforts by third-party candidates to prevent the debates in 1976 were extensive (Alexander & Margolies, 1978), but failed because the debates, as arranged by the League of Women Voters Education Fund were newsworthy events, exempt from Section 315 requirements. However, the 27 minute gap audio failure in the first debate exploded that notion, when the "spontaneous" news event was halted (despite the valiant efforts of certain production staffers) because news organizations could no longer broadcast it. Second, rather than providing forums for spontaneous debate, they appear as rehearsed performances. Responses differ little from those on the campaign trail, and above all, candidates tread gently to avoid making a costly slip or mistake. Finally, and perhaps most important, debates do not live up to their promise of providing voters with direct access to candidate statements. Candidates are guided (although not limited) by questions from journalists. But more important, journalists still serve to interpret debates for voters.

The best evidence of this interpretation comes from Lang and Lang (1978) and Steeper (1978). With two different methodologies, they have demonstrated how mass media interprets events such as debates. Lang and Lang, for example, noted that determination of who won the first 1976 debate varied significantly across groups surveyed immediately after the event, before exposed to any analysis, and groups surveyed a few days later when opportunities for media analysis and judgments intervened. Similarly, when exploring the so-called gaffe on Eastern European domination made by Ford in the second 1976 debate, Steeper found virtually *no* reaction by audience members responding on-line to the debates, and that those surveyed immediately after the debate but before exposure to media interpretation said that Ford "won." If stating Carter won, they made no mention of Ford's alleged blooper. As time wore on, more and more people cited Carter as the victor, referencing Ford's gaffe, so that among people surveyed late the next day after reading news accounts of the debate, virtually all cited Carter as winner, and almost exclusively because of Ford's gaffe. Such evidence is particularly supportive of the concept of a major role for journalists interpreting events, even ones to which audiences have complete access.

The richness of presidential debates underscores their value as important campaign communication events, if not to audiences, then researchers. They truly are multidimensional, for astute observers not only hear the candidates, but can observe their demeanor. The extent to which candidates, conduct themselves "presidentially," and maintain cool brows during heated questioning is part and parcel of the presidential package, and is available to voters only when there is relatively unhindered access to the candidates during events like presidential debates.

POLITICAL ADVERTISING

Although various forms of political advertising have long been with us (campaign buttons, posters, and billboards), only in the past twenty-five years, with the growth of televised political advertising, has advertising reached a true national audience. No level of government is immune; candidates from city council to president and even political issues such as those included in referenda all have had advertisements to publicize candidacies or positions.

Nowadays it is difficult to imagine how campaigns were conducted without political advertising, but politics itself has changed as much as our images of campaigning have. With the growth of radio, attempts were made by the Republican party to engage in the first political advertising (Jennings, 1968). Actors were hired to get the anti-New Deal messages across to voters in the context of a dramatic presentation, but the radio networks rejected the idea, arguing that drama was an irrelevant vehicle for presenting the weighty issues of the day. At the same time, a pseudodebate format between supporters of the Democrats and Republicans were also rejected. The attempts of the political parties in 1936 led the Association of Broadcasters to formally ban dramatic portrayals in 1939. By 1944, however, radio spot advertisements appeared as one minute dramas, although half hour dramas, the usual format for radio dramas, were still banned. Advertising was dominated by the Republican party, but by 1948, the Democrats used dramatization for the first time. Finally, by 1952, advertising on television became the norm, professional advertising agencies and consultants entered the fray, and modern political advertising came of age.

Qualitatively and quantitatively, television changed the nature of political advertising. Like radio, of course, it had mass appeal, and often was national in scope, but different variables became important. The visual dimension of television put a premium on looks and charm of the candidate, and on graphically slick productions. Although these tendencies were not apparent at the outset of televised political advertising, over time they became increasingly more important.

What, specifically are political advertisements intended to accomplish? For the most part, they are oriented to establishing or maintaining political images. Candidates for national office must appear as "presidential": intelligent, informed, just, fair, thoughtful, and articulate. Candidates for lesser offices have to contend with a larger problem: recognition. In primary elections, a recent phenomenon at the national level and for lower level elections, candidates must become known and create a favorable image, exuding those qualities perceived by the public as desirable.

Dan Nimmo (1978) has argued that there are two image dimensions with which candidates must be concerned: image creation and image reflection. Image creation suggests that what a candidate is, what he stands for, is less important than how he appears. It becomes possible to hide weak points and enhance strong points and, essentially, present a public face different from reality. Image reflection suggests that candidates can be reflected in the best light, in surroundings or with people supportive of the candidacy. Regardless of which image technique is employed, the goals, according to Nimmo, remain constant. Political advertising, much like advertising of consumer durables, is designed to: (1) make the candidate known to the voters; (2) lead voters to develop positive orientations to the candidates; and (3) lead voters to break traditional voting habits.

In short, political advertisements operate at psychological levels as many persuasive communications do. But the issue becomes clouded somewhat because political systems, at least in theory, do not operate the way purchases of consumer durables function. Consequently, there has been much criticism of political advertising and image creation because it "cheapens" democratic politics. Daniel Boorstein (1961), in one early critique, suggested that pseudoevents and pseudocandidates have emerged, turning politics into show business and public relations exercises. More popular accounts, such as McGinnis' (1968) *Selling of the President,* suggest that the public is deprived of full and accurate representations of candidates because of political advertising.

The issue then, would appear to be a simple one. Advertising of political candidates removes substance from political campaigns. Whatever issue content there is must be grossly oversimplified, for in sixty seconds, sophisticated multifaceted, complex treatment of issues is impossible. Second, advertising makes explicit appeals to images of candidates, or to a sense of party loyalty, or in other ways moves the voter away from issue voting.

The criticisms, however, although rooted in democratic theory, make assumptions about the extent to which issues play a role in voter decisions, and the degree to which voters have alternative sources of political information from which issue positions can be obtained. In many ways, political advertisements are similar to television newscasts. Newscasts, as has been previously noted, serve as the primary source of political information for most adults. They too are very short, image oriented, and not at all conducive to elaborate issue presentation. Indeed political advertisements provide candidates with opportunities to present those aspects of their candidacy (or the opponents) that they, rather than the gatekeepers, feel are important campaign elements. Moreover, advertisements allow candidates to keep in touch with the voter on his or her own terms.

Several recent studies on political advertising suggest that advertisements do play important roles in political campaigns and, moreover, do have potential for contributing to the issue information of voters. If this is the case, one of the most important criticisms of advertising—its demeaning of elections by shifting away from issues—becomes muted. The evidence from three studies is quite consistent: there is much issue content—however simplified—to political advertising on television.

Buss and Hofstetter (1976) focused on the formal logic of political spot advertising. In general, whereas the advertisements they considered focused on only a limited set of attributes, there was considerable emphasis on issues. Research by Atkin and Heald (1976), and Patterson and McClure (1976) focused more on the impact of ads on voters, but still noted the issue content of ads. Atkin and Heald found advertising to be quite important for their sample, especially for those without exposure to television news or newspapers. In general, knowledge of candidates and issues was correlated with exposure to political advertising, and consistent with agenda-setting notions, the highly exposed placed greater priority on those issues discussed in the ads than the less exposed.

Patterson and McClure (1976), in the most extensive research on political advertising to date, found political advertising to have important effects on voters beliefs about candidates i.e., their substantive issue positions, but *not* on candidate preferences. In other words, advertising served as an important source of political information. Ads have no power to overcome voter predispositions or views of the candidates, but ads were found to provide more information on issues than regular news programming.

If the conclusions of these studies are correct, we can say that political advertising does make a contribution to voter information. Candidates are kept in the public eye, the unknown is made known, and those without issue knowledge from other sources have a chance to gain information.

In terms of the "effects" on voters that political communication researchers are always seeking when they consider electoral politics, the conclusions are a little less certain. Information gain is of course one effect. But are votes changed? There is no evidence to suggest that they are, or that in fact, advertising is viewed differently than any other electronic political message in which principles such as selective perception and retention operate. One minute spots, which form the bulk of electronic political advertisements can only be avoided by the nonviewer or the nonlistener, so selective exposure may not operate (as it does for half hour ads, or five minute hitchhikers ads), but in general they serve a useful function in the context of current electoral politics.

CAMPAIGN REPORTING

In information loaded political environments, citizens become dependent on mass media. People use mass media for various purposes, as the sociologists of the 1940s told us, ranging from surveillance of the environment to entertainment. But the role of mass media is most heightened during election campaigns. In an era of issue voting, this dependence gains particular significance.

Several reasons can be cited for the importance of mass media during election campaigns. First, the scale of society is now too large for personal campaigning. Even with rapid means of transportation, there are simply too many places to go during the course of a campaign. Consequently, candidates rely on mass media coverage of their campaigns to bring the campaign to geographically remote or sparsely populated areas where personal appearances are of little value. Second, the size and inclusivity of the electorate have expanded as well. The ease of registration, the lowering of the voting age, enfranchisement of women and minorities throughout this century, as well as the virtual elimination of literacy requirements, all serve to include those on the periphery of politics in the electoral process. Many of those unaccustomed to participation and less involved attend only to mass media, and particularly to television news for political information. For candidates to bring their messages to the periphery requires wide campaign reporting to familiarize voters. Finally, isolation of the candidates following many assassination attempts has removed candidates from the campaign trail.

Regardless of which reason is more accurate, mass media have reshaped political campaigning. Several aspects, both positive and negative, can be cited. It can be argued that mass media have stimulated a great deal of interest in election campaigns. Describing them as horse races (Carter, 1978) and treating them as such has, if nothing else, engendered a sporting interest (so to speak) in election outcomes. More important however, is the fact that candidate visibility has been dramatically enhanced by political campaign coverage. Each day, in sections of newspapers under specially designed logos or in virtually reserved segments of air time, reports from the campaign trail are made available to audiences. Opportunities for image formation as well as issue information gathering are made available daily to even the most passive citizens.

Alternatively, of course, one can argue that mediated politics is disruptive of democratic processes. Candidates develop skills less than important for the presidency. Emphases are placed on television and media skills rather than substance. The nature of campaigning changes too, as candidates fit their schedules around news deadlines rather than vice versa.

Whether or not mediated election campaigns are dysfunctional or functional may not be the real issue. Instead, what is crucial is how the coverage of campaigns (the nature of campaign reporting) provides a framework for the election itself. Basically this occurs in one of two ways; through agenda-setting, or through gatekeeping. Mass media, it is argued, selectively report aspects of the campaign, those issues and topics raised in media accounts become salient to the voters.

It is clear that politicians feel that media accounts of events are important to the voters. Most notable perhaps was former Vice-President Spiro Agnew's charge that mass media biases were responsible for social turmoil. In response, as noted in Chapter 9, several studies of bias in the news were conducted (Frank, 1973; Hofstetter, 1976). Fortunately, these were conducted during election campaigns. These studies in particular employed methods allowing us to explore the dimensions of campaign reporting.

Since 1937 (Stene, 1937), scholars have attempted to quantify the dimensions of news coverage to compare the proportions of coverage to each candidate during the election period. Most of these studies were conducted during the 1950s and 1960s (Graber, 1971; Higbie, 1954; Klein & Maccoby, 1954; Kobre & Parks, 1953; Stempel, 1961, 1965, 1969), and concentrated on newspaper coverage, although more recent studies (Meadow, 1973a) included television news. Other research, primarily from Shaw and McCombs (1977), but also including Graber (1976a), Funkhouser (1973), and Meadow (1976b), demonstrated the issue content of television news.

Taken together, all of these studies yield several conclusions about media reporting, and hint at its relevance for voters. Campaigns are covered in some detail, but usually as campaigns. Evidence from several of these studies suggests that the campaign itself is often the most frequently described item in the news. Up to about half of all campaign news is devoted to discussions of where the candidates are going, where they have been, or other campaign hoopla. The remainder is devoted to the presentation of issues. Whatever material is presented is not found to be biased ideologically, according to several studies. Apparently attention to the candidate is divided equally—despite different levels of intensity of campaigning—in an effort to present the candidates fairly. What the voters do with this information is another question, but campaign reports are available to which voters can turn during election campaigns.

With campaigning itself less relevant to voters now than in the past, media have taken on new roles. Voters depend on media, so do candidates. But mass media do not serve only as megaphones to reach wider audiences. Candidates may issue statements along the campaign trial, but they are digested and presented by news teams which introduce news values or biases. The extent to which there is media fidelity to candidate statements depends on which reporters are assigned to the beat, rituals of objectivity and even economic constraints imposed by a stringent page limit or air time limit. Even aesthetic constraints intervene, especially in television news (Frank, 1974). For example, candidates may be shown in crowds, with different camera angles, with or without voice overs, each image presenting a different picture of the candidate.

If there was a bullet or hypodermic effects, of course, these considerations would increase in importance. Images of candidates would flow directly from mass media intact to the voter. But messages do not lead to votes. Patterson and McClure (1976) argued, for example, that news has little effect on voter beliefs. To some extent, there is infomation overload during the campaign, so voters screen and limit their attention to the news. Or, it may be that people find other sources of information in their environment, falling back on group affiliations or party identifications when they must think about the vote decision. So it is possible that there is only a limited influence of mass media. But, as issues resurface as the primary factor in voting, the information sources bringing these issues to the voter can't help but take on important new roles.

ISSUES IN DEMOCRATIC POLITICS

Lingering in the background of any inquiry into the role of mass media in electoral politics are questions that are raised for both governments and citizens alike. The basic criticisms repeatedly heard, revolve around political advertising and image campaigning. Candidates are argued to be packaged to look good, issues are said to be oversimplified for a graphic twenty second spot. The 1952 poem by Marya Mannes perhaps sums up the image problem:

> Hail to BBD and O
> It told the nation how to go
> It managed by advertisement
> To sell us a new president
>
> Eisenhower hits the spot
> Five Star General, that's a lot
>
> Feeling sluggish? Feeling Sick?
> Take a dose of Ike and Dick
>
> Philip Morris, Lucky Strike,
> Alka Seltzer, I like Ike

More broadly, people are said to be pushed away from issues toward superficial images, particularly since the growth of television. Physical appearance takes on a new importance as evidenced in the difficulties Nixon encountered with his perspiration and five o'clock shadow in the presidential debates. The days of the unattractive candidate or the boring speaker are probably numbered as candidates take elocution lessons or undergo surgery for such cosmetic reasons as repairing a drooping eyelid (Senator Henry Jackson) or having a hair transplant to combat baldness (Senator William Proxmire). More of a premium is now placed on wit, charm, and television personality than even before.

Even if this new emphasis on the physical were not enough, the nature of electronic campaigning has minimized the depth of issue discussion. Most campaign news is limited to mentioning who was where on the campaign trail; candidates become masters of the two minute news conference. In general, the criticism goes, too much power is concentrated in the hands of media people, and candidates and parties have lost control of the electoral process.

The problems these issues raise for democratic theory are significant. Voters presumably make decisions based on informed understanding of candidates and issues. At least this is the common understanding for some rational voters. The campaign process, however, requires candidates to develop skills not necessary for leadership as much as popularity. These problems are joined by several others that have risen as a result of videopolitics.

The first of these problems is the increasing use of campaign surrogates. Candidates, aware of local and national media sensitivity to politics during election campaigns, increasingly are sending surrogates in their place during campaigns. Not only does this include cabinet officers and other high ranking officials, but motion picture and television stars and other media heroes capable of attracting large audiences and media coverage. Data from the 1972 election for example (Meadow, 1973a) showed considerably more time on network news devoted to spokesmen for one presidential candidate than the candidate himself. Surrogates indeed do exhibit some competence to speak for the candidate, but the extent to which they do so varies considerably. In an effort to fill local pages and air time, such surrogates are becoming frequent.

A second problem to arise is the advantage of incumbency. Without doubt, incumbent presidents are always better known than their opponents. But in election campaigns, they are somewhat handicapped and relatively immobile because their duties prevented them from stumping during campaigns while the challenger traveled about. Nowadays, incumbency provides greater opportunity for incumbents by providing them with dual access to mass media, once as president, once as candidate, whereas the opponent has only candidate access. In 1972, for example, this served Nixon well during his relatively inactive campaign. As a campaigner, McGovern received about sixty percent of the time or column inches across several news media, compared to Nixon's forty percent. When considering how infrequently Nixon campaigned, the figure is not unreasonable. However, when his time/space as incumbent was added, he received 53 percent of the total coverage compared to 47 percent for McGovern. Similar findings reported by Repass and Chaffee (1972) underscore the media advantages of incumbency.

Beyond these shifts to the photogenic and the incumbency advantages, are the problems generated by media development of "viable" candidates (Arterton, 1978). Potential candidates with national rather than local constituencies are likely to receive early media attention, enhancing opportunities for national politicians such as leading U.S. Senators, and diminishing the prospects for local officials, such as governors or mayors. Even with more and more primary elections, voters arguably have a limited choice, because only a few candidates are considered by mass media reporters as serious contenders (as opposed to those "testing the waters" or happy for a spot on the ticket as vice-president). In particular, widely disseminated polling results have made candidates enter or withdraw from races without feedback from voters. Candidates vie as much for air time as for voters for two reasons: first, name recognition when the field is crowded; second, there are advantages of front running status in terms of fund raising or volunteer efforts. Although mass media forecasts can certainly be inaccurate (witness Carter early in 1976), the process of gaining the nomination is made more difficult.

A final problem is one gaining more and more attention as election night coverage becomes more and more sophisticated: the California poll-closing problem. Election hours thoughtout the country are roughly from 6 am to 8 pm, local time, which means that the polls on the West Coast of the United States (as well as Alaska and Hawaii), are open until 11 pm Eastern Time. Combined with the instant analysis and numerous projection techniques, voters on the West Coast can have some inkling of the size of the turnout, and even the success of the candidates.

Potentially, this situation is troublesome in democratic theory. First, voters on the West Coast are more subject to either "underdog" or "bandwagon" effects if those factors exist. Second, they have access to more information, other things being equal, than their East Coast counterparts. Thus far, evidence collected on this issue has minimized the impact of these time differences. First, it can be argued that if underdog and bandwagon effects exist, they cancel each other out. There is no evidence to date suggesting that voters feel sorry for a potential loser. Inevitably in post-election polls more people say they voted for the winner than his actual percentage would suggest, but this is always after the outcome is certain, and requires only a verbal statement rather than a behavioral commitment.

Second, only a handful of individuals, according to Tuchman and Coffin (1971), and Mendelsohn and Crespi (1970) are exposed to early returns. Most people have voted by the time they become available; if not, they vote before they attend to mass media. Thus only a few people potentially can be influenced, and they report that the information had no bearing on their decision. Of course, it is not only the "for whom" decision that is relevant, but whether to vote at all. In a close election the greatest effects can thus occur, as individuals misled about the victor may fail to vote, potentially changing the outcome.

All of the issues discussed in this chapter reflect the problems of mass mediated electoral politics. But rather than criticize their effects, perhaps we should accommodate them, for mass media coverage will surely change as new technologies become available. For the time being, we must view elections within the framework established by mass media as we look to the future.

IV
COMMUNICATION AS A POLITICAL ISSUE

11

LANGUAGE AND POLITICS

In Chapter 3, the centrality of language in political systems was underscored. The minimum requirement for participation is linguistic competence to articulate demands in the political arena. Recognizing this, leaders of inarticulate groups, as well as the leading decision-making role occupants have devoted considerable attention to the issue of language. The failure to accept, as Edelman (1977) puts it, chronic inequalities established through linguistic differences, leads many systems into divisive social conflict. As a result, language as a form of communication has been the subject of political attention.

There are several levels at which the social problems of language emerge. The first level is the attainment of linguistic competence for political participation as just described. Second, are the questions of social prestige and language. Often language has been used to differentiate social groups, to control and subordinate (Tonkin, 1979). Finally, at another level, language is reflective of limits to crosscultural communication. Domestically, linguistic differences indicate social cleavages. Internationally, linguistic homogeneity often defines the nation-state. As a result, in bi or multilingual systems, problems of national identity and loyalty grow.

Language and linguistic self-determination has been an important force in many political struggles historically as well as in contemporary society. Conflicts and cleavages often have been only temporarily submerged under certain governments, only to resurface after periods of dormancy. One particular problem— bi or multilingualism—has emerged in a host of political systems, making language policy (Mackey, 1979) itself a political issue.

Language in politics may be explored at several different levels: its general functions in the political world, the implications of the use of certain vocabulary forms and through a variety of narrow political conflicts resulting from different uses of language. These latter conflicts raise a number of policy issues discussed later in this chapter.

Language is how humans (and nonhumans) communicate. It may be verbal or nonverbal, meanings may be shared or different, but attempts to exchange information must be made through language. Too often, perhaps, we think only of talk and word play, but stated most generally, language should be viewed as a medium of exchange.

Politics interfaces with language because the context in which messages are received has great bearing on the meaning of messages. The same message passing between two international allies and two international enemies has radically different implications; a disagreement in one context is a provocation in another. Diplomats are extremely sensitive to the language of international diplomacy, so much so that journalists reporting on diplomatic niceties, such as official dispatches reaching "a frank exchange of views," automatically interpret that there were open disagreements during the discussions. In other circumstances a "frank exchange of views" might have a very different meaning.

Edward Sapir has written extensively on the importance of contexts. He asks whether concepts such as time, or space, or matter always have the same meaning because they are rooted in experience, or if our understanding of events is limited by the conceptual framework established by languages available to us. This is problematic when outside observers (i.e., those without the requisite vocabulary) try to comprehend nonverbal communications. Because we have so little facility in nonverbal language, arguably much of a conversation is missed. It also poses a particularly complex question when trying to translate across languages in which such concepts may not exist.

In Chapter 2, some of the general functions of language in politics were offered. Nimmo (1978), for example, argues that the essence of politics is talk. Political relations are expressed through various vocabularies such as those of power, influence, authority, or conflict. As with any forms of talk, there are a variety of characteristics and functions of political talk, but overall, political languages, like others, are largely symbolic with common meanings derived for all. The functions of political language parallel those offered by Robinson (1972) for general language: (1) to avoid certain activities (such as negotiate rather than fight); (2) to accept or reject social rules; (3) to promise and assure; (4) to regulate the behavior of others; (5) to mark role relationships; (6) to express social identity, and several others. Each of these functions help government decision makers as well as private individuals maintain political relationships.

The style of language used in political environments has frequently been explored by rhetoricians. But recently, political scientists, such as Graber

(1976b) and Edelman (1977), have looked at the use of different styles in varying political environments. Politicians, in fact, have been accused of using language pathologically, given the verbal distortions and fabrications accompanying political dialogue.

The functions of language—for social systems as well as individuals—are many, but for our purposes, only a handful are explored. Obviously, there is a social communication function (Le Page, 1964) through which the individual is linked to others and the broader social environment. This linkage is made possible by the common significance of the symbols employed (Robinson, 1972). Simultaneous with this social purpose is the individual function; language plays a major role in conceptualization and cognitive development, serving as a filter through which the environment is viewed. Mead (1956) and others have argued that language provides a basis for self-regulation and self-reflection, and assertion of one's identity.

In a more explicitly political setting, language has a certain relevance in the transmission or reception of information. Information is currency in the political world; in its absence political effectiveness is limited (Halperin, 1972). And as Mueller repeatedly indicates, if elites employ a linguistic code with which a community is unfamiliar, it is possible to deprive the community of political access.

LANGUAGE AND NATIONALISM

Among the other factors underlying nationalism (geography, commonality of outlook, ethnicity), Deutsch has cited common linguistic and cultural patterns. A bond of language is enduring (Pride, 1971), linking otherwise isolated individuals. As a very simple example, one need only consider the ease with which tourists strike up conversations with anonymous or unknown compatriots simply because their commonality of language provides them with an identity as well as a basis for sharing information. More political examples are found in colonists' practice of imposing language on vanquished peoples. Throughout history, it has been a consistent practice to suppress national languages of the defeated, partially to prevent unity, and partially to underscore symbolic dominance. Indeed this practice still continues with governments as diverse as Spain, the U.S.S.R., and France, each in a struggle to suppress certain minority languages. The effects of this linguistic repression are enduring. In nations of Africa and the Indian subcontinent, excolonies are occasionally engulfed in turmoil as a result of the search for new national languages to unite the people and discard the colonial linguistic yoke.

Language is a potentially divisive force for a nation if there is conflict over which language should be the official, dominant language. Nations ranging from Canada and Belgium, to India and newer nations in Africa have all experienced this problem. Even nations with a well established official language such as the United States have experienced internal conflicts over the extent to which minority languages are entitled to be acceptable in education, voting, and so forth. Only occasionally do nations escape the multilingual problem. Switzerland, for example, has managed to minimize divisive language conflict, in part because each language is accorded official status and an equal place in national government, and because external threats necessitated suppressing linguistic supremacy in favor of national unity. Decision makers, when given a chance, prefer homogeneous linguistic communities. Subcommunities governed through a language other than their own, potentially feel disenfranchised and ineffective, feelings not conducive to national unity.

LANGUAGE AND SOCIAL IDENTITY

Social identity, according to Robinson (1972) can be said to consist of three separate parts: nationality, ethnicity, and social class. In recent years, since the emergence of new nation-states and the decline of colonialism, the use of national and ethnic consciousness and an interest in ethnicity and cultural heritage has been widespread. Indeed, even popular culture has romanticized these heritage concerns with the dramatization of *Roots* and similar phenomena.

Many factors influence the feeling of ethnicity; those with similar ethnic origins tend to have similar socialization experiences and a common experiential core (Migus, 1975). Language, too, becomes an important unifying force, just as powerful in maintaining ethnic group cohesion as it is in maintaining national unity. Indeed, sustaining a living language is often seen by ethnic groups as crucial to the survival of the group as a separate entity. When the language of an ethnic group is threatened, so too is the group itself. Consequently, as Burns (1971) suggests, language provides a rallying point for issues other than language, which are joined to a group's struggle to survive.

Political authorities ordinarily hold out the possibility of assimilation to nonmajority language speakers. Three models of what occurs when the threat of assimilation appears have been offered by Migus (1975). First is the conformity model. Dominance by the majority group is maintained by pressure on the minority to conform to the majority's standards and norms. Often the conformity model is used to maintain numerical dominance of a group through policies such as selective immigration. Second, there is the melting pot approach. The combined characteristics of all ethnic groups are used as a standard and minority groups are encouraged to simply blend in by jumping into the pot. However, melting pots often do not conform to reality. Countries such as the United States and Canada, for example, have long been considered as nations of immigrants. Yet the dominant culture remains English, Anglo-Saxon, Protestant, and middle-American, with only occasional tolerance for new ethnicity (especially for foods, long the only visible element of melting pot theory).

The third model has gained most favor today. This calls for an integrated, yet multicultural society. Ethnic groups may retain certain defining characteristics while adjusting to the broader culture of which they are a part. Within this society, an ethnic group may sustain its language. Although potentially, this approach offers the most linguistic preservation, there are still considerable demands for integration and assimilation of majority language and culture, with multiculturalism reserved for "colorful ethnic festivals" or parades one day a year. Integrated multiculturalism is not likely to succeed in the absence of a single dominant group or long standing cultural heritage.

Faced with professed multiculturalism, a member of a minority language group has essentially three responding choices. One can rebel against his or her linguistic background, rejecting it and accepting majority culture in its totality. At the other extreme, one may rebel against the majority group, and identify completely with the minority group to the ethnocentric exclusion of the majority. Between the two extreme positions, one can assume a bicultural or bilingual identity, receptive to messages from both cultures. This bicultural state, however, is difficult to achieve and sustain, particularly in view of its unidimensionality: majority culture members rarely attempt to learn the minority culture, the flow is only one way.

LINGUISTIC CONFLICT

Contemporary political systems are often marked by linguistic conflict or at least bifurcation, but historically this was not always the case. Elites often spoke one language, nonelites another. For example, Tsarist Russian aristocracy spoke French, ordinary citizens spoke in their own Slavic languages. In agricultural and illiterate societies, such divisions had little significance, for groups tended to remain in isolation with little interaction. Democratization of politics, combined with industrialization, urbanization, and advances in transportation and communication changed this. Knowledge and competence in a specific language, or literacy, became vital to careers offering lucrative livelihoods and social status. In systems with a dominant language, majority language familiarity (Lieberson, 1970; Savard, 1975) became a currency in economic competition, and conflict over linguistic dominance expanded. Simultaneously, increasing popular participation in political decision-making rendered political articulation more necessary than ever.

Unlike other conflicts, linguistic conflict is not functional for the whole system. Looking back on Chapter 4, for example, we argued that lines of communications are opened. In the case of linguistic conflict they are being closed. Alternatively, the conflict itself is over the failure to keep lines of communication between groups open. Moreover, linguistic conflicts occur when there already is a high level of interaction between language groups; the integrative function of linguistic conflict is not very great. The resolution of linguistic conflicts is also somewhat different from that of other conflicts. The whole system can not be divided into units satisfactory to each group. Compromises are difficult to work out because of the totality of language and its centrality to everyday life. One group clearly is inconvenienced by any solution if forced to learn a new language or bear significant costs. As a result, resolutions are often unsatisfactory to all parties, but more often for minority language speakers on whom assimilation is imposed. Where other solutions have been attempted, political feedback from majority language users has been largely negative (i.e., Canada).

Because of the linkage between social class and language, linguistic conflicts tend to intensify with the extent of class differences. The issues at stake include economic and political access, and prestige within society. Although Basel Bernstein's (1962) analysis is not offered with regard to wholly different languages, many of his principles concerning elaborated and restricted codes do apply across languages. Simply stated, those of lower social class (i.e., users of a minority language in our case) have less access due to their linguistic code, and this code confines them to the lower class in a self perpetuating process. The outcome is always the same: the linguistic minority is relegated to lower class position economically and politically. The only solution for those ordinarily employing a minority language often is bilingualism.

BILINGUALISM AS A POLITICAL ISSUE

Bilingualism (and its associated concept of multilingualism) is a psychological as well as a political issue. Different sets of values, attitudes, and world views exist across languages, indeed certain concepts are not translatable because they require different conceptualizations of the nature of the world (Boudewyn, 1973). Moreover, as Gumperz (1970) states, different languages have different communicative norms, further complicating the issues.

Bilingualism can either be social or individual. For individuals it is the use of two languages by the same persons; for societies it is the recognition and equality of two official languages. The proximity or coexistence of two languages in the same political or geographic area frequently results in bilingualism. Individuals as well as societies experience certain communicatory limitations not faced by monolinguals: they must select among alternate codes when communicating. This code switching requires learning two verbal responses for each referent without interfering between codes. At the same time, bilingual individuals face conflicting social pressure uncountenanced by monolinguals. Multiple loyalties to each language group are straining, bilinguals (biculturals) are not always easily assimilated into either culture.

Because of this assimilation problem, bilinguals often operate with different language domains. Similarly, governments accept bilingualism on some occasions, yet prohibit it on others. A language domain (Ghosh, 1972) refers to those occasions or situations in which one language is habitually employed over another; for governments, it refers to the circumstances appropriate or acceptable for each language. In bilingual societies, the lower language is used for situations of spontaneity, intimacy, and solidarity, used with family and friends. Lower languages often survive even in monolingual, assimilation societies in which secrets are shared or codes of intimacy are needed. The high language is observed in formal situations where ritual and status are demanded, such as in the commercial or political worlds. Where high language is used for both official and intimate languages, ordinarily they are in dominant, elite communities within society. English spoken in the home of elites in former colonies, where tribal languages are ordinarily spoken, is one example of dual purpose high language. Speakers of the lower language must learn the high language for political and economic dealings, speakers of the high language have no such requirement (or incentive) for learning the low language.

Conflict is inherent in this bilingual situation. Unequal weighting of languages deprives the minority and low language speaker of equal access; dominant language users seek to defend their privileged status and language. Three solutions exist paralleling the multiculturalism options noted earlier: the minority group can evolve toward the majority language at the expense of reduced ethnic identity. Social institutions can be reformed to reduce handicaps facing the speakers of the minority language. Finally, and particularly if minority language speakers are clustered and isolated within a contained geographical region, separatist movements (negative integration or disintegration) can appear, demanding independence from the majority group.

The relationship between bilingualism and nationalism has been discussed in some detail by Kloss (1967) and Fishman (1971). For a variety of reasons, some nations have encouraged a high and low language, be it because of former colonial ties or modern necessity. Kloss has suggested that nations use "link" languages for international communication for one of three reasons. Historically, religion was a factor in intercultural communication, hence a high language of state politics, religious matters, and educational institutions evolved. More modern reasons are the remaining two factors. To gain access to political or commercial powers, certain languages have been encouraged. Finally, some nations have encouraged a high link language simply because of the multiplicity of nations already employing that tongue.

Nationalist attitudes have had several effects on the use of second languages. In former colonies, English and French have been widely adopted as second languages by all linguistic subgroups in their respective former colonies. Convenience is partially a factor. Bureaucracies already established in colonial tongues could continue to function. But intense rivalries between ethnic groups and tribes historically in opposition prevented the adaptation of one of the native languages as the official language, making colonial languages a middle ground compromise. At times, second languages have been specifically rejected because of nationalism. Kloss (1967) cites Holland and Denmark's refusal to recognize German as a second language as examples. Nationalism, similarly, has led language, as a symbol of nationhood, to be used to reject a colonial past. In Algeria, for example, all road signs in French (or even in Roman alphabet) were ordered removed in an "Arabfication" drive, despite the fact that of those literate in the country, more were literate in French than Arabic. Again, at the opposite pole, some nations have rejected multilingual tribalism in an effort to compete in the world economy. Two-tiered language systems emerge with a low language for cultural autonomy, and a high language for economic and political interaction.

Of course, not all system participants adapt a two-tiered linguistic structure. Minority language speakers form national minorities, which at times assert themselves and make demands on the system, engendering linguistic factionalism. Even among well established nations, such as Canada, Spain, France, Sweden, Belgium, and the Soviet Union, occasional difficulties have arisen among linguistic minorities. Kloss (1967) cites three ways in which nations have attempted to deal with linguistic minorities—dialectize, replacive bilingualism, and distinction.

In dialectizing, decision makers attempt to accord some status to a language, but largely as a historical relic. Languages become folk languages for retaining cultural heritages, but they are unacceptable for official purposes and are not supported by public institutions such as language instruction in school. Instead, instruction depends on at home use or private cultural organization. Languages such as Catalan in Spain and Provençal and Breton in Frence have been dialectized. In the Soviet Union, in all but a handful of the autonomous republics, local languages have been dialectized except where strong opposition (e.g., Armenia and Georgia) helped maintain local languages as official.

Replacive bilingualism occurs when the minority language is imposed on the majority language speakers in conjunction with minority learning the majority language. The goal in such situations is complete bilingualism. Also, under this category is the imposition of an external compromise language to serve as a bridge between a number of linguistic groups. Most recently, Canada has moved in the direction of replacive bilingualism, much to the dismay of western Canadians. (see d'Anglejan, 1979) Civil servants and bureaucrats were required to be bilingual or undergo training. Road signs, food labels, and so forth must be in English and French regardless of the percentage of French speakers in the province. In the western provinces, where there are almost no native French speakers such initiatives have been unwelcome. In other areas such as India, English has been accepted as the *lingua franca*, so to speak, as a common second language to all dialects.

Destruction and suppression of language has also been used to cope with linguistic factionalism, particularly when such factions move their cause into political as well as cultural affairs. In Spain, for example, Basque language and song had been outlawed because of its association with various liberation movements in Northern Spain and its system threatening use.

The key issue in the decision by government officials as to which road to take rests on the distinction between political and cultural nationalism. Movements by linguistic factions that proclaim an integral relationship between language and national identity are, as a simple hypothesis, more likely to be suppressed than those seeking cultural privileges. Of course, there is no guarantee that granting cultural rights to minority language users will avoid political confrontations at another point, but to suppress minority languages almost certainly guarantees linguistic conflict.

POLICY ISSUES IN BILINGUALISM: CANADIAN NATIONALISM

The real question for political communication researchers is how does language—as a basic means of human communication—in itself become a political issue? In other words, under what circumstances do the political system and political officials have to make decisions concerning the rights, privileges, or obligations of people with respect to language use? Two case studies provide good examples of the nature of language as a political issue: bilingualism and separatism in Canada, and the bilingual education controversy in the United States. Each is examined in some detail here.

French has been spoken in Canada for some 350 years; English for about 200. From the time of the British colonial victory, English has been the high language, French the low language, at least until 1969 when French was accorded status as an official language. Approximately one quarter to one third of Canadians are Francophones, the remainder are Anglophones, American Indian, or other foreign. The structure of government in some ways has been responsible for linguistic conflict in that the federal government's language policy of official bilingualism was not accompanied by provincial government policies similarly promoting bilingualism (Porter, 1958). Further complicating the issue is the relationship of the economic system to the linguistic order. English firms dominate the economy, indeed even major sectors of Quebec Province's economy are dominated by Anglophones (Royal Commission, 1965), so much so that the language of commerce and banking at the highest levels remains English. Thus, Rioux (1972) has argued that Francophones even in Quebec, where they number 80% of the population, must sacrifice linguistic and cultural identity for professional advancement.

Were differences between English and French cultures purely linguistic, the intensity of the conflict at the present time might be lower. However, political styles of the two groups differ greatly, further cleaving the society.

French political style is traditional and parochial, with a strong heritage of personal politics and patronage; somewhat less oriented to democratic participation than the English (Savard, 1975). Thus, conceptualizations of political issues are bound to differ, as are solutions. Indeed, the vocabulary for conflict resolution may not even exist.

All of this is compounded by long-standing patterns of discrimination against Francophones; only 14 percent of the bureaucratic elite are French speaking, in military units there are no monolingual French high officers (Lieberson, 1970), per capita income is lower for French speakers, English is a requirement for executive positions. In general, the burden of bilingual living has been placed on French rather than English speakers to the extent that Francophonic children until recently (when Bill 22 was enacted) had to attend English school even at the elementary school level (although this was not the case for Anglophones in Quebec). Mass media, of course, in search of large markets, were exclusively English outside of Quebec, although even within Quebec they were disproportionately English.

Such limitations on French spill over into other areas including personal and political identities. Lambert (1972) reports the results of English and French bilinguals responding to a series of semantic differential questions asked concerning audio tapes. The subjects were asked to rate the speakers on attractiveness, desireability, class, friendliness, leadership, and a variety of other personal characteristics, using only the sound of the voice as a guide. English bilinguals, as expected, rated the English speakers higher on most scales. However, the French bilinguals similarly gave high ratings to English speakers.

Against this background, demands for equality have been pressed in recent years, and in the latest turn of events, a push towards political independence for Quebec has been mounted. Not since 1830 had there been a rebellion against the English majority, but the "Quiet Revolution" of the 1960s, and the rise of ethnic pride in Canada as elsewhere in North America ended Francophonic passivity. Among other factors was the French-Canadian birth rate, which until the 1960s, had allowed French Canadians to keep a constant proportion of the population despite the almost universal preference of millions of immigrants to settle in English Canada or at least choose English as their language of instruction in Canada. The decline of the birth rate jeopardized the existence of the Francophonic community.

Political solutions for the long term threat to the continuity of the French community were sought at both the federal and provincial levels. The national government promulgated an act making Canada officially bilingual, allowing court proceedings in either language, government publications in both languages, and establishing preferential civil service hiring for bilinguals and language training for monolingual bureaucrats. Although the legislation itself might seem benign, the net effect on Anglophonic Canada was considerable, particularly in provinces with almost no French speakers. Bilingualism was expensive, and, what was more problematic, amounted to a preference for native French spakers for civil service positions because French Canadians were far more likely to be bilingual (as speakers of the low language) than were English Canadians.

At the provincial level, the Quebec government passed legislation requiring all new immigrants to attend French language school instead of offering a choice between English and French (most chose English). Such a law (which also happened to raise the issue of school busing in Canada) was only an outward manifestation of difficulties between Quebec and the rest of Canada since the Quiet Revolution of the 1960s. In 1967, the Parti Quebecois was founded by Rene Levesque, now head of the provincial government. The party advocated separatism and an independent Quebec, in part motivated by a linguistic unity suggested by Charles de Gaulle in his "Vive Quebec Libre" speech. Although at first the party's growth was slow, recent years have shown a shift away from support of Liberal candidates toward Parti Quebecois control of the provincial assembly.

The selection of the Parti Quebecois candidates did not in itself mean that sentiments of the Quebec residents were for secession from Canada. Indeed, in a plebescite concurrent with the elections, only 18 percent of the Quebec population voted for secession. But a changing leadership suggests policy shifts toward increasing home rule, self-determination, and autonomy—despite federal attempts to reverse this trend.

The question underlying the shifting sentiments of Quebecois is, "why?" What difference does it make to conduct commercial or political business in French rather than English, particularly if both languages are officialy acceptable for the monolingual? It is fairly clear that official status of a language is less than meaningful in social systems in which political power is derived from economic strength and social status. In other words, linguistic parity by no means assures economic, social, and political parity, or even participation. Under the present system, French Canadians not only must fear for the continuity of their ethnic identity, they must also face continuing discrimination. Independence means French used as both low and high language, moved out of the home and into the marketplace.

Still, it might be argued that success in Canadian society required knowledge of English, so to improve socially and economically, one need only acquire command of English. Role models certainly exist (e.g., ex-Prime Minister Trudeau), so another question that arises is, given a cultural homeland sure to remain predominantly French (Quebec), why should political demands be issued? Loh (1975) has offered some explanation through the linkage of linguistic and political nationalism to status inconsistency theory. In particular, French Canadian elites continuously confronted English Canadians in authoritative decision-making positions. As a result, they felt an achieved status inconsistent with their ascribed status. Separatist ideology grew among those eager to balance the two. A new political order where ascribed status (i.e.,

French origin) was irrelevant was envisioned. Alternatively, political nationalism might be said to emerge from class conflict rather than pure linguistic conflict. According to Porter (1965), French economically mobile new elites are moving as much against English elites as they are against traditional French religious-aristocratic dominance at Quebec politics. The conflict is manifest in linguistic terms against the highly visible English and enables the new elite to mobilize the masses under a cultural symbol—language—despite its class conflict origins. Alternatively, it may be that the conflict is purely ethnic, and that animosities have simply become more visible under new leadership. Regardless of individual economic or social status within the French community, all felt treated as subordinates by the English Canadians.

Loh's findings, although only suggestive, revealed several patterns, among them that political commitments to Quebec were higher than to Canada as a whole, largely because of the linguistic homogeneity. But more interesting, the most economically mobile felt more politically nationalistic about Quebec than the masses, suggesting either a desire to retain leadership within their own framework or a recognition of the barriers imposed to mobility beyond a certain limit in English society. Yet, there remain prospects for political stability in Canada, for those most committed to the federal government were bilinguals (both native English and native French). They also were committed to both cultures, and not to political nationalism. Thus if Loh's findings are accurate, bilingualism promises to be an important factor in preventing the dissolution of a political union. It is not too late for policies oriented toward French and English bilingualism to stabilize the system.

BILINGUAL EDUCATION

At the core of Canada's recent linguistic turmoil was recent legislation on the language of instruction in Quebec schools. In countries such as the U.S., however, where linguistic minorities are considerably smaller than in Canada, bilingual education still exists as a problem. The status of bilingual education in most countries, however, is quite simple: children must be taught literacy in the national language. Inasmuch as achievement and mobility in industrial societies are linked to competence in the official language, educational processes stress proficiency in the official tongue. On occasion, however, the result is a child without proficiency in native or official language. Arguably, the result is an inability to articulate economic or political demands in either language. At the same time, the ambitions and aspirations of parents to integrate their children into the cultural mainstream motivates parents to comply with government educational policies and isolate them from their cultural and ethnic origins. Again, recent ethnic pride movements combined with increasing evidence of the difficulties of monolingual education have raised the issue of bilingual education as a political concern.

Three types of bilingual education exist, each with a different objective. Transitional bilingualism advocates teaching in the minority language until adjustment to and fluency in the majority language occurs. The goal of mono-literate bilingualism is to assure fluency in the ethnic language but not literacy. Both fluency and literacy are taught in the majority language. Finally, biliterate bilingualism advocates both literacy and fluency in both languages. Of course, in addition to these bilingual education modes, is a strict monolingual education in which minority language speakers are treated no differently than majority language speakers and simply forced to learn the full range of subjects in a language with which they are unfamiliar.

The failure of the latter approach led to the development of the bilingual education modes cited above. In the United States, it was in 1968 that the Congress passed the Bilingual Education Act, providing for study in native languages. This was in marked contrast to the dominant philosophy earlier in the century when waves of immigrant children were ushered into monolingual classes. Indeed, twenty-two states even prohibited teaching in foreign languages.

The issues in bilingual education would seem straight-forward were they limited to whether children learn more quickly and completely under bilingual education or in monolingual programs. But at stake are other issues including community control of educational systems, cultural pluralism, minority rights, and ultimately, full social and political participation. It has even been argued by some minority language speakers that bilingual programs are designed to assure political dominance by existing elites by limiting the capacity of minority language speakers to become politically articulate. This latter issue becomes particularly salient when considering that most bilingual program students come from one linguistic group—Spanish—representing a significant percentage of the U.S. population (about 10%).

The central focus of the controversy is what is the goal of the bilingual education program? Attainment of competence in English? Imparting an under-standing of a wide variety of subjects in the language with which students feel most comfortable? Developing an appreciation for native culture? Although these goals are not always mutually exclusive, programs are dominated by one of the three orientations. On one level, wide instruction in a minority language is designed to overcome the cultural biases creeping into majority language texts, and to assure that children's self-esteem is not deflated by an inability to keep up in the classroom with native speakers where not only the language but the culture is entirely different. On another level, however, inequality may be perpetuated because students fail to progress in English sufficiently to join the majority culture at a later date.

As of now, the evidence is simply insufficient to support any of the positions fully. What is known, however, is that bilingual classrooms perpetuate segregation and moreover, are only unidirectionally bilingual. Only in the most unusual programs are majority language speakers required to learn minority language and culture. In addition, a conflict has emerged even within minority language communities, where some individuals with strong cultural pride seek to develop bilingual programs, and others fear their children will not be assimilated. In a sense, there is an imposition by the politically articulate within a community to dominate the inarticulate.

The arguments for bilingual versus monolingual education, and its correlates will no doubt continue until the evidence is more conclusive (Anderson, 1971; Pousada, 1979). Yet even in the absence of such knowledge, one can consider why bilingual education has been the focus of linguistic struggles between majority and minority languages. Politically, it seems highly unlikely that a push for official bilingualism would succeed. Not only is the linguistic minority too small in number to either wield influence or merit official status, but it also reflects new immigration rather than long standing cultural tradition. Unlike French speakers in Canada or Belgium, or even dialect speakers in Spain, there is no long tradition of native language use. Moreover, given melting pot mythology so pervasive in the United States, there is strong pressure to assimilate as other immigrating minorities had done in earlier generations.

Perhaps a more important reason for the focus on the classroom as the arena for bilingual conflict is the symbolic importance of education. For many parents schooling represents not just social mobility for their children. It is also an area of their lives over which they like to have maximum control. Traditionally, education took place in the home, in modern society, schools may be viewed as extensions of the home with a specialized function. Education is where much acculturation and socialization occurs. In short, it serves as a government directed intergenerational transfer of information. Thus, what kind of information is transferred becomes a salient issue. Will it be culturally biased, irrelevant for minorities, or will it have relevance to their lives and be supportive of the culture? At the same time, education, one of the most visible services of government, serves as an appropriate arena for political participation, even for the least articulate. Various structures exist, such as parents associations, in which those ordinarily not participating politically are given a chance and encouraged. In this way, people are mobilized more than usual. For aspiring articulates within a community, education is an important issue, largely because of its visibility, salience, and core of interested parties.

OTHER ASPECTS OF LANGUAGE

Earlier, we argued that language was a minimum requirement for participation. Thus, language has become a policy question in many political systems. But this only refers to literal language rather than speech codes which also are a part of language as a political issue. Developing the skills to participate, learning bureaucratic language, separating political cues and buzz words from empirical distributive politics, still is an important issue. Differences between social classes in their use of language, differences between men and women in the power style of their vocabularies serve to heighten political inequalities as much if not more than differences in literal language. Foreign language policy (Hayden, 1979) has implications for international and cross-cultural understanding. Domestically, political supremacy and dominance is obscured by carefully chosen language, so the political order remains the same beneath a veneer of change. Finally, language helps to structure all of our perceptions of politics. Vocabularies are created, as Edelman (1977) suggests, to bind our wounds, break promises, or otherwise avoid substance. Applied to minority languages or even to the demands of the politically inarticulate, there is little question why language is such an important political issue.

12

POPULAR CULTURE
AND POLITICS

In the discussion of political socialization in Chapter 7, it was noted that fiction programming on television often portrayed political leaders and relationships implicitly or explicitly. Other popular cultural media, ranging from commercial motion pictures to best selling novels, and even music, similarly provide politically relevant information. Controversies over children's television, book banning, and censorship of popular media reflect how communications become politically significant. In this chapter, linkages between popular media and political understanding and action are explored.

ELEMENTS OF THE POPULAR CULTURE

Popular culture refers to those aspects of human entertainment or activity which are not narrowly or creatively elitist and which are generally (although not exclusively) distributed through mass media. Popular culture is widely received and has mass appeal. Certainly it is pervasive in any culture, but it can be studied systematically despite the width of audiences. In many academic contexts, popular culture is studied by folklorists or anthropologists, but the political implications of popular culture make it worthy of our attention.

As a focus of inquiry, popular culture is justified in several ways. First, the political (and nonpolitical) media of elites within a society differ from those of the masses. Examining only "high" culture or elite media provides less than a complete understanding of the sources of information and opinion serving as stimuli for nonelites. In many ways, popular culture is more relevant to the

194

empirical world of mass taste than any other of the cultural forms. Second, its import is for reasons shared with virtually all other socializing agents. Popular culture is pervasive; it is an indirect form of socialization, and virtually an unlimited range of values is presented. Third, popular culture is multidimensional, including even some of the elements of elite culture, such as music and dance, but in different forms. Finally, it is multimedia, and can be found across media. Indeed, sometimes the creation of a new medium is necessary for popular taste media, such as the comic book or underground press.

The elements of the popular culture of most concern to us from the viewpoint of political socialization are varied. There are popular motion pictures, dramatic and comedic television programming, popular music and dancing, certain forms of popular art (not necessarily avant-garde, but perhaps Norman Rockwell), cartoons and comics, certain hobbyist magazines and newspapers, and books, particularly certain best sellers and mass market paperbacks.

For our purposes, some of these elements are more relevant than others, in large part because their importance differs at various stages in an individual's life cycle, and across historical periods. An important indicator of how something is popular culture is reflected in how enduring over time a form of popular culture is; the more popular (mass) its appeal, the less enduring it is across time. In any case, each popular cultural form previously mentioned is examined in a following section, with emphasis on the political messages of each.

FILM AND POLITICS

Over the eighty year history of the cinema, its use as a political tool has been manifest. On one level, the political environment has constantly provided a backdrop against which films were made. Government encouragement, censorship, or other action has left its mark on the film industry in many cultures. At the same time, the role of the film as an agent of socialization and a source of political beliefs has been widely recognized. Thus, there is an interaction of the two politics and film dimensions, for the recognition of the power of film has made political authorities view the film industry carefully.

Histories of the film are plentiful and available elsewhere. However, before focusing on one particular type of film—the commercial war film—explicitly portraying one very political institution, a brief review of the political context of film making and its role portraying sociopolitical reality is offered.

Work by Huaco (1965) and Jarvie (1970), among others, writing on the sociology of film art has made substantial linkages between the political world and the film industry. Certainly at the first stage, there must be the necessary technical capacity—directors, actors, equipment, editors, and so forth. But beyond that, there must be a social system sympathetic to (or at least permissive enough for) film making as a vehicle for social change. Huaco goes on to analyze three schools of films: Soviet Realism, German Expressionism, and Italian Realism in these terms, each time finding a relationship between external politics and the growth of the film industry. Indeed, indirectly, political turmoil in Europe was largely responsible for the growth of Hollywood as a motion picture capital and was even important in making war a focus of many commercial films.

In the Soviet Union, for example, the desire to spread the theory and principles of revolution necessitated a strong film industry. In 1919 the industry was nationalized, but unlike other industries was never returned to private hands during Lenin's New Economic Policy of the 1920s. Formerly Russia had relied on imported films or on tsarist urban-oriented cinema, but following the revolution, schools for film making of newsreels (for agitation purposes) developed. Overall, the goals for Soviet cinema were quite clear: help eliminate bourgeois culture.

Following the outbreak of World War I in Germany, the demand for morale-restoring patriotic films was high. Films from the West had been boycotted, yet demand for films was high, so new studios emerged, focused on what Hollywood had ignored: Germany. War documentaries were produced for the troops at an incredible rate, providing a training ground for film makers. In Italy, following World War II, an industry developed from the skills acquired in wartime documentary production. In particular, entertainment films were quite popular as a response to fascist censorship, which abhored realism.

Overall, the relationship between the political environment and the production of film in these three examples is quite clear. Even in the present U.S. film industry, there is a relationship between political climates and popular film in the area of pornography. Although many of the issues revolve around those of free speech (Chapter 13), to some extent the publicity surrounding the suppression of films has encouraged the proliferation of certain film subjects.

THE PORTRAYAL OF SOCIOPOLITICAL REALITY

When considering the socialization aspects of film (aside from the direct propaganda film), the actual question is, what are the consequences of the portrayal (or failure to portay), the political system? As always the consequences may be indirect, although as noted in this section, several researchers have tried to make the linkage more explicit.

In reality, there are at least four subjects of politics upon which popular motion pictures can focus. First, there are political processes in which the theme is intrigue and the drama based on politics or political processes. Examples include films (many of which are adaptations from books) such as *Advise and Consent, All the President's Men,* and *Inherit the Wind.* Second, films may focus on political actors, real or imagined, such as *Che, Patton,* or *Citizen Kane.* A third group of films includes those emphasizing political events, such as the *Potemkin,* or *Executive Action* (a film on the assasination of John F. Kennedy).

Fourth, are films dealing implicitly with politics, or in which politics forms the context for action, such as *Joe, Medium Cool, Coming Home,* or even the Wertmueller films in which the working class/bourgeois conflicts are omnipresent. Of course, in addition there are documentaries and straightforward propaganda films, which may or may not be fictionalized, and may be produced privately or through governments. Each of these film types raises questions: who is the audience; what does each type of film demand from the audience; what are the effects?

Early assumptions of the effects of movies on audiences were assumed to be the same as the more modern criticisms of television: it is detrimental to health, morals, and so on. No one argued that there were implications for politics, but the issues of health and morality became in themselves political, nearly resulting in government control until self-regulation by the movie industry increased. At the time of the original research into film, unfortunately, methodology was not very sophisticated, so little data are reliable. Recent research (Jowett, 1976) has had the benefit of more developed scientific techniques.

The first studies such as Alice Mitchell's (1929) *Children and Movies* linked juvenile delinquency to movie going, presumably because of movie content and the atmosphere at the theater. These studies inspired the Payne Fund studies, a series of twelve field studies, which fundamentally culminated in a simple formula for the effects of film: General Influence x Content x Attendence = Influence. All in all, the Payne Fund studies suggested "harmful effects" of films, particularly for children. Adults were not found to be emotionally possessed by films.

Children, however, were vulnerable. Overall, of course, the studies were quite limited in focus, concentrating on superficial relationships, and good/bad dimensions, rather than on the impact of film on beliefs or knowledge. In addition, several other dimensions of effects have been left untouched: the relationship between the desire of a film maker to see his or her work as political, and the audience response to those desires. Moreover, there is the question of the extent to which commercial films, in a patently fictional space, can have significance for the audiences.

Independent of this information, we can examine the potential of one popular genre of film—the war film—in terms of its portrayal of sociopolitical reality and its implications for political systems.

THE WAR FILM

The Hollywood war film is clearly as much a film category as romance, westerns, or crime and gangster films. War films exist at three levels of reality—documentaries purporting to depict historical events, glory/action films portraying acts of heroism, and war protest films showing the more painful sides of conflict. Traditionally, emphasis in the commercial war film has been on the glorification of the fighting soldier, but the result is that many actual dimensions of conflict resolution are ignored. Much of war, for example, is conducted on the diplomatic front rather than on battlefields. Only in the rarest case (e.g., *Tora! Tora! Tora!*) are both diplomatic and military factors treated simultaneously. Political crises are notoriously absent, suggesting either that they do not exist, or that they are less important than physical combat. Regardless of which is the case, less than full treatment is given.

Perhaps the most important aspect of the war film is the interaction between the real political and military worlds and the fictional or semifictional film world. Since 1923, over five hundred feature films produced in the U.S. have enjoyed the assistance and cooperation of the Pentagon for battle scenes, technical advice, and actual troops and equipment. Among these have been films ranging from D.W. Griffith's *America,* in which one thousand cavalry and marching band troops were borrowed; to *Wings,* in which virtually the entire American Army air force was used to recreate World War I battle scenes; to *The Longest Day, The Green Berets* and *Midway.* Many of the efforts to assist production have been criticized, for example when several sailors were injured filming *Tora! Tora! Tora!* and when troops actually needed during the Berlin crises of 1961 were busy on exercises being staged for the producers of *The Longest Day.*

Several important policy issues are raised by government assistance to film makers. In general, the justification for such aid has been the assumption of significant socialization consequences to audiences of such films. During the filming of *America*, for example, President Coolidge argued that the effects would be wholesome for the country, and, moreover, would help officers learn about the Revolutionary War. Even today, when assistance is somewhat more closely regulated, the Pentagon argues that movies help inform the public and thus serve a critical public relations function for the armed services. Recruiting too is made easier (and costs lowered) by glorification films. And, finally, the actual filming often is done during regular military maneuvers, so there is no cash cost.

The arguments for government aid are strongest before consideration of the content limitations often imposed by the need for government assistance, which raise serious questions about the role of government in helping produce private films. Indeed, because the military usually has objectives served by commercial films, when these needs are not met, assistance is denied. In other words, there is for all practical purposes, prior censorship when films do not promise to portray the military in a favorable light. The military becomes the final judge of whether or not to contribute its assistance. Several films failing to meet requirements have been denied help, other films have failed to seek assistance recognizing their unwillingness to be subject to Pentagon censorship. During the 1960s for example, *Fail Safe* was refused aid because it suggested that, in fact, the systems designed to prevent accidental war were not fool-proof. Often, there is considerable pressure to change scripts because of the risk of losing Defense Department support. Recent examples include *Cinderella Liberty*, in which changes requested were so extensive that the producer/director decided to abandon all hope for Pentagon aid despite the increased costs of about ten percent. More successful was the Pentagon in having certain objectionable parts of the book *From Here to Eternity* moderated or eliminated in the film version in return for technical assistance. All of these examples suggest the premium placed on favorable portrayal of the military, based on presumed (or desired) effects on audiences.

Not all war films are about combat, although combat does provide a legitimizing context for violence. Spy films, for example, became increasingly popular during the Cold War between 1945 and the mid-1960s. In addition, there were some successful anti-war films as early as 1930 (*All Quiet on the Western Front*), continuing through several contemporary films focusing on the Vietnam War. Several recent research efforts have documented these trends. Shain (1974) for example, cites numerous cold war movies ranging from films dealing with infiltration (*The Iron Curtain,* and *I was a Communist for the FBI*) to the merits of the material world (*Silk Stockings*), to tales of merciless barbarians (*Night People*). Isenberg (1975) looked at pacifist films, noting in particular a strong period during 1930-1938 when they were produced, even by major Hollywood studios. Nevertheless, he states that such movies were not condemning all wars, nor were those responsible for war identified. Because the plight of the soldier was emphasized more than anything else, it was easier to swallow the message.

The periods of anti-war films (a booming business again today) and Cold War/spy film suggests again that films are more reflective of the historical time periods in which they are made than that they lead public conceptualizations of events. Indeed, filmmakers seem to read the mood of the audience with respect to the production of war films. Films about war suffer from the same problems as most commercial films. They are simplified, stereotypic, and predictable, and, most important, temporary diversions—entertainment. But they are carefully reviewed by government officials seeking to promote or uphold an image for the military. As always, no explicit effects can be identified, but as long as government officials perceive effects they continue to have an active interest in actual message production of potentially patriotic films.

MUSIC AND POLITICS

As with other elements of the popular culture, the relationship between music and society is observed from several disciplinary perspectives and from numerous ideological viewpoints. In general the depiction of the political system is simplified in popular lyrical music, and the content may either be explicitly focused on social issues, or escapist. Lyrical music has been around for centuries, but our emphasis is on music of this century and its implications for political socialization (rather than the religious learning or folk acculturation of yesteryear).

Popular music serves as an appropriate subject for three basic reasons. First, it is mass based, widespread, and not elite. Although focused on mass audiences, its broadest appeal is to teenagers reaching the critical period described in Chapter 7. Second, the key to popular music is that it is frequently repeated through recording devices, offering opportunities to hear the words and listen (or memorize the lyrics) in different contexts. Third, for certain music of this century, secondary associations in which the sing-out has been used, has provided a political use for music.

The study of music and politics has its roots in ethnomusicological research in which culture, society, and music are linked. The main areas of ethnomusicology ordinarily include instrumentation, lyrics, status and role of musicians, typology and classification of music, audiences, and other dimensions, but for this section, the focus is primarily on lyrics, with emphasis on the twentieth century protest song. To be sure, earlier analysis took a broad cultural approach without looking at the purely political implications, but recently (beyond historical war chants, etc.) popular music emerged with several complicated relationships between music, the performer as hero, audiences, and explicit linkages to political countercultures. In addition to widely listened to popular music, protest music has also become significant in the U.S. during this century.

Almost of necessity, the political protest song must be viewed in a historical context. Classical elite music was largely irrelevant in the U.S. Culturally, and geographically, the pioneering spirit dominated musical developments. Arguably, the first political songs in the U.S. were Negro spirituals, protests against isolation and disrupted culture, which if not political songs, were protest songs. In more modern times, the labor movement gave rise to modern political songs. Beginning in 1904, song books of the International Workers of the World were written for a variety of targets from industry to the church, with the avowed purpose of sowing the seeds of rebellion. By 1915, there were some fifty songs in the IWW song book.

The prosperity of the 1920s minimized protest songs until the depression, when protest songs emerged anew, written as parodies of popular songs. During that period song writers such as Woody Guthrie wrote firsthand descriptions of underprivileged America, and songs in celebration of the common man. At the same time again, albeit less intentionally than in other areas, the federal government became involved in subsidizing song writers through the Federal Arts Project.

World War II halted much of the protest songwriting, although the merger of urban and rural folk songs began to mix protest and traditional music. But following the war, the range of songs began to widen to include war, free speech, and civil rights issues. Some song writing groups were investigated by the House Un-American Activities Committee and were forced underground until 1960, when the protest song again emerged in the work of Peter, Paul, and Mary, Bob Dylan, Judy Collins, Joan Baez, and the Kingston Trio. Songs, such as "We Shall Overcome," reemerged as songs to be sung in a very political environment, fostering symbolic unity, rather than simply to be heard. Still, the wide attention to such songs was limited by little radio play and virtually no television exposure, which instead went to rock and roll musicians.

In 1965, popular rock music began to turn away from teeny bop and love ballads to British style music and, later, folk-rock, in conjunction with both the expanding Vietnam War and the excursion of the Beatles into countercultural areas. Arguably, however, the popularization of folk themes of protest was linked to the decline of the politics/popular music linkage. Dancing to pacifist and integrationist music somehow made it less urgent as a social demand. Message songs and singers, although commercially successful, became stereotypes, vulnerable to symbolic ridicule by opposing political forces, reduced to long-haired objects of political animosity. Eventually the protest song moved away from explicit politics to life style freedoms and more to personal laments than those characterizing politics.

Research from the past decade has offered insights into the relationship between certain forms of popular music and political orientations. Speaking generally, Denisoff (1969) has argued that despite the explicitly political lyrics of modern folk and rock music, it manifests the characteristics of expressive, rather than instrumental politics. In other words, music often was protest for its own sake, although attention was drawn to issues raised. More empirical work by Denisoff and Levine (1971), and Fox and Williams (1974) looked specifically at the music/politics relationship.

As a simple hypothesis, Fox and Williams asked if styles of music pre-ferances were linked to political orientations. In general they found liberalism associated with a preference for rock music, but the relationship was not very strong. More significant, perhaps, was the fact that liberal students listened more to records (protest, rock), and conservatives had a preference for radio (popular hits, easy listening). Further findings dispelled the notion that modern music was preferred more by one political group than another. In Denisoff and Levine's analyses of popular protest songs, they found that only a small minority of a sample of students interpreted a particularly explicit anti-war song ("The Eve of Destruction") "correctly," and a somewhat greater number interpreted the song partially correctly. However, compared to another explicit song, repeated airplay of "The Eve of Destruction" greatly increased popular understanding. Overall, Denisoff and Levine suggest that protest music is more than simple background noise, but less than a full cry for justice.

Largely because modern protest music (on Top 40 lists) is not always heard in the appropriate context for political action, it may be that its significance has been overestimated. The absence of group cohesion, interaction, and identity among many members of a listening audience prevents much of the message from being transferred and meaningful. Essentially, effectiveness of songs requires the material to be recognized as significant, that it be understood and legible, and that there be opportunities to act after the message is received (as the early union songs provided).

The analysis of the role of music in politics is, like all dimensions of the popular culture, difficult. Underlying the analysis is an assumption that music effects the audience, without any knowledge of the significance of music to the audience.Clearly, class consciousness has been a theme of much protest music, yet there is no evidence to suggest that such a consciousness exists. Perhaps the significance of music in politics is symbolic both for citizens and officials. For citizens, there is a constant reminder of dissatisfaction, a chance to increase group identity, if not solidarity. For officials, not all subjects should be taken as complacent, although officials may take heart that there has been relatively little durability of protest songs across generations. In fact, protest music, like broad social discontent, has been episodic.

CARTOONS AND COMICS

More than one politician has echoed the sentiments of Boss Tweed of New York when referring to the political cartoons of Thomas Nast: "I don't care a straw for your newspaper articles; my constituents don't know how to read, but they can't help seeing those damned pictures." Actually, there is more to cartoons than the political cartoon, including the caricature and the comic strip, but political cartoons have long been a part of the popular culture.

Each of the three major cartoon modes has a different style and political relevance. Caricatures are simply grossly exaggerated drawings without verbal commentary, but with exaggerations rooted in the object of editorial criticism. Comic strips (and the extended version, the comic book) ordinarily present a narrative in serial format, with the characters speaking for themselves. Used at first to encourage newspaper purchases (and to some extent this is still true), the comic strip was limited to amusing situations or one-liner jokes, but eventually became politicized to the point where several newspapers moved at least one strip, Doonesbury, to the op-ed page because of its continuous, hard-hitting politics. Strips also evolved into comic books around the time of World War II when many soldiers read them. Once out of the realm of newspapers, comics became much more violent, and, incidentally, more politically relevant as they included crime stories or military affairs, and war hero stories. Comics were perceived to have such a strong influence on children that several times during the

1950s, Congressional hearings were held that ultimately led the industry to develop its own code. The thrust of comic books thereafter shifted (until the countercultural underground comic) back to comedy and love, with an occasional strip on sociopolitical affairs particularly from the realm of justice and military conflict (Leab, 1965). Indeed, many of these latter strips eventually became spinoff television series such as *Batman* and *Superman*, figures always in search of law and order.

As a socialization force, comics were presumed to be important in that they provided a mirror for the hopes, values, and concerns of society. And certainly in their new form, comix, they provide a medium for bringing socially disapproved topics to the public consciousness. But comic strips and books as well have been politically less significant than the editorial cartoon.

In the United States, it is accepted that Benjamin Franklin was the first editorial cartoonist, depicting a severed snake (in 13 parts) each labeled with the name of colony, and captioned "Join or Die." Despite this early contribution, editorial cartoons became important only with the development of the penny press and wide circulation. Following the Civil War, newspapers began to carry political cartoons regularly, in part because of new technology (engraved plates rather than woodcuts) that simplified pictorial reproduction. According to Dennis (1974), later growth occurred during the 1880s when political cartooning came of age during the muckraking era, particularly with the biting work of Thomas Nast's cartoons of Boss Tweed. Certain symbols of enduring value emerged at that time, many of which are still in use. Among these are the Democratic donkey and Uncle Sam, dressed as he is today.

At the present time there are approximately 100 cartoonists, some of whom are syndicated. Again, they develop characteristic styles and symbols. Indeed, without the presence of certain accepted symbols, cartooning is a very limited art. Herblock's five o'clock shadow on Nixon, (despite the free shave when Nixon was inaugurated), the large and prominent teeth on Jimmy Carter, all came to symbolize individual leaders, and to some extent, public perceptions of them. Political cartoonists are in the difficult position of continuously criticizing, moving from issue to issue, but they must consider many issues only superficially. Cartoons are often used outside of the editorial page context, including in news weeklies and even civics textbooks, giving them wide audiences. As elements of the popular culture, they are among the most explicitly political. But to the extent they offer only a passing chuckle rather than a deep reflection on government, political cartoons and comics offer limited political significance compared to other elements of the popular culture. Often subject to editorial decisions, if they become too offensive or take positions contrary to those espoused by the host news organization, they simply are not printed. Thus, the extent to which cartoons are important depends on the willingness of gatekeepers to cooperate.

UNDERGROUND PRESS

During the past twenty years there has been a considerable growth of underground newspapers. Unlike virtually any other medium, newspapers cost relatively little to start and print, and a skeleton staff can put together a paper, especially as wire services emerge. The underground press is virtually the only medium consistently opposed to the political status quo, but given technical constraints, low circulation, and a certain absence of professionalism, suffers from many of the same problems as the traditional press.

The theory behind underground newspapers is quite simple. As we have seen elsewhere in this volume, the political system and news gathering organizations have common interests and are mutually supportive, hence traditional news is constrained. In addition, the format of modern newspapers is not appropriate for modern news, given the interrelationship of all political, social, and economic institutions. Similarly, the hierarchy of news organizations is irrelevant for most news collection and dissemination. As a result, underground papers emerged to provide a different conception of news.

At their peak, according to Glessing (1970), there were approximately two hundred underground papers with a circulation of nearly two million. Since the peak in 1972, there has been a decline, partially related to trends in politics and various subcultures. To some extent, they have been replaced by more specialized newspapers and magazines for specialized community interests, such as women's interest, drug interest, or the gay community. The relative ease of distribution to these specialized communities is partially responsible for their growth, as it was at first for underground newspapers. Head shops, record shops, radical bookstores, political rallies were natural distribution points for underground papers, but later placed a ceiling on the extent to which the papers could expand their circulation.

At the outset many underground newspapers were successful in part because of the affluence of youth and youth culture and because of the low overhead of offset press. But more important was the failure of traditional news organizations to report news of the growing countercultural movement and anti-war news. Thus in some ways, the life of underground papers was tied to the then current political culture and the failures of traditional press. When these changed, underground papers were jeopardized. Some underground papers managed to survive, but at considerable cost in terms of their founding principles. *The Village Voice*, for example, has changed considerably since its founding in 1955, to the point where now, as part of the chain of publications, it has become quite established, oriented more to the middle-class, urban, young professional than to countercultural types. Perhaps it was the very success of the paper, in financial terms, that led to this shift. Advertising by record companies and classified ads generated substantial revenues, and soon advertising and promotion staffs were created. Recently the *Village Voice* has even taken to promoting itself through ads in the New York *Times* and elsewhere, using advertising copy describing its ability to deliver "upwardly mobile audiences" at so many dollars per thousand!

The reasons for the decline of underground newspapers do relate to the decline of underground issues and changing lifestyles of former readers, but they also reflect institutional and organizational factors concerning the papers themselves. In particular, staff were less than completely reliable, often consisting of transients and individuals more dedicated than competent. Life styles of staff members did not lend themselves perfectly to punctuality and to meeting deadlines. Similarly, buyer loyalty was rather low, from week to week the press run would vary greatly.

One interesting facet of underground newspapers was the extent to which they were modeled after more traditional news organizations. They developed two news services, the Liberated News Service, and the United Press Syndicate. These two services were sold to underground and college newspapers. The Liberated News Service was well developed, including overseas correspondents, photography service, and other materials; the United Press Syndicate provided mostly technical help with actual layout and production. Unlike traditional news services there were explicit political criteria for covering events: does it further the goals of the movement? Such criteria led to a split between underground papers more oriented toward radical politics, and those more concerned with the general counterculture.

Certainly, problems unique to the underground press contributed to their later demise. In general, there was considerable opposition to them in many communities, creating difficulties in distribution. In some communities, news dealers were harassed with obscenity charges, making them somewhat reluctant to display, if not carry, underground papers. Printing companies were not always cooperative, requiring advance payment and leaving underground papers precariously financed. In some circumstances, random publication hurt sales considerably, whereas revenues were further limited by advertisers reluctant to purchase space because they were offended by the content. And finally, many staffs were so concerned with democratic participation by the staff, that decisions often were nonoptimal from an economic perspective.

Nevertheless, there were contributions made by the underground press. Clearly it pointed out many of the weaknesses of the establishment press— largely how system-supportive the press is, and how dissent and alternative life styles are largely ignored. Underground papers directed their attention to minorities and youth, two groups with less than full access to traditional press. Underground papers served to tie the radical and countercultural communities together, providing shared information and even a radical calendar of events. Ironically, in some ways, underground papers served the same functions as suburban community presses.

The prospects for underground newspapers as an important political force now seem rather limited. Many have disappeared, others have become trendy. The issues responsible for generating underground news are no longer as immediate. There is no supportive environment for the press. And finally, perhaps cynically, there never were real prospects for an enduring underground printed press in a generation weaned on television. Perhaps in looking toward the future, one might, with the growth of new technologies and expanding cable television, see the emergence of underground television with guerrilla theater, liberation news, and so forth. Of course, this would depend on the renewed conflict of generations or life styles, and on the failure of traditional media to cover the multidimensionality of politics.

TELEVISION ENTERTAINMENT

In Chapter 7, we touched on television as an important provider of information in the socialization process. Ordinarily, we think of television news playing this role with respect to politics. However, dramatic and comedy shows have as much or more political content than news programs. For example, political leaders, past or present, are often explicitly portrayed in dramatic fare ("King," "The Adams Chronicles"), or political situations are presented ("The Missles of October," "The President's Plane is Missing," "Grandpa Goes to Washington"), which often provide the only insights adults have to political decision-making processes. Although over-simplified and stylized for dramatic appeal, they are realistic enough to provide a framework for understanding the role of personalities in political leadership, or how decisions are made. Even in comedy fare, as Robinson (1977) points out, politics has a place. The conflict between hardhat and hippy (Archie Bunker and his son-in-law on "All in the Family") or between blacks and whites ("The Jefferson's") are routinely presented behind the mask of comedy.

Besides all the identifiable political figures in entertainment programming, there are the marginally political: lawyers, police officers, sheriffs, and teachers who, although not in themselves political figures, represent government agencies, law enforcement, or authority. Frank and Meadow (1974) for example, found that important political values were represented in entertainment programming even by the marginally political in terms of the extent to which they work within the system or bend the rules to see that justice triumphs. Social and political values are not so subtly presented even by those outside of the political arena. Merelman (1968) showed that Western heroes could be typically classified as either working with the community in a collective effort to rid the West of evil, or as loners, working alone because they found the system a hindrance. Spy and crime shows had even a stronger message about the effectiveness of political systems: private eyes are often employed to work outside the legal system, suggesting the system itself is unable to do the job. The glamour and gadgetry of spy shows suggest that technology shapes or even determines outcomes—perhaps with implications for defense of C.I.A. operations. Most important, perhaps, is the message throughout, that power—be it in spy shows where people plot to rule the world (and where the enemies always have Slavic accents) or in a small western town where the gunslinger terrorizes the townspeople—is evil, and a negative value to be sought only by villains. Indeed, though power is emphasized in entertainment programming, it is not held by politicians or even bureaucrats, both of whom serve only to impede the containment of evil.

Earlier, it was noted that much of politics in television is hidden or latent, masked behind comedy. For that very reason, the potential effects or impact of dramatic programming is heightened. Political messages are transmitted when audiences least expect them, when defenses and perceptual screens are dropped. Concepts such as selective exposure (at the foundation of the limited effects model) simply do not apply to entertainment programming. Moreover, the characters bringing the masked message have the characteristics associated with successful persuasive communicators; they are valued and trusted "friends" in a manner of speaking, bringing political messages directly into the home.

CONCLUSION

Looking back on the elements of the popular culture examined in this chapter, it becomes abundantly clear that politics surrounds us in our everyday lives. Even when trying to avoid politics with escapist entertainment diversions, the hidden politics of entertainment emerges. Some media specialize in predominantly supportive portrayals, others are not supportive, and some show the full range of political beliefs. Some portrayals are explicit; some are latent, such as power relationships in drama; still others, such as cartoons, are in between. Obviously, across cultures there are as many differences in political portrayals as there are across media within a culture.

If we are going to explore popular media as a socialization (information) source, there are a number of key variables that must be explored. Does the portrayal of politics, political actors, and political relationships make a difference to individuals? Is the context important? To what extent do discontinuities within and across media, as well as between media and other sources of information, minimize the importance of media? In addition, there are questions that touch on the role of the political authorities (the government) in media portrayals by aiding the production of such content, for example.

Ultimately, the question is, how does content link to beliefs? Are popular media, in fact, escapist or informative? Even if, as yet, there are no conclusions, the answers to four questions help explain the mass culture-socialization linkage. How do individuals use media, what role do content discontinuities play, what is the relative impact of each medium and, most significantly, what are the enduring effects and linkages to political behavior and exposure to the popular culture?

13

COMMUNICATION AS A POLITICAL ISSUE: REGULATION

Throughout most of this volume we considered the political system and political behavior from the perspective of dependence on the communications environment. Certainly, the political environment and political institutions help to establish new communication channels, but the thrust of the argument heretofore demonstrates that patterns of information exchange and language use within a political system shapes political behavior. When considering activities such as regulation of communication, we are looking at the other side of the coin, the extent to which communicatory activity is shaped by the political environment. Thus, the emphasis shifts to communications as dependent and political environments as independent variables, rather than vice versa.

What this implies, of course, is a concern for the politics of communications; what kinds of political processes, decisions, and institutions shape patterns of human information interchange? Broadly, there are two ways in which governments play an active role in communications processes: governments may communicate directly with individuals or other political actors (government as communicator), or governments may prevent, encourage, prohibit, or otherwise regulate communications among private parties. This chapter considers the regulation of communication activity, whereas Chapter 14 considers the role of government as communicator. Specifically, the present chapter describes regulatory institutions, and, within the context of the United States, constitutionally imposed constraints on communication that lead to government policies in communication. Without doubt, these two issues raise a host of constitutional and legal questions well beyond the scope of this volume. But without dealing broadly with communication issues, an important aspect of political communication would be missed.

REGULATION

In the United States, one political body charged with regulating communication is the Federal Communications Commission (F.C.C.), with its jurisdiction over broadcasting and interstate telephone, telegraph, and other telecommunications operations. To some extent much of the work of the F.C.C. is simply to provide order in the technology intensive fields of communication: assuring nonoverlapping frequency allocations, establishing rates in monopolistic industries, certifying the qualifications of technical personnel, and so forth. However, inevitably the decisions made regarding so-called technical issues have significant political and policy implications. These are combined with the more explicit political overtones of international regulation of communications technologies where order and noninterference are sought. In addition to the formal, legal regulation of certain communications industries there is supervisory regulation by professional organizations and governing bodies within each industry providing standards for production, content, dissemination, and so forth. Further regulations derive from the economic limitations on each component of the communications industry, which further serve (implicitly if not explicitly) to regulate information flow. Whether we focus on legal or nonlegal constraints, the flow of information, even in the most sympathetic of political environments is controlled and regulated. Precisely because of this control or regulation, information delivery is a scarce resource; the allocation of it becomes a political activity. Moreover, increasing evidence and widespread assumptions of the importance of information in the socialization processes, social movements, and even in traditional electoral politics, has made information flow almost as political as it is technical.

Regulatory bodies such as the F.C.C. are described in detail elsewhere (Cole & Oettinger, 1978; Mosco, 1979), but the highlights of the F.C.C. as a political body underscore the degree to which communication regulation is political. Institutionally, the F.C.C. operates in a manifestly political environment. Besides Cole and Oettinger, Krasnow and Longley (1978) have explored the political institutions in considerable detail, concluding that there are six actors determining F.C.C. broadcasting policy. Interactions among the F.C.C., the broadcast industry, citizen groups, the courts, the White House and Congress ultimately shape F.C.C. regulatory policy. Many aspects of communication policy making are thus no different than any other policy making in an institutionally pluralistic setting; the interplay of competing forces and actors presumably serves the public interest.

Within the F.C.C., decisions are reached through internal politics: the staff bureaucracy withholding information from the commissioners, squabbles between commissioners, and so forth. Appointments to the F.C.C. are as political as any other: they are made by the President with ratification by the Senate. In a sense, members of the Commission serve at the pleasure of Congress (which created, and can eliminate the F.C.C.), but in all but the most serious matters, Congressional oversight has been limited.

Further description of the regulatory environment as political would belabor the obvious: regulation, particularly when the explicit goal is to further the public interest, and when the arena to further these goals is a creation of the political system, is bound to be "political." A more serious question that is raised, however, is whether the purpose of communication regulation is to regulate the flow of information (communication as the political issue), or to regulate scarcity (monopoly as the political issue). To some extent, Congress tried to make clear that availability of information to the widest possible audience, at the least cost and greatest convenience was the goal of the regulations, and moreover, that the F.C.C. was to avoid any action that could be construed as censorship. Because the limitations on the availability of information are a by-product of the struggle for monopoly regulation, arguably, one must look elsewhere for arenas wherein the control of communication is a political issue. Regulatory environments created because of technology (e.g., limited spectrum space) become politically charged as interest groups seek to preserve their monopoly, but the language in which the conflict is waged carefully avoids any hint that the conflict is over information rather than information *policy*.

To be sure, there are cases that come before the regulatory bodies that concern information or content, but more often issues of censorship and limitations on the availability of information come up before courts of law or quasi-regulatory bodies. Informal codes exist within industries, for example, that have the effect of limiting the availability of information. The rating board of the Motion Picture Association of America, for example, passes judgment on the suitability of films for family or adult viewing audiences, the results of which have considerable implications for film profitability. Scenes are cut or lines looped to acquire a different rating. Similarly, the Comic Authority seal of approval is sought by many publishers of comic books, again constraining the range of topics or vocabulary employed in the comics.

Although these regulatory authorities may ultimately alter the availability of certain (fictional) content, they may be less significant than accountants as information regulators. In the private sector, information availability to the public depends on profitability. Books are not published, films not produced, nor newspapers printed (in the long run) without the expectation of revenues in excess of the cost of producing and distributing the material. For electronic broadcasters, even the disappearance of the sponsored show in favor of the spot-advertised network of independently produced shows, has not eliminated control of programs. Perhaps more now than ever, broadcasters are sensitive to Nielsen and other audience rating services; shows failing to attract audiences that can be sold to advertisers are quickly cancelled. Only public broadcasting enjoys the luxury of a nonprofit status, although its budgets too are constrained by an ability to solicit contributions. Such economic regulation virtually assures that message content is such that the lowest common denominator principle applies to attract the widest audience.

Although profit criteria virtually assure that highly esoteric programming and books are not produced except in nonmarket contexts (university presses, state controlled broadcasting, etc.) different cost factors, as well as legal constraints, do provide for some cross-media differences. Indeed, each medium plays a different role in forming the total information environment. Considering only the two most popular visual media, film and television, vast differences emerge. Motion pictures offer considerably more latitude in their content, partially because they face no "public interest" requirement, but also because they are more voluntary, requiring more activity (as well as cash outflow) on the part of the audience, and enjoy a more limited distribution than television. For its part, television is a "family" medium with suggested guidelines for family viewing hours, and habitual audiences for dramatic programming. At the same time, regulatory requirements (absent in the cinema) impose on television news programming the airing of community controversies or candidate equal time access, among other obligations. The result, almost inevitably, is a specialized role for each medium to contribute to the total information environment. Indeed when the roles are intertwined (through such developments as Home Box Office, pay television, interactive cable systems, or even home video recorder/players) the objections raised are economic, although often couched in language suggesting that their introduction would narrow the informational environment by eliminating one of the specialized industries.

By this logic, regulation—be it governmental or industrial—is a blessing in disguise, allowing and encouraging diversity and specialization. For the political system as a whole, however, the result is a conservatism and bias toward stability. Given a strict regulatory environment, innovation within media is strongly discouraged. Economically, the costs of innovation are high, and the potential for financial loss substantial. Politically, avoiding controversial issues in all but the most compelling circumstances assures compliance with fairness arguments. In short, all parties have an interest in maintaining the status quo and in preserving the values and the system that enables their success. As long as alternatives are limited by regulations developed in an environment in which the regulatory agency is captured, profitability is assured. The delayed growth of cable television systems, for example, is only one of many examples of alternative information sources less than acceptable to entrenched interests.

As indicated at the ouset of this chapter, formal political regulation as well as constraints imposed by the marketplace are only two dimensions of communication as a political issue. The other dimension, which for the present is termed the free press issue, is closely linked to democratic theory. The issues raised under this concept extend not only to the press, but to all news media and, to some extent, non-news media and individual free speech as well. After a brief note on the international scope of the problem, the remainder of this chapter is devoted to opening this issue within the framework for analysis offered in Part I.

INTERNATIONAL REGULATION
OF COMMUNICATION

The United States, of course, is not the only country wherein the regulation of communication is a political issue. Globally, spectrum space must be allocated and divided by neighboring countries, all of which have competing needs for civil and military broadcasting. At the same time, domination of international communication services by Western countries has increasingly come under attack by developing nations seeking greater control of their own news as well as high technology information hardware. Conflicts over these and similar issues have emerged in international political bodies over the past few years, as the new international information order has taken shape.

To address the first of these issues, World Administrative Radio Conference (WARC) has again convened to allocate spectrum space in light of changing technology and new political entities arising since 1959 (Howkins, 1979). In particular, developing nations seeking telecommunications facilities to enhance literacy, national integration, and other development goals are likely to present a unified voice against the more developed systems currently controlling much of the resources (Hudson, 1979). Equally important politically, are the implications that WARC outcomes have for other international social and political negotiations (Pool, 1979). Communications policy is now regarded as so significant to new nations, that the information have-nots will employ whatever resources they have to assure the most favorable outcomes possible.

The domination of international communication services by Western nations is the second international political issue. The concepts raised in Part II, particularly power, integration, and political socialization are the concepts of concern to emerging nations. Without control of information, national integration, social contr ' and socialization are limited. So too, is national sovereignty (Nordenstreng & Schiller, 1979). The result is a heightened concern among developing nations for the new information order. Given that news coverage from wire services and network television broadcasts do not cover Third World news adequately nor discuss Third World events outside of the context of U.S. policy (Charles, Shore, & Todd, 1979; Larson, 1979), developing nations have sought to increase control over foreign generated news. When the world is viewed through foreign eyes, developmental goals are affected.

Control of news raises issues that are culturally linked. Western and, particularly, U.S. journalists are distressed by the questions of censorship, government licensing, and compeling news organizations to print official replies to stories deemed to be unfair by sovereign governments. At the same time, where the media are political tools for civic education, where unique national identities are being forged, the demands of developing nations are not without merit. To some degree, the rights of access to information and freedom to inform are the areas of agreement, but to assure these rights in societies where communications facilities and networks are foreign dominated may require seemingly radical solutions. Although it seems unlikely that the West will yield its control, the fact that the issue is raised serves as an example of the cross cultural concern for the regulation of communication as a political issue.

TOPICS IN FREE PRESS AND PRIVACY

In recent years few topics in communication as a political issue in the United States have been more in the public eye than those issues surrounding the rights and privileges of mass media concerning news gathering and dissemination, and the rights of individual citizens to privacy of their own communications. These controversies appear in a chapter on regulation in the sense that they reflect constraints on communication imposed by statute or judicial interpretations, although not by technology or requirements of the marketplace. This regulation derives almost exclusively from constitutional rights and, as often as not, conflicts over competing constitutional rights. Among the goals of the Bill of Rights is the maximization of information dissemination, yet frequently this yields to other rights when they come into conflict.

Few find it hard to disagree with recognizing limits to free speech. After all, the dangers of unrestrained free speech at times outweigh the need to have completely unconstrained verbalizing. Slander and libel laws similarly place limits on free expression because of the need to protect other individual rights. But more recent controversies appear less clear in terms of the protection of rights gained at the expense of more controlled communications, particularly those limiting the privileges of the press. Referring to the model in Chapter 3, the strategic location of mass media at the interface between citizens and the government requires a degree of independence from each, at least as much as possible, given the limitations discussed in Part III.

Specifically, the controversies to be explored in the remainder of this chapter are rights of news gatherers to protect source identity and information, the sanctity of news rooms as refuges from government inspection, the conflicts between rights of the criminally accused and the public to be informed, and the attempts of government to prohibit publication of illegally acquired government documents from time to time. Individual privacy of communication rights, particularly with respect to eavesdropping and wiretapping, and rights to information contained in certain centralized files are also briefly addressed.

The issues in a discussion of the free press are closely linked to those of democratic theory, where participation is said to depend on an informed citizenry. Not only is the press needed for the exchange of ideas, but it must serve as a "fourth estate," capable of checking and calling attention to government excesses. Often systems with tightly controlled communications are those with limited public input into government. Nevertheless, increasingly even in open systems, mass media feel they are coming under attack.

In the United States, for example, controversies over the free press have moved away from the exclusive focus on pornography and obscenity (although clearly these remain issues, particularly for entertainment media) of the 1960s to more fundamental questions, such as what aspects of "news" can be reported. News blackouts and censorship for topics of national security have long occurred, but more recently, news publishers have had to respond to attempts to "gag" them. News disseminators have argued that the ability of mass media to perform the "watchdog" function, overseeing government, is undermined as its ability to independently generate and present information is constrained. These attempts to silence media operate at various levels, from the case of individual criminal defendants seeking to assure an unprejudiced jury, to the government's efforts to prohibit publication of classified memoranda or studies.

Cases from the past decade abound, but the best example is that of the Pentagon Papers. In 1971, the federal government sought to prohibit the New York *Times* and the Washington *Post* from publishing a secret Pentagon study of American participation in the Vietnam War. The contending positions taken and the decisions reached in Court (the *Times* and the *Post,* were permitted to publish the papers after a short delay) reveal their opinions on the regulation of the press and the implications this has for the political system. The *Times*, for example, noted in a June 16, 1971 editorial:

> A fundamental responsibility of the press in a democracy is to publish information that helps the people of the United States to understand their own government, especially when those processes have been clouded over in a hazy veil of public dissimulation and even deception.

Explicitly, the *Times* suggested its role was critical at the interface between government and the public, with responsibilities and "obligations under the First Amendment" to publish. In later days the *Times* indicated that permission to publish was "a significant victory for press freedom," and that it was "a ringing victory for freedom." In a July 1 editorial, the *Times* extended its success even further "reaffirming the guarantee of the *people's right to know implicit* (my emphasis) in the First Amendment." Although the newspaper introduced a new dimension into the controversy—the right to know—the message was clear, in that the *Times* hoped for total revision of government secrecy and classification laws (see Chapter 14). Perhaps the most lofty lesson learned from the Pentagon Papers case was by the citizenry, not so much about the war as about the self perceived role of the prestige press, such as the *Times* (July 1, 1971):

> Out of the publication of this material, the American people emerge the gainers . . . They have gained an understanding of their rights under the Constitution. And they have gained in the personal effort of free men to control their government rather than vice versa.

Clearly the *Times* as watchdog was proud of its self-proclaimed role and indispensibility.

Fact or myth, this understood role was recognized by the judges involved in the case. District Judge Murray L. Gurfein, in denying a government injunction to prohibit publication, wrote:

> A cantankerous press, an obstinate press, an ubiquitous press, must be suffered by those in authority in order to preserve the even greater values of freedom of expression and the right of people to know . . . There is no greater safety valve for discontent and cynicism about the affairs of government than freedom of expression in any form.

This view of an opposition press conflicts somewhat with our discussion of the mass media as merely a filtering agent. The indispensibility of an unhindered press, however, to aggregate interests of the community and vigorously assert itself was not shared by the Supreme Court in upholding the lower court decisions:

> . . . the only effective restraint on executive policy and power in the areas of national defense and international affairs may be in an enlightened citizenry— in an informed and critical public opinion, which alone can here protect the values of democratic government. For this reason, it is perhaps here that a press that is alert, aware and free most vitally serves the purposes of the First Amendment. For without an informed and free press, there cannot be an englightened people.

Stewart's concurrence, suggests less an advocacy role than a mediating one. The primary agent making demands on government is the citizenry, not the press, which serves only as a vehicle for citizens to be informed of government activity. The end result of course, is the same—a free press is acquired—but the perceived role of the public vis-à-vis the press is different.

The Pentagon Papers case was somewhat unique in that the New York *Times* had possession of the purloined documents for some three months before publication and the materials involved were somewhat dated. The Pentagon Papers decision and other judicial decisions on the side of a relatively unhindered press involve the public's right to know the acts of a faceless government, which seeks to limit the flow of information. The question here, with due respect to

Shakespeare, is to publish or not to publish. More recent decisions by judicial bodies, however, have dealt with the question of gathering information.

Proponents of the free press argue that unhindered access to information sources is as much an element in the free press concept as is the right to print collected information. Underlying this notion is the premise that citizens must feel free to express themselves to journalists without fear that their identities will be known. In other words, journalists are arguing for a news gatherers privilege, comparable to that the law recognizes between attorney and client, priest and confessor, or husband and wife, to assure their source access.

The growth of investigative journalism has been a significant factor behind the growth of litigation over news privilege. Indeed the role of the press (written) has changed considerably with popular devotion to electronic journalism. Although hard news on a day to day basis may make good print copy, it is dated for individuals using electronic media. Consequently, more resources have been devoted to long term investigative journalism, as well as more analysis and news commentary. In addition, columnists (e.g., Jack Anderson) relying on inside tips from disgruntled government employees or reporters relying on detective techniques in the Watergate era have become outlets for the disenchanted to present their observations outside of a courtroom or a prosecutors office. Combined with a fear of government suppression of mass media engendered with the Nixon-Agnew criticisms of news gatherers, the new journalism resulted in a heightened concern for the legal implications of news gathering and source confidentiality.

Two recent cases call attention to this problem, one again involving the New York *Times*, (the "Dr. X" or the *"Farber"* case), the other the *Stanford Daily* (*Zurcher*) case concerning the files of a college newspaper. One distinction in these two cases is that in the Farber case the confidentiality of a reporter's sources was at issue; in the Stanford case, the sanctity of the newsroom from government searches was of primary importance. Both cases, however, raise the question of whether or not sources will bare themselves to reporters if their identity becomes known through reporter testimony or newsroom searches. These cases are only the most recent over the past decade in which reporter privilege has been raised.

In the Farber case, a reporter gathered material and reported it in the pages of the New York *Times*. Subsequently, the subject of the articles (Dr. X) was indicted and tried. During the trial, he sought to have Farber's notes subpoenaed, thinking the material would be useful for his defense. Despite a "shield" law in the state in which the trial was taking place, the judge required Farber to release his notes. Farber refused and was sent to jail; his employer, the *Times* faced heavy fines daily. Farber and the *Times* claimed his notes were privileged, subject to First Amendment protection.

Other cases have dealt with this concept of newsperson privilege in which reporters claimed their trade depended on free access to information. However, a 1972 decision (*Branzburg*), was firmly against a strict constitutional guarantee of an absolute privilege for news gatherers, or even a conditional privilege. Part of the problem, the Court reasoned, was the definition of who is a reporter—a journalist? a scientific investigator? a lonely pamphleteer?

Dissenting opinions offered some insights into the "regulatory" implications of such a decision. The press would be tempered because the reporter would "cease to investigate and publish information about issues of public impact." In particular, Douglas' dissent hinted at the role of the press as advocate rather than disseminator in the context of a democratic system:

> Effective self government cannot succeed unless the people are immersed in a steady, robust, unimpeded and uncensored flow of opinion and reporting ... A reporter is no better than his source of information ... If he can be summoned to testify ... his sources will dry up, and the attempted exposure, the effort to enlighten the public, will be ended ... If what the Court sanctions today becomes settled law, then the reporter's main function in American society will be to pass on the public the press releases which the various departments of government issue.

Clearly Douglas sees newsperson privilege as a necessary tool for advocacy and "watchdog" journalism.

Despite the Court's invitation to Congress to develop guidelines for a limited newsperson privilege, Congress has been unable to develop such a law. Only on a case by case basis, using ordinary judicial proceeding, can newspeople hope to have any privileges.

In the *Stanford Daily* case, decided in 1978, the Supreme Court ruled that police were allowed to search a newsroom (with a valid warrant) to search for evidence of crimes committed by others. The newspaper had a file of photographs of demonstrators it had refused to turn over to police. At the demonstration, nine policemen were injured. Although the decision noted that magistrates granting warrants were to pay careful attention to the First Amendment rights of news media, fears arose that some judges, more concerned with law enforcement than constitutional privileges, would not be so careful. Combined with the political disclosure of sources and other rulings such as the KQED ruling, in which the Supreme Court ruled that the press had no greater right of access to public facilities than private citizens, special access to information can no longer be counted on by the press.

The issue of access to public activities and events is still unsettled. Despite a recent Supreme Court ruling is the question of whether or not pretrial proceedings should be open to the public and mass media remains unsettled. Under these conditions, information prejudicing individual rights to a fair trial may be published, so again the conflict between individual rights and media rights will emerge. Courts have held individual rights to be more sacred, and although the press usually has been free to publish whatever information it gathers (with exceptions such as the *Progressive Magazine* article on atomic weapons), there have been limits placed on information to which it can gain access. Thus, because information possessed by the press cannot be restrained from publication, courts, and particularly trial judges, have sought to limit information access two ways. One is to close the courtroom to the press and public during sensitive testimony; the other is to prohibit courtroom actors such as lawyers, witnesses, jurors, or employees from speaking with the press. Increasingly, the weight of the law is for individual rights of the accused to a fair trial rather than the public's "right to know."

Another related area of individual rights that comes into conflict with the press is privacy. Although this issue is significant to the press seeking to publish information on public figures, privacy also has relevance for individuals or even businesses whose information transmission may be subject to loss of privacy. Specifically, eavesdropping, wiretapping, and other forms of electronic surveillance serve to limit the extent to which citizens can freely exchange information. On the one hand, the possibility that an information disseminator may be sued for libel limits his initiative to pursue information in some circumstances. On the other hand, patterns of litigation in recent years have suggested that information published must not only be known to be false but must be presented with intended malice, or reckless disregard for libel suits to proceed successfully. Thus, a news organization merely amplifying data has little to fear if it is reasonably prudent in reporting on a public figure's private life. (The standards, however, are different for the private lives of nonpublic figures.)

The technology of secrecy (Westin, 1971) and eavesdropping is changing so rapidly that old laws limiting wiretapping and eavesdropping are ineffectual. Electronic intelligence equipment is available to private and government users for purposes ranging from personal entertainment to business espionage and crime detection. Although unresolved, these problems are significant issues, because they relate to fundamental privacy rights as much as to national security. Telephone and similar communications companies are working on the problems, but resolution is still some distance away.

CONCLUDING NOTES

Taken together, all of the issues presented in this chapter constitute very real political and social issues. Certainly explicit forms of regulation sanctioned by law involve communication actors in political controversies. Bodies like the Federal Communications Commission or the World Administrative Radio Conference clearly are political in nature. Processes of lobbying, persuading, threatening, cajoling, and arguing, all political processes, are encouraged by these bodies.

Less obvious, however, are the other forms of regulation that control or limit the flow of information. Subsidies for publishers in the form of lower postage rates, industry standards and seals of approval that have an impact on the marketability or availability of information, similarly involve political decisions and solutions. Finally, many of the controversies that strike at the core of the role of mass media, particularly news media in democratic societies, are also political in nature. The rights of people to know versus the rights to secrecy, questions surrounding newsperson's privileges to keep sources confidential, censorship and prior restraint, the sanctity of the newsroom, all are political, because the strategic location of mass media between government and the citizenry has the effect of limiting the willingness and ability of the media to look both ways by reporting mass concerns to government and reporting the outputs of government to the citizenry. In a sense, by continuously going to court, the media have become politicized, advocating for their own interests and aligned against government. The implications of this shift are not yet apparent, but the changing of roles is emerging.

The question of government regulated communication has a close relative: government communication itself. Perhaps because mass media are no longer simple mechanisms to amplify government outputs or citizen inputs, governments have taken to disseminating information (or seeking to hide it) more aggressively. The role of government as communicator is the subject for the final example of communication as a political issue in Chapter 14.

14
THE GOVERNMENT
AS COMMUNICATOR

In the preceding chapter it was demonstrated that governments (and other institutions) may treat the transmission and exchange of information as a political issue. Through administrative regulation, judicial decisions, and other mechanisms, governments become involved in communication. However, in those instances, the government's major role is establishing a framework for private communications agents to conduct their affairs. In other words, the information environment is shaped by such actions of government; no direct action by government is involved.

There are, however, certain activities in which the government actively participates in generating, transmitting, and receiving information. Under the circumstances, the government acts as communicator, bypassing independently controlled mass media in the search for an audience. When governments produce messages directly, gatekeeping roles are minimized. European models of broadcasting, for example, have the government as a producer of messages through nationally owned channels. In the United States, commercial, private broadcasters dominate, although quasigovernment organizations, the Corporation for Public Broadcasting and the Public Broadcasting System supplement broadcasting.

Outside of broadcasting, there are other areas where the government serves to disseminate information directly. More generally, there are other areas where the flow of communication involves the government directly. Perhaps the most obvious is the production of propaganda by governments through public service announcements or through publicly financed patriotic campaigns. In addition, recent actions, ranging from expanded broadcasting of sessions of the U.S. House of Representatives through House owned and operated television equipment, to the increasing frequency of televising court cases, have expanded the potential of government as communicator. Moreover, beyond these public activities are numerous activities in which governments engage in communicatory behaviors more private in nature. Among these are government surveillance, eavesdropping, and covert intelligence collection. Equally significant are government policies surrounding the quantity of government communication including policies on secrety and document classification systems, and even topics such as executive privilege to withhold information. All of these areas reflect on the government's role as information provider, and are discussed more fully throughout this chapter.

GOVERNMENT AS ARTIST

Governments acting as communicators can follow two basic approaches. First, they may subsidize the production of messages by others. Second, they may actually produce messages. Each of these approaches has had its supporters and detractors.

The classic argument, based on free market principles, is that government ought not produce messages or subsidize them. If no one wants the messages produced, (nor is willing to pay for their production), they ought not be produced. However, even this most fundamental argument has its limits. If "the public good" is not served by private media, then government must step in. Moreover, in the event that media do not present information required to assure system support or the transmission of demands, governments often must see to it that messages are presented.

Although these contingencies must be considered, the dangers to all communication should governments produce or heavily subsidize message production, are equally real. Governments have such resources that they can politically control all media. Secondly, government produced messages are likely to be supportive of the status quo rather than critical or revolutionary. Combined with the monopoly on the aspects of the political socialization process that governments already enjoy through schools, the significance of ongoing government information in adulthood is increased.

Nevertheless, governments have a need to communicate. Perhaps only facts need be promulgated, with official announcements to keep the polity informed, in which case government information bureaus might well be justified. But fictional productions, for reasons cited earlier (see Chatper 12), are a different matter because of the propaganda implications of government messages.

To a limited degree, the federal government already engages in some message production, although usually for educational and training purposes. Explicitly political messages, however, are produced by offices such as the U.S. International Communications Agency (formerly the United States Information Agency). Although such messages are prohibited by law from dissemination within the United States, occasionally there has been litigation over this limitation (such as the film documentary about John F. Kennedy, *Years of Lightning, Days of Drums,* eventually shown in this country). Regardless of the artistic merits of such materials, the assumptions of a propagandistic motivation outweigh other merits. Much of the history of government film productions is documented by Purcell (1956), and McCann (1973).

Alternatives to government message production, of course, do exist. Subsidies can be offered, licenses granted, censorship imposed. Governments can contract for services, and other direct and indirect action can be taken, including providing or hindering new technologies. But these alternatives appear to be less controversial and threatening to the system than government message production. Perhaps only the "safest" productions of governments will be tolerated by the private sector, provided they enhance democracy. One such example is the televising of government proceedings—although some have argued that even this is the first step in total government message production.

TELEVISED PROCEEDINGS
OF GOVERNMENT ACTIVITIES

Throughout much of the history of modern human societies, decisions have been made by governments. In only a handful of circumstances, however, have the deliberations prior to final decisions been made in the public arena. Tribal councils met in sacred temples, Roman senators met behind closed doors, monarchs met with advisors in secret, and other decision makers kept out of public view. From time to time, governing bodies have met for public sessions, and, more frequently, the public has witnessed judicial proceedings or their aftermath (beheadings, hangings, pillories, etc.). Certainly, these have provided opportunities for citizens to observe their government in action, but until recently the opportunity was available to only a very limited proportion of the population. Passive governments permitted those willing to pay the costs (travel to the seat of government, take time from laboring) to observe judicial proceedings, recognizing that few were prepared to do so. At the same time, a government could hold itself out as open and accessible.

Modern technology has changed all this, in potential if not in practice. No longer must a curious citizen go to arenas of government decisions, instead the government can come to the citizen. Broadcast technology and the availability of cable systems now make it feasible to transmit the activities of government directly into the homes of citizens. However, despite this capacity for widespread access, self-imposed regulations have, until recently, severely curtailed broadcasts of government activities. Only in the past two years have governments begun to permit live televised coverage of legislative sessions and judicial proceedings without special permission.

The issue, of course, was not public access to government action. Court transcripts, though costly, could be procured and were a matter of public record. Similarly, the *Congressional Record* was available to document legislative activities completely. These records, however, in written form, fail to capture the emotion with which the words are uttered, and, moreover, they are dated by the time they are generally available. Finally, these documents fail to include the visual dimension of political activity. Nevertheless, these materials were considered to meet the public's need for access to government, supplemented by digested media reports or occasional visits to the spectator's gallery.

Recently, steps have been taken to increase public access to legislative and judicial proceedings. The U.S. House of Representatives instituted televised coverage of House proceedings in February 1979. In that same month, the American Bar Association voted to continue the ban on television and radio in courtrooms, a ban in force for forty-two years. This action was taken despite endorsement by state court chief justices of removal of the ban (Federal judges remain opposed). At the time of this writing, six states have permanent rules permitting electronic coverage; thirteen others are experimenting and considering new rules.

For trials, the issues seem clear cut: the very presence of mass media, particularly electronic media with their cumbersome equipment and lights (even in the era of the lowlight, portable mini-cam) will alter the event, creating a festive atmosphere, intimidating witnesses, jurors, defendants, and attorneys alike. Arguably, mundane trials will be ignored and emphasis given to trials of notorious criminals, with a distortion of the judicial process certain to follow. Proponents of televised trials argue that the status of the profession will be enhanced, that judicial performance, subject to little routine scrutiny today, will be upgraded with judges' behavior more visible.

In Florida, the most comprehensive experiments with cameras in the courtroom (Whisenand, 1978) were conducted and concluded. Media were allowed unlimited access to civil and criminal trials, as well as appellate arguments, subject only to restrictions on noise, lighting levels, or other disruptive behavior, and to the same rules applicable to the inclusion or exclusion of the public. Methods used to assess the value and problems associated with press presence included questionnaires administered to two thousand participants in trials during which cameras were present. Overall, according to Whisenand, nearly five hundred courtroom photographs were published in eleven newspapers during the experimental period, and one Miami TV station broadcast courtroom coverage virtually daily. Most proceedings were visited to produce footage for spot TV coverage, but two murder cases were extensively televised, and one of them was broadcast on radio. The judges in the cases reported more annoyance with the shutter noise of still cameras than with TV cameras, but argued that there was no risk of creating a theatrical appearance. However, there was some judicial concern expressed over the impact of broadcasting proceedings on the attention of jurors, the quality of testimony, administrative burdens on judges, and, to some extent, prejudicial publicity in multiple defendant trials.

Hard evidence addressing the problems is scarce, but from surveys conducted within the judiciary (Whisenand, 1978), those who have had experience with cameras in the courtroom have not been displeased, and are more supportive than those without such experiences. Similarly, the Florida State Court survey supported continuing coverage. Although these data suggest behavior is not modified by the presence of cameras, they are unable to address one significant question: whether as a matter of policy, judicial bodies should seek to expand public access.

One question, of course, is whether or not there is any prejudicial effect on jurors or witnesses. As yet there is no evidence on this question, and, outside of carefully controlled conditions, it is not likely that there can be evidence. The rights of a defendant or complainant to a fair trial (in the sense of an equivalent trial had there been no coverage) may be jeopardized. But more important are the long term consequences for the system of justice when the aura of the courtroom is changed, and when the courtroom is demystified. At the present time, familiarity with judicial proceedings is limited. Perhaps a citizen has served on a jury, perhaps not. Maybe he or she has been issued a traffic ticket or parking summons and is compelled to go to court. Under these circumstances, the citizen is intimidated by the formality and awesomeness of the judicial system.

These experiences are only enhanced by fictional exposure to legal proceedings. Courtroom dramas on television and film have helped to assure courtroom mystique—grey haired, attentive judges, well-scrubbed defendents, packed gallerys, thoughtful jurors listening to every word, ornate courtrooms all contribute to an image of a powerful, yet fair process. Fiction though it may be, this image maintains the strength of the court. Televised proceedings, where defendants do not break down and admit their guilt on the witness stand, where jurors doze off, where judges read behind the bench, and where other image breaking activities occur, ultimately may have implications for the power of the courts to assure compliance or maintain myths essential to society.

These problems are not unique to televising courtroom trials, but extend to legislative sessions as well. In 1979, the House of Representatives began broadcasting its sessions (both for benefit of the members not on the floor and for news feed for commercial television), but only after considerable debate as to the merits of such a plan. Televising is considered experimental, and does not extend to both houses of Congress at the present time.

The current broadcasting of House sessions is by no means a first. In 1947, television was permitted to broadcast the opening session of the 80th Congress. Subsequently, speeches such as the State of the Union address have been broadcast, as have special sessions and hearings such as the McCarthy hearings in the early 1950s, the Ervin Watergate hearings in 1973, and the House Judiciary impeachment hearings in 1974. However, ordinary legislative sessions have been excluded.

Outside the United States, legislative sessions are broadcast and have been for some time. Stewart's (1974) review indicated that New Zealand authorized broadcasts of selected debates as early as 1936, but since 1962 has operated a continuous broadcast service of all legislative debates. Broadcasting of Austrian legislative work is more carefully controlled. All proceedings are videotaped, and excerpts are made available for evening news programs. In Australia, since 1946, broadcasts have been made under the supervision of a Joint Committee on the Broadcasting of Parliamentary Proceedings, to assure equal coverage for both opposition and government parties. In the West German Bundestag, permission is routinely granted for the major television networks to cover important debates, provided that certain guidelines concerning camera location are met. The networks retain editorial responsibilities for legislative coverage. In the Scandanavian countries, tapes are made available for regular and special news programs, except when important debates warrant live coverage. Finally, Canada recently has instituted coverage of the House of Commons.

Beyond these national legislative broadcasts are those in the various states. Forty-nine states permit broadcast coverage of the state legislature, although in many, only ceremonial sessions may be broadcast. However, nearly half the states routinely permit reports on legislative proceedings. For the most part, public broadcasting has provided the most extended coverage. One state in particular (Florida) has been unusually aggressive in broadcasting its legislative sessions, providing half-hour or hour long reports of legislative activity, including analyses and highlights of debate.

In their research on the Florida broadcasts, LeRoy, Wotring, and Lyle (1974) raised the most important issue. Although an overwhelming majority of the viewing audience found the broadcasts informative and worthwhile and believed the broadcasts should be continued, a majority of state legislators, as well as majority of state house journalists, felt that the broadcasts caused some of the legislators to do their work differently. In other words, the effects of the broadcasts are felt in two areas: effects on audiences, and effects on political actors.

For audiences, broadcast legislative sessions yield new insights into the legislative process. Evidence from numerous content analyses (Frank, 1973) shows that the preponderance of political reporting goes to the executive branch (the presidency) at the national level, with Congress and the judiciary far behind. Undoubtedly, the nature of the executive underlies this emphasis; there is a visible leader who is generally accessible to the news, the leader is widely recognized by audiences, and plays a multiplicity of roles. But just as important is the notion that Congress is too complex. Shrouded in electronic secrecy, hidden behind parliamentary rules, with committee operations and procedures and rituals bewildering to the general public, it is not surprising that Congress is so poorly understood. Yet, with exposure to the workings of the legislature, as in the Florida case, citizens come to understand and appreciate the subtleties of legislative action, the essence of deliberation, the need for specialization and committee work, and, in general, the legislative process. Respondents in the LeRoy, Wotring, and Lyle study found broadcasts informative (85%), had increased their understanding of the legislative process (67%), and had let them know, at least a little better, what their legislature does (67%). There is no reason to believe the same results would not be found at the national level.

The cost of this increased citizen awareness is in terms of the effects of broadcasting on legislators. Two effects cited most frequently are "grandstanding" (playing to the cameras) and increasing attendance. Whereas the latter effect may be viewed as desirable in some circles, clearly it takes members away from other activities because of the need to be seen on the floor.

The long term consequences of this may be significant. As suggested in Chapter 8, much legislative activity is not visual, nor is it conducted on the floor of the legislature. Committee meetings, cloakroom encounters, closed-door meetings with lobbyists and staffers, all are part of the legislative process and cannot be replaced by floor activity. Perhaps equally significant can be the strengthening of certain roles in Congress—the party leaders, presiding officers, and so forth, in the eyes of the viewers. Overall, the factors that make legislatures suitable for broadcast coverage in parliamentary systems—lively partisan debate and discussion of fundamental policies of the ruling government—are inapplicable to the American legislators who are charged with technically drafting legislation, listening to expert testimony, or otherwise responding to executive initiative.

To some extent, the fears of those who oppose televised legislatures have already been realized. A number of legislators have mastered the art of the two-minute interview, suitable for editing into a brief policy statement. Others have had (when cameras were permitted into the hearing rooms) charts, models, and other graphics or visuals prepared to entice camera coverage. Still other legislators have taken to wandering the halls in search of television lights. And finally, events are scheduled during the day to assure that material can be incorporated in the evening newscasts.

Although this discussion of televised government may seem remote from our concern with government as communicator, the recognition of some of the potential effects on audiences and legislators has led the House to devise its own system for broadcasting House sessions. After considering a number of options, which included pool coverage by the commercial networks, intermittent coverage by interested commercial networks, owning and operating its own system; the House opted for installing and operating its own television system, staffed by employees of the House. Material would be made available to be excerpted on a daily basis, and taped highlights would be prepared by the House staff.

Under this system, the government itself serves as communicator in two ways. First, if sessions of the Congress are shown without gatekeeping journalists intervening, government officials serve directly as the sources of political messages. Only rarely does this happen. The Committee hearings noted above were unusual exceptions. For the executive, only during televised news conferences and major speeches are presidential utterances transmitted directly to voters. Even during the most recent televised presidential debates between Jimmy Carter and Gerald Ford there were limits placed on commercial networks covering the debates, including prohibiting certain camera angles and even shots of the audience. In fact, one of the reasons the House chose to hire its own staff was to maintain control of shots included in the broadcasts. Commercial networks were reluctant to have any news source (i.e., Congress) dictate the content of visuals or in any way impair its press freedoms. For its part, the House was unwilling to risk cameras zooming in for tight shots of row after row of empty desks or members reading newspapers or opening mail, rather than attentively listening to debate. Such fears, it should be noted, were expressed in Florida as well. Once television cameras were permitted, the members banned newspaper reading and lunching in the legislative chambers.

Criticisms of Congressionally controlled broadcasts have focused on two areas. First have been the implications of a House operated system for nationalized news. Under a media domino theory, the development of a capability to present government activity directly to home audiences is only a step away from blaring loudspeakers with patriotic songs and government propaganda entering our daily lives. Although the government, of course, has long had this capability, until the House system was installed, with its potential for continuous floor coverage on cable systems, if not broadcast systems, the potential was unrealized. Although not widely known, there already was considerable control of commercial broadcasters in Congress. Committee work required permission of the Chairman, even shooting film from other than specific sites on the Capital lawn required permission of the Architect of the Capitol or the Sergeant-at-Arms.

More serious, perhaps, are the implications for public perceptions of the operation of Congress, and the workings of Congress itself. Congress, as with other government institutions, is cloaked in secrecy and surrounded by myth. To see the dull, day to day activities on the floor of the House would certainly dispel the mystique, and yet it would provide little insight into the workings of Congress, indeed might misinform viewers. Because relatively little occurs on the floor, including attendance, floor coverage understates the dimensions of Congress. At the same time, in the omnipresent search for publicity, members of the House may be drawn away from Committee work toward the television cameras hoping for exposure and favorable clips for the constituents. Although too early to tell, rule changes are possible to shift the focus of legislative effort to the floor, with accompanying dislocation for staff, lobbyists, and others. Finally, televising Congressional sessions may not lead to parity with the executive, and enhanced respect for or attention to the legislature. Whatever strength Congress has as an institution may be derived from the lack of knowledge of its inner workings. As suggested earlier, the work of Congress simply does not lead to visual presentation. Other than as a matter of record, televising sessions is not likely to prove very helpful to legislators or constituents beyond resolving certain curiosities about a day on the floor of the House.

PROPAGANDA

Most widely considered when contemplating government as communicator is propaganda. Originally a term derived from religious missionary work designed to help propagate the faith, propaganda now is associated largely with government message production. These messages may be directed to domestic audiences to enhance patriotism and villify enemies, or to foreigners to convert their loyalties or demoralize them. Broader definitions of propaganda include any persuasive messages, but our concern here is only with government action. Excluded from our consideration would be commercial speech, as well as persuasive political messages emanating from nongovernmental sources.

The fundamental purposes of propaganda campaigns are two. First, there is the socialization goal of citizen (or enemy) education, and particularly adult reeducation. A second purpose is government public relations, to demonstrate that government is functioning and deserving of support.

Examples of socialization propaganda abound. In the United States, there have been a variety of government sponsored information (propaganda) campaigns ranging from projects designed to minimize smoking, or at least call attention to its effects, to patriotic appeals to purchase savings bonds. The anti-smoking campaigns notwithstanding, most campaigns have been over consensus issues such as the prevention of forest fires. In other countries, reeducation propaganda campaigns have been more complicated. The Cultural Revolution in China during the late 1960s was one such cumbersome task, the acceptability of cooperation with capitalist countries in the late 1970s requires a similar effort. All revolutions, in fact require significant reeducation projects, often at the expense of economic productivity (e.g., Cambodia).

Propaganda for international consumption is more well known, it not widespread. Radio broadcasts are routinely beamed overseas or to neighboring countries in a number of foreign languages. International propaganda is also more widely recognized as legitimate, even in countries such as the United States. Following World War II, the State Department built on the precedents of the Office of War Information, to form the United States Information Agency. This agency and its foreign counterparts had major responsibility for foreign policy propaganda or, as President Truman stated in Executive Order 9608:

> . . . it will endeavor to see to it that other people receive a full and fair picture of American life and of the aims and policies of the United States Government.

Public relations programs of government agencies must tread a thin line between information dissemination and self-aggrandizing propaganda. Government programs often require instructional materials to accompany them. Government research programs publish their reports, public information officers dispatch press releases and government publication centers distribute free pamphlets on everything from fixing home appliances to canning home grown vegetables. Although there may be few who criticize the Government Printing Office for providing pamphlets promoting health and safety, the excessive zeal of some public information offices has been widely criticized. Perhaps the most popular example was the material presented in a CBS television documentary, *The Selling of the Pentagon,* in which large expenditures to promote popular support for large defense budgets and the Vietnam War were revealed. What this suggests is that for propaganda public relations purposes, government communication must be limited to the noncontroversial and nonpartisan to assure popular receptivity.

PROPAGANDA AND LEGITIMACY

Although theories of the persuasiveness of certain communications may in themselves be interesting (see Chapter 6) the use of persuasive communications in political contexts is even more intriguing. Indeed, as mentioned at the outset of this volume, much impetus for political communication research derives from the study of propaganda. And propaganda itself is linked to problems of legitimacy and loyalties arising in mass societies. In other words, propaganda as it is known today consists of persuasive communications (i.e., influence attempts) to establish (or reestablish or disestablish) legitimacy and authority for future communications to result in outcomes desired by the propagandist.

Organizational theorists (Barnard, 1938; Simon, 1957) have long argued that organizations—be they as large as political systems or as small as nuclear families—must maintain "zones of acceptance," wherein subordinates yield to their leaders. These zones define the parameters of legitimacy (the scope) wherein followers are obedient. Thus, an essential ingredient for assuring the success of preferred outcomes is maintaining a high degree of legitimacy.

From a communications perspective, legitimacy becomes important. Defined as the belief among members of a system that it has authority (be it through power resources, terrorism, habit, custom, or consent of the governed), at the very least legitimacy determines those actions and symbols that merit responses by subordinates. Distinguished from legality (a function of sovereignty) legitimacy involves a series of expectations about the system. Moreover, a high degree of legitimacy is important to political systems because it enhances political stability, and assures that channels of communication between leaders and subordinates are kept open. Ordinarily, legitimacy generates respect, if not admiration, and assures a certain authority and orderliness in systems.

Legitimacy is usually vested in roles and hierarchies, but it can break down if alternatives arise. Hence, political systems operate partially to establish, increase, or maintain their legitimacy through active propaganda campaigns or other communication manipulation. It is often argued in democratic systems that staying in office is the most important goal of a politician. But to remain in office, politicians must maintain their legitimacy and the belief that they are best for the constituency. Thus, politicians may engage in public relations campaigns. For example, at construction sites, there are inevitably signs that civic progress is brought to you by the mayor or governor, assuring citizens that something is being done for them. Similarly, public ceremonies are often held to reassure citizens symbolically that their leaders are caring for them. Be it the annual parade on November 7 in the Soviet Union, with military might rolling down the streets, or the President visiting a nuclear reactor accident site, events and ceremonies symbolically reinforce perceptions of authority—particularly in the absence of competitors for legitimacy.

Even when competitors for a given role exist, legitimacy is not called into question if the selection process is sufficiently routinized. During presidential election campaigns, for example, candidates try to win both the electoral and popular vote to assure their legitimacy in a system where the principle of majority rule is cherished. But perhaps more important is the fact that during campaigns few candidates are considered legitimate by mass media. The two major party candidates receive essentially all media coverage, and other contenders—though legal—are not given legitimacy by having their status enhanced through mass media (Barber, 1978). Campaign rituals therefore establish contenders, but the system legitimacy is not called into question. And, after the election, legitimacy is no longer an issue, because the winner has virtually unlimited access to the media, and the loser fades away.

In general, several modes of legitimacy assurance have been developed. First, politicians may assure that desires and demands are met either symbolically or with tangible rewards. Second, they may limit the flow of information about competitors for legitimacy. Third, even when not limiting the amount of information about pretenders to legitimacy, the type of information may be constrained.

Examples of the limitations to the amount or type of information available to enhance legitimacy are plentiful. Although cost of establishing communication systems is one factor for government control of electronic media, it may be argued that many governments retain control as a tool of propaganda, and to exclude the presentation of alternatives. Censorship in conjunction with propaganda campaigns can severely restrict options.

All governments engage in propaganda campaigns of one form or another. Explicitly in the United States, official propaganda may be unrelated to system legitimacy. We see, for example, Smokey the Bear instructing us to be careful with fire, or posters telling us to drive safely. But implicit propaganda takes a different form. As noted earlier, only a limited range of alternatives are made widely known. Government leaders have virtually unlimited access to mass media through speeches and press conferences to present their points of view and, in *bona fide* news events, do so in the absence of competition. To be sure, there are commentaries and analyses accompanying many of these events, interpreting their significance. But the point is that the range of phenomena—the agenda—discussed is already determined.

Opposing messages are also excluded. There is relatively little access to alternatives to ordinary news coverage. There may be regulation in some areas (broadcast) or high start up costs, but the effect is a limited flow of information. To some extent the growth of the underground press during the 1960s recognized this limited access and tried to present alternatives. But establishing their own legitimacy was difficult, and with few exceptions (perhaps those coopted?) most failed to survive.

Other political systems have different methods. In Eastern Europe broadcasts of Radio Free Europe or the Voice of America were often jammed electronically to limit knowledge of the alternatives. Control of media is more explicit; systems maintain their strength in the absence of competition. In lesser developed countries, propaganda may be equally explicit since legitimacy of national governments (in contrast to more localized units) is in itself a major issue.

During wartime, propaganda has had different uses. In such circumstances there is an unusually strong need for the government to secure the loyalty of its citizens or, alternatively, to weaken ties with the enemy. Propaganda campaigns occur at many levels in society, including messages designed for political leaders, the military, and ordinary civilians, largely because all society is involved in modern conflicts. In such conflicts, success depends as much on productive capacity as a power resource as on military strength. And productive capacity is a function of civilian moral and productivity.

The fundamental premise in all the early propaganda campaigns was quite simple: individuals would be exposed to persuasive messages, their beliefs and attitudes would shift (and be reinforced) accordingly. In other words, early campaigns were based on a strict stimulus-response paradigm. (Indeed, these early assumptions gave rise to a number of early direct-effects models of communication that ultimately were incorporated in radio research and the first election studies.)

To be sure, the stimulus-response notion for propaganda was too limited, given the variability of the contexts in which messages were received and even differences among the human characteristics of audiences. By the time of World War II, the result was far more sophisticated propaganda campaigns. These campaigns were rooted more in the development of symbols in full recognition of the strength (and consensus) in ambiguity. Moreover, during this second major wave of propaganda campaigns some of the social psychological principles of communication began to emerge as, increasingly, the group bases and sociological/psychological underpinnings of opinions and behaviors were recognized.

Among the more interesting ruses employed during World War II campaigns were those dependent on women and music to draw large audiences. Gordon (1971), and Brown (1973) both have demonstrated how such figures as Tokyo Rose would be able to attract audiences with popular American music while intermittently suggesting that the girlfriends and wives of American soldiers were unfaithful back home. Nevertheless, little evidence has been produced to suggest that propaganda campaigns directed at enemy soldiers have been successful. Shils and Janowitz (1948) for example, have shown that the highly regimented, tightly knit military are exceptionally psychologically unreachable. However, when political propaganda is oriented toward the whole group—or cuts across group loyalties, there is potential for imapct.

THE FLOW OF GOVERNMENT INFORMATION

The need for privileged communication in government often constrains the amount of information made available to the public. At times, the needs of individual citizens (not to mention their rights) for privileged communications have often come into conflict with government needs for information. Consequently, there has been significant conflict in a number of areas including government secrecy and classification systems, intelligence collection, centralized data banks, electronic surveillance, freedom of information, legislative secrecy, and executive privilege. Although many of these issues were smoldering for some time, during the Watergate period they became widely discussed. At that time, evidence from the Pentagon Paper revelations, the My Lai incident, and Nixon's refusal to yield tapes and documents, brought forth these issues. The philosophical as well as the legal subtleties of these issues require far more discussion than can be provided here. The descriptions that follow serve only to illustrate the controversies.

Executive privilege has a long history in the U.S. and in common law (Berger, 1974), but only with Watergate did its importance become renewed. As a communication problem, the issue is clear: Congress needs information to carry out its constitutional duties, the president seeks not to present counseled information. Although the rationale behind a president's decision may vary from case to case—one time it may be to preserve the independence of the executive branch, another time to hide illegal activities—the end result is an impasse with Congress over rights to information. The justification for privilege makes sense in the abstract because it is the only way a president can assure his aides or even visiting foreign leaders of the confidentiality of their counsel. Yet more often than not, political expediency over policy differences is the underlying reason for chief executives hiding behind the cloak of executive privilege. Since 1952, in fact, the privilege has been invoked over 50 times, with justification ranging from military secrecy to privilege of counsel to pending litigation (Dorsen & Shattuck, 1975). But always the issue is the same: information is required for the exercise of government, its absence cripples the decision-making body without it.

General secrecy in government is a second issue in the flow of government information. Widely accepted is government's ability to prevent military secrets from falling into enemy hands, government secrecy and classification systems now include certain "sensitive" nonmilitary areas, including legislative hearings. Three questions generally underlie secrecy of information as a political issue: (1) who has a right or need to know; (2) what are the systemic consequences of open discussion; and (3) who controls those controlling access to classified government information?

As a political issue, secrecy became significant largely in the post World War II era as spying and Cold War conflicts heightened official paranoia. Phillips (1975) describing the history and dimensions of classification notes that despite many efforts to limit the proliferation of classified documents, more and more documents, not only of the Defense but of State and Commerce Departments, were classified. Beyond the issue of general public and mass media access to these documents, were the problems created for Congressional oversight. Transmission of classified documents is much more cumbersome and expensive than transmitting unclassified materials. Similarly, even locating such documents in the absence of indexes limits their availability. Despite repeated reforms and executive orders to limit classification, no incentives have been provided by assessing penalties to those who overclassify. Emphasis for punishment still is placed on those who leak or reveal classified documents.

Interesting examples of overzealous secrecy abound, but many from the Vietnam War years are particularly instructive, because they point out the limited rationality of secrecy. The invasion of Cambodia and the bombing of Laotian territory were originally conducted secretly; i.e., hidden from Congress and the public, but were not really secret. How could they be when Cambodian radio, freelance reporters, and wounded soldiers provided ample evidence of the invasions? In a sense, the purpose of the secrecy was not to assure the success of the planned missions, but to obscure the action from Congressional and public critics of Administration policy. These examples, and others, graphically illustrate some of the points raised in Chapter 6: location in the information environment leads to heightened power and limited criticism. Classification of action or documents serves to artificially protect such locations.

Outside the national security and defense areas, secrecy has had less historical standing in democratic contexts. Closed meetings, of course, are not the only contexts in which deals and bargains can be struck, but they do keep such agreements out of public scrutiny. Markup and conference committee sessions in particular—where bills take their final form—are often closed. Certainly such sessions may operate more efficiently, but at a cost of public visibility and accountability. In local government, where the citizen participation ethic is strongest (as is the myth of accessibility), similar problems of secrecy exist. Stein (1975) cites the proliferation of special committees and sessions to limit public input. The extraordinary growth of local (and state) governments combined with a slower recognition of citizen rights to access, has made local government fall behind federal government openness. At the local level, secrecy problems are further compounded by inadequate records and transcripts, even of official meetings. The smaller size of decision-making bodies also permits more informal gatherings rather than meetings, further discouraging access.

One reason for the problems engendered by secrecy, as well as the Freedom of Information Act, is that requests may result in the invasion of privacy of both citizens and bureaucrats. The question of privacy and its related problems (intelligence collection, electronic surveillance, centralized computer files, etc.) is yet another political issue in the flow of government communication.

Many of the issues of secrecy and openness in government have increased in intensity since the Federal Freedom of Information Act and various sunshine laws and their state equivalents were enacted. These statutes entitle citizens, or media to attend meetings of public bodies, subject to certain limitations, and gain access to certain "identifiable" documents. Immediately after the enactment of these laws, however, numerous problems arose. Deliberative bodies conducted more of their business in closed "executive sessions." Documents now open for public scrutiny were unindexed, hence unidentifiable. In other words, to access a document, one had to be aware of its existence.

With the possible exception of the discussion of the free press and regulation in Chapter 13, perhaps no laws recognize the importance of information to the citizenry as do the freedom of information laws. As a symbolic commitment to open government, this legislation is unsurpassed. It commits the decision makers to share with the control objects. But because of administrative barriers, the law remains essentially symbolic. Costs of retrieval are high, decisions must be made as to whether or not a document must be made available essentially on a case by case basis, legal appeals are cumbersome, and delays substantial. Attorneys have linked the search for documents to pretrial proceedings in terms of complexity. Overall, despite the symbolic commitment to openness, it is arguable whether or not citizen efficacy participation, and "democracy" is enhanced by the Freedom of Information Act. Indeed, frustration may increase and participation decline in response to the maze of regulations surrounding free information. Moreover, evidence suggests that Freedom of Information requests are most likely to come from the corporate sector seeking discovery and business secrets, or interest groups rather than individual citizens (Wellford, 1975).

Returning to the model in Chapter 3, filtering mechanisms enhance their power to the exclusion of individual citizens. No doubt, the motives of many bureaucrats may be more mundane (to protect themselves) then to systematically exclude citizens from information, but the net effect is that bureaus are as possessive as ever about files. Again, because there are punishments for disclosure of information acquired as a public servant, but none for refusing to release information, there is little question as to disposition of borderline requests.

Again, for national security purposes, debate over intelligence collection has been less controversial than when collection is for individual criminal activity or other purposes. Earlier limited to wiretapping, new technologies have resulted in a variety of electronic snooping and eavesdropping gear, enabling almost any private communications to be more or less publicly heard. Even the very highest public officials (i.e., Morton Halperin, Henry Kissinger) have at times been subjected to such surveillance. The availability of the technology, however, provides incentives for public officials to attempt to gather information secretly rather than openly, if there is a possibility of doing so without being caught. In particular, according to Halperin and Stone (1975), the executive branch thrives on such information gathering for purely bureaucratic reasons: information so gathered is hidden from Congressional or other oversight. With exclusive possession of data covertly gathered, the executive branch alone is in a position to claim knowledge.

Westin (1971) has considered an increasingly important dimension of government intelligence-computer systems. On the one hand, are the problems of personal liberty raised by the centralization of information and the accessibility of such information to computer system operatives. Building strict access limitations into software might minimize this problem. On the other hand is the information advantage given to decision makers compared to individual citizens. Despite Freedom of Information Act provisions, computer stored records make it very difficult for individuals to ever familiarize themselves with documents, let alone acquire them.

Without doubt, computer systems have increased certain aspects of government efficiency or enhanced its ability to deliver certain services. Managerial control over documents is broadened. And as Westin (1971) argues, computers are only tools that increase ability to process information, they do not alter the purposes for which files have been kept in precomputer days (secret files, official lying). But what they can do is make it simpler for otherwise unwieldy bureaucracies to marshall resources in defense of certain policies, or weight the pursuit of tax evaders or criminals decidedly in favor of the government rather than the individual, and so forth. With developments in the field, however, it is possible to balance this strength with new public policies benefiting individuals or groups seeking access to nonprivate files.

CONCLUSION

All of the topics discussed in this chapter are serious issues confronting public policy makers and citizens alike. Governments do communicate, people and groups do seek access. Undoubtedly these issues will be important agenda items in the future as technology changes and public expectations concerning secrecy, privacy, and openness of government change. To some extent, governments may make themselves more open symbolically, if not tangibly, in the coming years. Televised government proceedings are only a single example. But the real questions are whether these innovations will make a difference for citizens as well as policy makers, whether they will be merely window dressing, while the real decisions are made elsewhere, or whether a balance can ever be struck between the information and communication needs of governments compared with those of citizens. In many ways, the burden for citizens is clear: they must learn new languages, new skills for communicating with governments. Governments, with access to information virtually unlimited, are likely to retain the upper hand unless new policies emerge. Whatever the case, there is little doubt that communication itself will remain a political issue in the years to come.

CONCLUSIONS

The central thesis of this book is that a variety of political concepts can be understood best as communications phenomena. Looking at several of the most central concepts—conflict, integration, development, participation and socialization—as illustrative examples, I have tried to demonstrate how there can be no politics independent of communication processes. What this requires is not so much a different view of the political system, but first a recognition of the importance of the internal communication and information processes of political institutions. Secondly, it requires that we recognize the importance of communication and information exchange among the components of the system.

When viewed this way, the major political concepts take on new meaning. Power is not merely an outcome variable resulting from successful domination, but is explained more generally as a result of information exchange. Among power resources are information and strategic location within a political environment. What is offered in this volume with respect to understanding power, as political scientists use it, is a return to fundamental notions of social system control. In the model in Chapter 3, for example, power has several centers. The filtering mechanisms are one locus, narrowing demands or gatekeeping outputs. Decision systems may be another, potentially refusing to act.

In general, there are power relations to be understood internally for the components as well. Overall, we have drawn on diverse literatures and approaches to power and influence to yield a communication view of political power. First, power can exist only where there is information exchange. Second, strategic location in relationships in which an actor is in a position to control the flow of information is essential to understanding power. With these two communication based notions, political scientists and communication researchers, perhaps, can offer theories explaining empirical findings from community power, agenda-setting, and opinion leadership.

Social conflict, too, was explained from a communication perspective. Within groups, conflict is functional because it serves to bind the membership together by providing an identifiable enemy around which to communicate and about which symbols may be developed. Group cohesion is fostered. Across groups, conflict may not disrupt channels but may revive them where dormant or create them where nonexistent.

Political integration can be viewed in terms of people uniformly responding to stimuli. In developing systems, the major burden of communication institutions is to establish nationhood and reorient individual loyalties to the national level, generally mobilizing the population. Linked to political power, development requires that control of the channels of communication be centralized.

Similarly, for the two other major concepts discussed, a concern for communication variables offers new insights. Participation is linked to communication not only through presentation of candidates in mass media, but as a general mode of expression of views. Socialization is linked to communication in two ways. First as a general concept, we can consider socialization to consist largely of the transmission of information. Second, we can understand the process of socialization through our knowledge of sources of messages, receptiveness of audiences and the content of messages themselves.

Each of the institutions and issues raised in Parts III and IV of this volume are keyed to the concepts of Part II. Decision-making institutions reveal their strength as rooted in location within the system, and the extent to which they are dependent on external information. News organizations similarly derive their perceived power from access to decision makers, combined with gatekeeping policy outputs. Elections and electoral behavior provide one example of participation for which communication and information are crucial. Language use has provided an example of social conflict and the relationship of commonality of symbols to system integration and development. The popular culture provides information as part of the package available to the developing individual to incorporate into his or her view of politics during critical periods of political socialization. And finally, in our consideration of communication as a political issue, it becomes clear, that to maintain political dominance and legitimacy, information is at times controlled by public officials.

What is suggested in this volume is that political scientists may not have a full grasp of political communication. At the same time, neither do communication researchers. Both perspectives must be combined, recognizing that communication shapes political processes and institutions, and, reciprocally and dynamically, communication shapes political institutions and processes.

Political scientists deal with human interaction and political institutions, but generally in terms of institutional processes, behaviors, or outputs. The exchange of messages *per se* is less important than the social and institutional framework, which allows the communication relationship to be established and the policy output that follows from the exchange. Of course, political scientists have considered the extent to which political systems shape the communications environment, but usually as a philosophical question (e.g., the right to free speech), or in the context of public policy regulatory questions. But they rarely consider the possibility of looking at communication as the independent variable shaping the political environment. In other words, we know on the one hand that political communication is concerned with the way in which the political environment can shape the quantity and quality of communication. Communication can be said to vary with the constraints imposed by political regimes. On the other hand, political communication researchers must also consider the way in which the political world is shaped by the communication environment.

To some extent, this is already done. We look and see how electoral outcomes are shaped by mass communication. But we must move ahead toward greater theorizing about politics as a dependent variable, by considering political *concepts* to be the result of communications phenomena. To do so would not argue that all politics is communication, but would enable us to recognize that communication offers a process view of politics and that it creates, sustains, and contributes to understanding political phenomena.

BIBLIOGRAPHY

Aberbach, J. D., & Walker, J. L. The Meanings of Black Power: A Comparison of White and Black Interpretations of a Political Slogan, *American Political Science Review*, 1970, *64*, 367-388.

Adams, J. B., Mullen, J. J., & Wilson, H. M. Diffusion of a 'Minor' Foreign Affairs News Event. *Journalism Quarterly*, 1969, *46*, 545-551.

Adelson, J. & O'Neill, R. The Growth of Political Ideas in Adolescence: The Sense of Community. *Jounal of Personality and Social Psychology*, 1966, *4*, 295-306.

Aiken, M., & Mott, P. (Eds.). *The Structure of Community Power*. New York: Random House, 1971.

Alexander, H., & Margolies, J. The Making of the Debates. In G. F. Bishop, R. G. Meadow, & M. Jackson-Beeck (Eds.), *The Presidential Debates: Media, Electoral and Policy Perspectives*. New York: Praeger, 1978.

Allison, G. T. *Essence of Decision: Exploring the Cuban Missile Crisis*. Boston: Little Brown, 1971.

Almond, G. A., & Coleman, J. S. (Eds.). *The Politics of the Developing Areas*. Princeton: Princeton University Press, 1960.

Almond, G. A., & Powell, G. B. *Comparative Politics: A Developmental Approach*. Boston: Little Brown, 1966.

Almond G. A., & Verba, S. *The Civic Culture*. Princeton: Princeton University Press, 1963.

Althiede, D. *Creating Reality*. Beverly Hills: Sage, 1975.

Anderson, T. Bilingual Education: The American Experience. *Modern Language Journal*, 1971, *55*, 427-440.

Arnold, T. *The Symbols of Government*. New Haven: Yale University Press, 1935.

Arora, S., & Lasswell, H. D. *Political Communications: The Public Language of Political Elites in India and the U.S.A.* New York: Holt, Rinehart, & Winston, 1969.

Arterton, F. C. Campaign Organizations Confront the Media-Political Environment. In J. D. Barber (Ed.). *Race for the Presidency*, Englewood Cliffs, N.J.: Prentice-Hall, 1978.

Atkin, C., & Heald, G. Effects of Political Advertising. *Public Opinion Quarterly*, 1976, *40*, 216-228.

Bachrach, P., & Baratz, M. *Power and Poverty*. New York: Oxford University Press, 1970.

Barber, J. D. (Ed.). *Race for the Presidency*. Englewood Cliffs, N.J.: Prentice-Hall, 1978.

Barnard, C. I. *The Functions of the Executive.* Cambridge, Mass.: Harvard University Press, 1938.

Beck, P. A. Agents in the Political Socialization Process. In S. Renshon (Ed.). *Handbook of Political Socialization.* New York: Free Press, 1977.

Becker, L. B., McCombs, M. E., & McLeod, J. The Development of Political Cognitions. In S. H. Chaffee (Ed.). *Political Communication.* Beverly Hills: Sage, 1975.

Beebe, Marcelle (Ed.) *Literary Symbolism.* San Francisco: Wadsworth, 1960.

Benedict, R. *Patterns of Culture.* Boston: Houghton-Mifflin, 1934.

Bennet, W. L. *The Political Mind and the Political Environment.* Lexington, Mass.: D.C. Heath, 1975.

Berelson, B. R. What Missing the Newspaper Means. In P. F. Lazarsfeld, & F. N. Stanton (Eds.), *Communication Research 1948-1949.* New York: Harper, 1949.

Berelson, B. R., Lazarsfeld, P. F., & McPhee, W. N. *Voting.* Chicago: University of Chicago Press, 1954.

Berger, R. *Executive Privilege.* Cambridge, Mass.: Harvard University Press, 1974.

Bernstein, B. Social Class, Linguistic Codes and Grammatical Elements. *Language and Speech,* 1962, *5,* 221-233.

Bernstein, C., & Woodward, B. *All the President's Men.* New York: Simon & Schuster, 1974.

Best, J. J. *Public Opinion: Micro and Macro.* Homewood, Illinois: Dorsey, 1973.

Binder, L., Coleman, J. S., LaPalombara, J., Pye, L. W., & Weiner, M. (Eds.). *Crises in Political Development.* Princeton: Princeton University Press, 1966.

Bishop, G. F., Meadow, R. G., & Jackson-Beeck, M. (Eds.). *The Presidential Debates: Media, Electoral and Policy Perspectives.* New York: Praeger, 1978.

Bloomfield, L. *Language.* New York: Holt, 1933.

Blotner, J. *Modern American Political Novel.* Austin: University of Texas Press, 1967.

Blumer, H. *Symbolic Interactionism.* Englewood Cliffs, N.J.: Prentice-Hall, 1969.

Blumler, J. G., & Gurevitch, M. Towards a Comparative Framework for Political Communication Research. In S.H. Chaffee (Ed.), *Political Communication.* Beverly Hills: Sage, 1975.

Blumler, J. G., & McQuail, D. *Television in Politics.* London: University Press, 1969.

Boorstein, D. J. *The Image: A Guide to Pseudo-Events in America.* New York: Harper & Row, 1961.

Boudewyn, M. Societal Bilingualism. *Review of Applied Linguistics,* 1973, *20,* 1-9.

Boulding, K. *The Image.* Ann Arbor: University of Michigan Press, 1956.

Brody, R. A., & Tufte, E. R. Constituent Congressional Communication of Fallout Shelters: The Congressional Polls. *Journal of Communication,* 1964, *14,* 34-49.

Brown, J. A. *Techniques of Persuasion.* Baltimore: Penguin Books, 1963.

Burke, K. *A Grammar of Motives.* New York: Prentice-Hall, 1945.

Burns, R. *One Country of Two.* Montreal: McGill-Queens University, 1971.

Buss, T. F., & Hofstetter, R. C. An Analysis of the Logic of Televised Campaign Advertisements: The 1972 Presidential Campaign. *Communication Research,* 1976, *3,* 367-392.

Butler, D., & Stokes, D. *Political Change in Britain.* New York: St. Martins, 1969.

Butler, I. *The War Film.* Cranbury, N.J.: A. S. Barners, 1974.

Byrne, G. C. Mass Media and Political Socialization of Children and Pre-Adults. *Journalism Quarterly,* 1969, *46,* 140-141.

Campbell, A., Converse, P. E., Miller, W., & Stokes, D. *The American Voter.* New York: Wiley, 1960.

Campbell, A., Gurin, G., & Miller, W. E. *The Voter Decides.* Evanston, Illinois: Row Peterson, 1954.

Carter, R. F. A Very Peculiar Horse Race. In G. F. Bishop, R. G. Meadow, & M. Jackson-Beeck (Eds.), *The Presidential Debates: Media, Electoral and Policy Perspectives.* New York: Praeger, 1978.

Cartwright, D. Influence, Leadership and Control. In J. G. March (Ed.), *Handbook of Organizations.* Chicago: Rand McNally, 1965.

Cassirer, E. *An Essay on Man: An Introduction to a Philosophy of Human Culture.* New Haven: Yale University Press, 1944.

Chaffee, S. H. (Ed.). *Political Communication*. Beverly Hills: Sage, 1975.

Chaffee, S. H., Jackson-Beeck, M., Durall, J., & Wilson, D. Mass Communication in Political Socialization. In S. A. Renshon (Ed.), *Handbook of Political Socialization*. New York: Free Press, 1977.

Chaffee, S. H., Ward, L. S., & Tipton, L. P. Mass Communications and Political Socialization. *Journalism Quarterly*, 1970, *47*, 647-666.

Charles, J., Shore, L., & Todd, R. The New York *Times* Coverage of Equatorial and Lower Africa. *Journal of Communication*, 1979, *29*, 148-155.

Clark, T., (Ed.), *Community Structure and Decision Making*. San Francisco: Chandler, 1968.

Cobb, R. W., & Elder, C. D. *Participation in American Politics: The Dynamics of Agenda-Building*. Boston: Allyn & Bacon, 1972.

Cohen, B. *The Press and Foreign Policy*. Princeton: Princeton University Press, 1963.

Cole, B., & Oettinger, M. *Reluctant Regulators: The FCC and the Broadcast Audience*. Reading, Mass.: Addison-Wesley, 1978.

Coleman, J. S. *Community Conflict*. New York: Free Press, 1957.

Coleman, J. S. *The Adolescent Society*. New York: Free Press, 1961.

Coleman, J. S. (Ed.). *Education and Political Development*. Princeton: Princeton University Press, 1965.

Colin-Ure, S. *The Political Impact of Mass Media*. Beverly Hills: Sage, 1974.

Collins, B. E., & Guetzkow, H. *A Social Psychology of Group Process for Decision-Making*. New York: Wiley, 1964.

Converse, P. E. Information Flow and the Stability of Partisan Attitudes. *Public Opinion Quarterly*, 1962, *26*, 578-599.

Conway, M. M., Stevens, A. J., & Smith, R. G. The Relation Between Media and Children's Civic Awareness. *Journalism Quarterly*, 1975, *52*, 531-538.

Cooley, C. H. *Human Nature and the Social Order*. Boston: Scribner, 1902.

Coser, L. *The Functions of Social Conflict*. New York: Free Press, 1956.

Coser, L. *Continuities in the Study of Social Conflict*. New York: Free Press, 1967.

Crouse, T. *The Boys on the Bus*. New York: Random House, 1973.

Cutler, N. E. Toward a Political Generations Conception of Political Socialization. In D. C. Schwartz, & S. K. Schwartz (Eds.), *New Directions in Political Socialization Research*. New York: Free Press, 1975.

Cutler, N. E. Political Socialization Research as Generational Analysis: The Cohort Approach versus the Lineage Approach. In S. A. Renshon (Ed.), *Handbook of Political Socialization*. New York: Free Press, 1977.

Cutler, N. E., Tedesco, A. S., & Frank, R. S. *The Differential Encoding of Political Images: A Content Analysis of Television News*. Philadelphia: Foreign Policy Research Institute, 1972.

Dahl, R. A. *Who Governs?* New Haven: Yale University Press, 1961.

Dahl, R. A. *Modern Political Analysis*. (2nd ed.). Englewood Cliffs, N.J.: Prentice-Hall, 1970.

d'Anglejean, A. French in Quebec. *Journal of Communication*, 1979, *29*, 54-63.

Das Gupta, J. Official Language: Problems and Policies in South Asia. In T. A. Sebeok (Ed.), *Current Trends in Linguistics*. The Hague: Mouton, 1969.

Das Gupta, J. *Language Conflict and National Development: Group Politics and National Language Policy in India*. Berkeley: University of California Press, 1970.

Das Gupta, J., & Gumperz, J. J. Language Communication and Control in North India. In J. A. Fishman, C. A. Ferguson, & J. Das Gupta (Eds.), *Language Problems of Developing Nations*. New York: Wiley, 1968.

Davies, J. C. The Family's Role in Political Socialization. *The Annals*, 1965, *361*, 10-19.

Davies, J. C. (Ed.). *When Men Revolt and Why*. New York: Free Press, 1971.

Davies, J. C. Political Socialization: From Womb to Childhood. In S. A. Renshon (Ed.), *Handbook of Political Socialization*. New York: Free Press, 1977.

Davison, W. P. *Mass Communication and Conflict Resolution*. New York: Praeger, 1974.

Dawson, R., Prewitt, K., & Dawson, K. *Political Socialization* (2nd ed.). Boston: Little Brown, 1977.

Dennis, E. E. The Regeneration of Political Cartooning. *Journalism Quarterly*, 1974, *51*, 664-669.

Dennis, J. Major Problems of Political Socialization Research. *Midwest Journal of Political Science,* 1968, *12,* 85-114.

Denisoff, R. S. Folk Rock: Folk Music, Protest, or Commercialism? *Journal of Popular Culture,* 1969, *3,* 214-230.

Denisoff, R. S. Protest Songs: Those on the Top Forty and Those of the Streets. *American Quarterly,* 1970, *22,* 807-823.

Denisoff, R. S., & Levine, M. H. The Popular Protest Song: The Case of the Eve of Destruction. *Public Opinion Quarterly,* 1971, *35,* 119-124.

Denisoff, R. S., & Peterson, R. A. *The Sounds of Social Change.* Chicago: Rand McNally, 1972.

Deutsch, K. W. *Nationalism and Social Communication.* Cambridge: M. I. T. Press, 1953.

Deutsch, K. W. *The Nerves of Government.* New York: Free Press, 1963.

Deutsch, K. W., & Singer, J. D. Multipolar Power Systems and International Stability. *World Politics,* 1964, *16,* 390-406.

Dewey, J., & Bentley, A. F. *Knowing and the Known.* Boston: Beacon, 1949.

DeVries, W., & Torrance, V. L. *The Ticket-Splitter.* Grand Rapids, Michigan: Eerdmans Publishing Co., 1972.

Dexter, L. A. What Do Congressmen Hear: The Mail. *Public Opinion Quarterly,* 1956, *20,* 16-27.

Domhoff, G. W. *Who Rules America?* Englewood Cliffs, N.J.: Prentice-Hall, 1967.

Dominick, J. R. Television and Political Socialization. *Educational Broadcasting Review,* 1972, *6,* 48-56.

Dominick, J. R. Children's Viewing of Crime Shows and Attitudes on Law Enforcement. *Journalism Quarterly,* 1974, *51,* 5-12.

Donohue, G. A., Tichenor, P. J., & Olien, C. N. Mass Media and the Knowledge Gap: A Hypothesis Reconsidered. *Communication Research,* 1975, *2,* 3-23.

Dorsen, N., & Shattuck, J. Executive Privilege: The President Won't Tell. In N. Dorsen, & S. Gillers (Eds.), *None of Your Business: Government Secrecy in America.* New York: Penguin Books, 1975.

Ducat, S. B. Power Blackouts as Critical Events: The New York Case, Unpublished paper, Annenberg School of Communications, University of Pennsylvania, 1978.

Duncan, H. D. *Language and Literature in Society.* Chicago: University of Chicago Press, 1953.

Duncan, H. D. *Communication and the Social Order.* New York: Oxford University Press, 1962.

Duncan, H. D. *Symbols in Society.* New York: Oxford University Press, 1968.

Easton, D. *A Framework for Political Analysis.* Englewood Cliffs, N.J.: Prentice-Hall, 1964.

Easton, D. *A Systems Analysis of Political Life.* New York: John Wiley, 1965.

Easton, D., & Dennis, J. *Children in the Political System.* New York: McGraw Hill, 1969.

Eckhardt, W. War Propaganda, Welfare Values and Political Ideologies. *Journal of Conflict Resolution,* 1965, *9,* 345-358.

Eckhardt, W., & White, R. K. A Test of the Mirror Image Hypothesis: Kennedy and Kruschev. *Journal of Conflict Resolution,* 1967, *11,* 325-332.

Edelman, M. *Symbolic Uses of Politics.* Urbana: University of Illinois Press, 1964.

Edelman, M. *Politics as Symbolic Action.* Chicago: Markham, 1971.

Edelman, M. *Political Language: Words That Succeed and Policies that Fail.* New York: Academic Press, 1977.

Efron, E. *The News Twisters.* Los Angeles: Nash, 1971.

Ellsworth, J. W. Rationality and Campaigning: A Content Analysis of the 1960 Presidential Campaign Debates. *Western Political Quarterly,* 1965, *18,* 794-802.

Ellul, J. *Propaganda: The Formation of Men's Attitudes.* New York: Knopf, 1965.

Eulau, H., Wahlke, J. C., Buchanan, W., & L. C. Ferguson. The Role of the Representative: Some Empirical Observations on the Theory of Edmund Burke. *American Political Science Review,* 1959, *53,* 742-756.

Fagen, R. *Politics and Communications.* Boston: Little Brown, 1966.

Fathi, A. Diffusion of a 'Happy' News Event. *Journalism Quarterly,* 1973, *50,* 71-79.

Feshbach, S., & Singer, R. D. *Television and Aggression.* San Francisco: Jossey Bass, 1971.

Finifter, A. W. The Friendship Group as a Protective Environment for Political Deviants. *American Political Science Review, 1974, 68,* 607-625.

Fishkin, J., Kenniston, K., & MacKinnon, C. Moral Reasoning and Political Ideology. *Journal of Personality, 1973, 27,* 109-119.

Fishman, J. A. *Sociolinguistics: A Brief Introduction.* Rowley, Mass.: Newbury House, 1970.

Fishman, J. A. *Language and Nationalism.* Rowley, Mass.: Newbury House, 1971.

Frank, R. S. *Shifts in Symbolic Communication as a Result of International Crisis.* Unpublished doctoral dissertation, University of Pennsylvania, 1972.

Frank, R. S. *Message Dimensions of Television News.* Lexington, Mass.: D.C. Heath, 1973.

Frank, R. S. The Grammar of Film in Television News. *Journalism Quarterly, 1974, 51,* 245-251.

Frank, R. S., & Meadow, R. G. Hero Structure in American Television Programming: Authority and Power Symbolism in Prime-Time Entertainment. Unpublished paper, Foreign Policy Research Institute, Philadelphia, Pa., 1974.

French, J. P., & Raven, B. The Bases of Social Power. In D. Cartwright (Ed.), *Studies in Social Power.* Ann Arbor, Michigan: Institute for Social Research, 1959.

Friedrich, C. J. *Man and His Government.* New York: McGraw-Hill, 1963.

Frey, F. Political Development, Power and Communications in Turkey. In W. Pye (Ed.), *Communications and Political Development.* Princeton: Princeton University Press, 1963.

Fox, W. S., & Williams, J. D. Political Orientations and Musical Preferences Among College Students. *Public Opinion Quarterly, 1974, 38,* 352-371.

Funkhouser, G. R. The Issues of the 60's: An Exploratory Study in the Dynamics of Public Opinion. *Public Opinion Quarterly, 1973, 37,* 62-75.

George, A. *Propaganda Analysis.* Evanston, Illinois: Row Peterson, 1959.

Gerbner, G., Gross, L., Jackson-Beeck, M., Jeffries-Fox, S., & Signorielli, N. Cultural Indicators: Violence Profile No. 9. *Journal of Communication, 1978, 28,* 176-207.

Ghosh, S. K. *Man, Language and Society.* Paris: Mouton, 1972.

Gilman, G. An Inquiry into the Nature and Use of Authority. In M. Haire (Ed.), *Organization Theory in Industrial Practice.* New York: Wiley, 1962.

Glessing, R. J. *The Underground Press in America.* Bloomington: University of Indiana Press, 1970.

Gordon, G. *Persuasion: The Theory and Practice of Manipulative Communication.* New York: Hastings House, 1971.

Graber, D. A. Press Coverage Patterns of Campaign News: The 1968 Presidential Race. *Journalism Quarterly, 1971, 48,* 502-512.

Graber, D. A. Press and TV as Opinion Resources in Presidential Campaigns. *Public Opinion Quarterly, 1976a, 40,* 285-303.

Graber, D. A. *Verbal Behavior and Politics.* Urbana: University of Illinois Press, 1976b.

Greenstein, F. I. *Children and Politics.* New Haven: Yale University Press, 1965.

Greenstein, F. I., & Polsby, N. W. (Eds.), *Handbook of Political Science.* Reading, Mass.: Addison-Wesley, 1975.

Gumperz, J. J. Bilingual Education: Linguistic or Socio-Linguistic Bases. *Georgetown University Monographs on Language and Linguistics, 1970, 23,* 47-58.

Gurr, T. *Why Men Rebel.* Princeton: Princeton University Press, 1970.

Gusfield, J. *Symbolic Crusade.* Urbana: University of Illinois Press, 1963.

Harrison. S. S. *India: The Most Dangerous Decades.* Princeton: Princeton University Press, 1960.

Hacker, A. The Taxicab Rate War. In A. Westin (Ed.), *The Uses of Power.* New York: Harcourt, 1962.

Hall, R., & Hewitt, J. The Quasi-Theory of Communication and the Management of Dissent. *Social Problems, 1970, 18,* 12-27.

Halperin, M. H. *Bureaucratic Politics and Policy.* Washington, D.C.: Brookings, 1972.

Halperin, M. H., & Stone, J. J. Secrecy and Covert Intelligence Collection and Operations. In N. Dorsen, & S. Gillers (Eds.), *None of Your Business: Government Secrecy in America.* New York: Penguin, 1975.

Harik, I. Opinion Leaders and Mass Media in Rural Egypt: A Reconsideration of the Two-Step Flow of Communication Hypothesis. *American Political Science Review*, 1971, *65*, 731-741.

Harsanyi, J. C. Measurement of Social Power, Opportunity Costs, and the Theory of Two-Person Bargaining Games. *Behavioral Science*, 1962, *7*, 67-80.

Hattery, L. H., & Hofheimer, S. The Legislator's Source of Expert Opinion. *Public Opinion Quarterly*, 1954, *18*, 300-303.

Haugen, E. *Language Conflict and Language Planning.* Cambridge: Harvard University Press, 1966.

Hawley, W., & Wirt, F. D. (Eds.), *The Search for Community Power.* Englewood Cliffs, N.J.: Prentice-Hall, 1968.

Hayden, R. L. Toward a National Foreign Language Policy. *Journal of Communication*, 1979, *29*, 84-92.

Hess, R. D., & Torney, J. V. *The Development of Political Attitudes in Children.* Chicago: Aldine, 1967.

Higbie, C. E. Wisconsin Dalies in the 1952 Campaign: Space vs. Display. *Journalism Quarterly*, 1954, *31*, 56-60.

Hill, R., & Bonjean, C. News Diffusion: Test of the Regularity Hypothesis. *Journalism Quarterly*, 1964, *41*, 336-342.

Himmelstrand, U. Verbal Attitudes and Behavior: A Paradigm for the Study of Message Transmission and Transformation. *Public Opinion Quarterly*, 1960, *24*, 224-250.

Hirschman, A. O. *Exit, Voice, and Loyalty.* Cambridge, Mass.: Harvard University Press, 1970.

Hofstetter, C. R. *Bias in the News.* Columbus: Ohio State University Press, 1976.

Hollander, E. P. *Leaders, Groups, and Influences.* New York: Oxford University Press, 1964.

Hollander, N. Adolescents and the War: The Sources of Socialization. *Journalism Quarterly*, 1971, *48*, 472-479.

Holsti, O. R., Brody, R. A., & North, R. C. Measuring Affect and Action in International Reaction Models: Empirical Material From the 1962 Cuban Missile Crisis. *Peace Research Society Papers*, 1965, *2*, 170-190.

Holz, J. Media Coverage of Legionnaires Disease. Unpublished paper. Annenberg School of Communication, University of Pennsylvania, 1978.

Hovland, C. I., Janis, I. L., & Kelly, H. H. *Communications and Persuasion.* New Haven: Yale University Press, 1953.

Howkins, J. What is the World Administrative Radio Conference? *Journal of Communication*, 1979, *29*, 144-149.

Hauco, G. A. *The Sociology of Film Art.* New York: Basic Books, 1965.

Hudson, H. E. Implications for Development Communications. *Journal of Communication*, 1979, *29*, 179-186.

Hunter, F. *Community Power Structure.* Chapel Hill: University of North Carolina Press, 1953.

Hyman, H. *Political Socialization.* New York: Free Press, 1959.

Ingelhart, R. The Silent Revolution in Europe: Intergenerational Change in Post-Industrial Societies. *American Political Science Review*, 1971, *65*, 991-1017.

Isenberg, M. T. An Ambiguous Pacifism: A Retrospective on World War I Films. *Journal of Popular Film*, 1975, *4*, 98-115.

Jackson-Beeck, M., & Meadow, R. G. Content Analysis of Televised Communication Events: The Presidential Debates. *Communication Research*, 1979a, *6*, 321-344.

Jackson-Beeck, M., & Meadow, R. G. The Triple Agenda of Presidential Debates. *Public Opinion Quarterly*, 1979b, *43*, 173-180.

Janda, K. Toward the Explication of the Concept of Leadership in Terms of the Concept of Power. *Human Relations*, 1960, *13*, 345-364.

Janis, I. *Victims of Groupthink.* Boston: Houghton-Mifflin, 1972.

Jarvie, I. C. *Movies and Society.* New York: Basic Books, 1970.

Jennings, M. K. *Community Influentials.* New York: Free Press, 1964.

Jennings, M. K., & Langton, K. P. Mothers Versus Fathers: The Formation of Political

Orientations Among Young Americans. *Journal of Politics,* 1969, *31,* 329-358.
Jennings, M. K., & Niemi, R. G. The Transmission of Political Values from Parent to Child. *American Political Science Review,* 1968, *62,* 169-184.
Jennings, M. K., & Niemi, R. G. The Division of Political Labor Between Mothers and Fathers. *American Political Science Review,* 1971, *65,* 69-82.
Jennings, M. K., & Niemi, R. G. *The Political Character of Adolescence.* Princeton: Princeton University Press, 1974.
Jennings, R. M. Dramatic License in Political Broadcasts. *Journal of Broadcasting,* 1968, *12,* 229-246.
Johnson, L. B. *The Vantage Point: Perspectives of the Presidency.* New York: Harper & Row, 1971.
Johnson, N. R. Television and Politicization: A Test of Competing Models. *Journalism Quarterly,* 1973, *50,* 447-455.
Johnstone, J., Slawski, E., & Bowman, W. Professional Values of American Newsmen. *Public Opinion Quarterly,* 1972, *36,* 522-540.
Jowett, G. S. *Film: The Democratic Art.* Boston: Little Brown, 1976.
Katz, E., & Feldman, J. J. The Debates in the Light of Research: A Survey of Surveys. In S. Kraus (Ed.), *The Great Debates.* Bloomington: Indiana University Press, 1962.
Katz, E., & Lazarsfeld, P. F. *Personal Influence.* Glencoe: Free Press, 1955.
Katzman, N. Television Soap Operas. *Public Opinion Quarterly,* 1972, *36,* 200-212.
Kelley, G. The Status of Hindi as a Lingua Franca. In W. Bright (Ed.), *Sociolinguistics: Proceedings of the UCLA Linguistics Conference, 1964.* The Hauge: Mouton, 1966.
Kennedy, R. *Thirteen Days.* New York: Norton, 1968.
Key, V. O. *The Responsible Electorate.* Cambridge, Mass.: Belknap Press, 1966.
Klapper, J. T. *The Effects of Mass Communication.* Glencoe: Free Press, 1960.
Klein, M. W., & Maccoby, N. Newspaper Objectivity in the 1952 Campaign. *Journalism Quarterly,* 1954, *31,* 285-296.
Kloss, H. Bilingualism and Nationalism. *Journal of Social Issues,* 1967, *23,* 39-47.
Kobre, S., & Parks, J. How Florida Dailies Handled the 1952 Presidential Campaign. *Journalism Quarterly,* 1953, *30,* 163-169.
Kohlberg, L. The Child as a Moral Philosopher. *Psychology Today,* 1968, *7,* 25-30.
Kohlberg, L. State and Sequence: The Cognitive Developmental Approach to the Study of Socialization. In D. A. Goslin (Ed.), *Handbook of Socialization Theory and Research.* Chicago: Rand McNally, 1969.
Kovenock, D. Influence in the U.S. House of Representatives: A Statistical Analysis of Communication. *American Politics Quarterly,* 1973, *1,* 402-464.
Krasnow, E. G., & Longley, L. D. *The Politics of Broadcast Regulation.* (2nd ed.). New York: St. Martins, 1978.
Kraus, S. (Ed.). *The Great Debates.* Bloomington: Indiana University Press, 1962.
Kraus, S. (Ed.). *Great Debates, 1976: Ford Vs. Carter.* Bloomington: Indiana University Press, 1979.
Kraus, S., & Davis, D. *The Effects of Mass Communication on Political Behavior.* State College: Pennsylvania State University Press, 1976.
Kraus, S., Davis, D., Lang, K., & Lang, G. E. Critical Events Analysis. In S. H. Chaffee (Ed.), *Political Communication.* Beverly Hills: Sage, 1975.
Lakoff, R. *Language and Woman's Place.* New York: Harper, 1974.
Lambert, W. E. *Language, Psychology and Culture.* Palo Alto, California: Stanford University Press, 1972.
Lang, G. E., & Lang, K. The Formation of Public Opinion: Direct and Mediated Effects of the First Debate. In G. F. Bishop, R. G. Meadow, & M. Jackson-Beeck (Eds.), *The Presidential Debates: Media, Electoral and Policy Perspectives.* New York: Praeger, 1978.
Lang, K., & Lang, G. E. *Collective Dynamics.* New York: Thomas Y. Crowell, 1961.
Lang, K., & Lang, G. E. *Television and Politics.* Chicago: Quadrangle, 1968.
Langer, S. K. *Philosophy in a New Key.* Cambridge, Mass.: Harvard University Press, 1942.

Langer, S. K. *Feeling and Form.* New York: Scribner, 1953.

Langton, K. P. *Political Socialization.* New York: Oxford University Press, 1969.

Langton, K. P., & Jennings, M. K. Political Socialization and the High School Civics Curriculum. *American Political Science Review,* 1968, *62,* 852-867.

LaPalombara, J. (Ed.). *Bureaucracy and Political Development.* Princeton: Princeton University Press, 1963.

LaPalombara, J., & Weiner, M. (Eds.). *Political Parties and Political Development.* Princeton: Princeton University Press, 1966.

Larson, J. F. International Affairs Coverage on U.S. Network Television. *Journal of Communication,* 1979, *29,* 136-147.

Lasswell, H. *World Politics and Personal Insecurity.* New York: McGraw Hill, 1935.

Lasswell, H. The Structure and Function of Communication in Society. In L. Bryson (Ed.), *The Communication of Ideas.* New York: Harper, 1948.

Lasswell, H., & Kaplan, A. *Power and Society.* New Haven: Yale University Press, 1950.

Lasswell, H., Leites, N., & Associates. *Language of Politics.* New York: G. W. Stewart, 1949.

Lasswell, H., Lerner, D., & Pool, I. S. *The Comparative Study of Symbols: An Introduction.* Stanford, California: Stanford University Press, 1952.

Lazarsfeld, P. F., Berelson, B., & Gaudet, H. *The People's Choice.* New York: Columbia University Press, 1948.

Lazarsfeld, P. F., & Merton, R. Mass Communication, Popular Taste and Organized Social Action. In L. Bryson (Ed.), *The Communication of Ideas.* New York: Harper, 1948.

Leab, D. J. Cold War Comics. *Columbia Journalism Review,* 1965, *3,* 42-47.

LePage, R. *The National Language Question.* London: Oxford University Press, 1964.

Lerner, D. *The Passing of Traditional Society.* New York: Free Press, 1959.

Lerner, D. Mass Communication and the Nation State. In W. P. Davison, & F. T. C. Yu (Eds.), *Mass Communication Research: Major Issues and Future Directions.* New York: Praeger, 1974.

LeRoy, D. J., Wotring, C. E., & Lyle, J. Today in the Legislature: The Florida Story. *Journal of Communication,* 1974, *24,* 92-98.

Levin, M. L. Social Climates and Political Socialization. *Public Opinion Quarterly,* 1961, *25,* 596-606.

Lieberson, S. *Language and Ethnic Relations in Canada.* New York: Wiley, 1970.

Lindbloom, C. E. The Science of Muddling Through. *Public Administration Review,* 1957, *19,* 79-88.

Lippmann, W. *Public Opinion.* New York: MacMillan, 1922.

Lipset, S. M. *Political Man.* Garden City, New York: Doubleday & Co., 1960.

Lipset, S. M., Trow, M., & Coleman, J. S. *Union Democracy.* Glencoe: Free Press, 1956.

Lipsky, M. Protest as a Political Resource. *American Political Science Review,* 1968, *62,* 1144-1158.

Litt, E. Political Cynicism and Political Futility. *Journal of Politics,* 1963, *25,* 312-323.

Loh, W. D. Nationalist Attitudes in Quebec and Belgium. *Journal of Conflict Resolution,* 1975, *19,* 217-249.

Lovibond, S. H. The Effects of Media Stressing Crime and Violence Upon Children's Attitudes. *Social Problems,* 1967, *15,* 91-100.

Lowi, T. J. American Business, Public Policy, Case Studies and Political Theory. *World Politics,* 1963, *16,* 667-715.

Luckmann, T. *The Invisible Religion: The Transformation of Symbols in Industrial Society.* New York: MacMillan, 1967.

Lynd, R. S., & Lynd, H. *Middletown.* New York: Harcourt Brace, 1929.

MacCann, R. D. *The People's Films.* New York: Hastings House, 1973.

MacDonald, J. F. The Foreigner in Juvenile Series Fiction, 1900-1945. *Journal of Popular Culture,* 1974, *8,* 534-548.

Mackey, W. F. Language Policy and Language Planning. *Journal of Communication,* 1979, *29,* 48-53.

Malinowski, B. The Problem of Meaning in a Primitive Language. In C. K. Ogden, I. A. Richards (Eds.), *The Meaning of Meaning: A Study of the Influence of Lan-*

guage Upon Thought and the Science of Symbolism. New York: Harcourt, Brace, 1945.

Malinowski, B. *Magic, Science and Religion and Other Essays.* Garden City, New York: Doubleday, 1948.

March, J. G. An Introduction to the Theory and Measurement of Influence. *American Political Science Review, 1955, 49,* 431-451.

March, J. G., & Simon, H. A. *Organizations.* New York: MacMillan, 1958.

McCombs, M. E., & Shaw, D. L. The Agenda-Setting Function of Mass Media. *Public Opinion Quarterly, 1972, 36,* 176-187.

McCormack, W. C. Language Identities: An Introduction to India's Languages Problems. In J. W. Elder (Ed.), *Chapters in Indian Civilization Volume II.* Madison: University of Wisconsin Press, 1967.

McGinnis, J. *The Selling of the President, 1968.* New York: Trident Press, 1968.

McLeod, J. M., Becker, L. B., & Byrnes, J. E. Another Look at the Agenda-Setting Function of the Press. *Communication Research, 1974, 1,* 131-166.

McLeod, J. M., & Chaffee, S. H. The Construction of Social Reality. In J. T. Tedeschi (Ed.), *The Social Influence Processes.* Chicago: Aldine, 1972.

Mead, G. H. *Mind, Self and Society.* Chicago: University of Chicago Press, 1934.

Mead, G. H. *On Social Psychology.* Chicago: University of Chicago Press, 1956.

Mead, M. *Coming of Age in Samoa.* New York: Morrow, 1929.

Meadow, R. G. Cross-Media Comparison of Coverage of the 1972 Presidential Campaign. *Journalism Quarterly, 1973a, 50,* 482-488.

Meadow, R. G. Television Stereotypes and Foreign Policy. Paper presented to the International Political Science Association, Montreal, Canada, 1973b.

Meadow, R. G. *Information and Maturation in the Political Socialization Process.* Unpublished doctoral dissertation, University of Pennsylvania, 1976a.

Meadow, R. G. Issue Emphasis and Public Opinion: The Media During the 1972 Presidential Campaign. *American Politics Quarterly, 1976b, 4,* 177-192.

Meadow, R. G. The Content of Children's News Sources: A Comparative Analysis of the *Weekly Reader* and Television News. Paper presented to the International Communication Association. Berlin, West Germany, 1977.

Meadow, R. G., & Jackson-Beeck, M. A Comparative Perspective on Presidential Debates: Issue Evolution in 1960 and 1976. In G. F. Bishop, R. B. Meadow, & M. Jackson-Beeck (Eds.), *The Presidential Debates: Media, Electoral and Policy Perspectives.* New York: Praeger, 1978.

Mebane, R. *The Great Game of Politics: A Study of Metaphor in the Mass Media.* Unpublished master's thesis. Annenberg School of Communications, University of Pennsylvania, 1977.

Meier, R. L. *A Communications Theory of Urban Growth.* Cambrdige, Mass.: M.I.T. Press, 1962.

Mendelsohn, H., & Crespi, I. *Polls, Television and the New Politics.* Scranton, Pa.: Chandler, 1970.

Merelman, R. M. Power and Community in Television. *Journal of Popular Culture, 1968, 2,* 63-80.

Merelman, R. M. The Development of Political Ideology: A Framework for the Analysis of Political Socialization. *American Political Science Review, 1969, 63,* 750-767.

Merelman, R. M. The Development of Policy Thinking in Adolescence. *American Political Science Review, 1971, 65,* 1033-1047.

Merelman, R. M. Political Reasoning in Adolescence: Some Bridging Themes. Paper presented to the American Political Science Association. New Orleans, La., 1973.

Merelman, R. M., & McCabe, A. Evolving Orientation Towards Policy Choice in Adolescence. *American Journal of Political Science, 1974, 18,* 665-680.

Merton, R. K. Patterns of Influence. In P. F. Lazarsfeld & F. N. Stanton (Eds.), *Communication Research 1948-1949.* New York: Harper, 1949.

Migus, P. M. *Sounds Canadian.* Montreal: Peter Martin Associations, 1975.

Milbrath, L. W. Lobbying as a Communications Process. *Public Opinion Quarterly, 1960, 24,* 32-54.

Milbrath, L. W., & Goel, M. L. *Political Participation.* Chicago: Rand McNally, 1977.

Mills, C. W. *The Power Elite*. New York: Harcourt, Brace, 1956.

Mitchell, A. M. *Children and Movies*. Chicago: University of Chicago Press, 1939.

Mitchell, J. M., Mitchell, W. C. *Political Analysis and Public Policy*. Chicago: Rand McNally, 1969.

Mladenka, K. R., & Hill, K. Q. The Development of Political Orientations: A Partial Test of a Cognitive Development Hypothesis. *Youth and Society*, 1975, *2*, 130-147.

Morgenthau, H. *Politics Among Nations*. New York: Alfred Knopf, 1960.

Morris, C. *Signs, Language and Behavior*. New York: Prentice-Hall, 1946.

Mosco, V. *Broadcasting in the United States*. Norwood, New Jersey: Ablex, 1979.

Mueller, C. *The Politics of Communication*. New York: Oxford University Press, 1975.

Nagel, J. H. *The Descriptive Analysis of Power*. New Haven: Yale University Press, 1975.

Neustadt, R. *Presidential Power*. New York: Wiley, 1976.

Newcombe, T. M. *Personality and Social Change: Attitude Formation in a Student Community*. New York: Dryden, 1943.

Newcombe, T. M. The General Nature of Peer Group Influence. In T. M. Newcombe, & E. K. Wilson (Eds.), *College Peer Groups: Problems and Prospects for Research*. Chicago: Aldine, 1967.

Nie, N., Verba, S., & Petrocik, J. R. *The Changing American Voter*. Cambridge, Mass.: Harvard University Press, 1976.

Nimmo, D. *Newsgathering in Washington*. New York: Atherton, 1964.

Nimmo, D. *The Political Persuaders*. Englewood Cliffs, N.J.: Prentice-Hall, 1970.

Nimmo, D. *Popular Images of Politics*. Englewood Cliffs, N.J.: Prentice-Hall, 1974.

Nimmo, D. *Political Communication and Public Opinion in America*. Santa Monica, California: Goodyear, 1978.

Nordenstreng, K., & Schiller, H. L. (Eds.). *National Sovreignty and International Communication*. Norwood, N.J.: Ablex, 1978.

O'Keefe, G. Political Campaigns and Mass Communication. In S. H. Chaffee (Ed.), *Political Communication*. Beverly Hills: Sage, 1975.

Osgood, C. E. Meaning Cannot be r_m? *Journal of Verbal Learning and Verbal Behavior*, 1966, *5*, 402-407.

Ostlund, L. E. Interpersonal Communication Following McGovern's Eagleton Decision. *Public Opinion Quarterly*, 1973, *37*, 601-610.

Park, R. A. News as a Form of Knowledge: A Chapter in the Sociology of Knowledge. *American Journal of Sociology*, 1940, *45*, 669-686.

Parsons, T. *The Social System*. Glencoe: Free Press, 1951.

Patrick, J. J. Political Socialization and Political Education in Schools. In S. A. Renshon (Ed.), *Handbook of Political Socialization*. New York: Free Press, 1977.

Patterson, J. W. Moral Development and Political Thinking: The Case of Freedom of Speech. *Western Political Quarterly*, 1979, *32*, 7-20.

Patterson, T. E., & McLure, R. D. *The Unseeing Eye*. New York: Putnam, 1976.

Phillips, W. G. The Government's Classification System. In N. Dorsen, & S. Gillers (Eds.), *None of Your Business: Government Secrecy in America*. New York: Penguin, 1975.

Piaget, J. *The Origins of Intelligence in Children*. New York: Norton, 1952.

Piaget, J. *The Construction of Reality in the Child*. New York: Basic Books, 1954.

Piaget, J. *The Child's Conception of the World*. Totowa, N.J.: Littlefield, Adams & Co., 1965.

Piaget, J. *The Moral Judgment of the Child*. New York: Free Press, 1969.

Pool, I. S. The problems of WARC. *Journal of Communication*, 1979, *29*, 187-196.

Porter, J. Higher Public Servants in the Bureaucratic Elite in Canada. *Canadian Journal of Economics and Political Science*, 1958, *24*, 483-501.

Porter, J. *The Vertical Mosaic: An Analysis of Class and Power in Canada*. Toronto: University of Toronto Press, 1965.

Pousada, A. Bilingual Education in the U.S. *Journal of Communication*, 1979, *29*, 84-92.

Pride, J. B. Customs and Cases of Verbal Behavior. In E. Ardener (Ed.), *Social Anthropology and Linguistics*. London: Tavistock, 1971.

Prothro, J. W., & Grigg, C. M. Fundamental Principles of Democracy: Bases of Agreement and Disagreement. *Journal of Politics*, 1960, *22*, 276, 294.

Purcell, R. *Government and Art.* Washington, D.C.: Public Affairs Press, 1956.
Pye, L. W. (Ed.). *Communications and Political Development.* Princeton: Princeton University Press, 1963.
Pye, L. W., & Verba, S. (Eds.). *Political Culture and Political Development.* Princeton: Princeton University Press, 1965.
Radcliffe-Brown, A. On the Concept of Function in Social Science. *American Anthropologist,* 1935, *37,* 394-402.
Rahudkar, W. B. Impact of Fertilizer Extension Programmes on the Minds of the Farmers and Their Reaction to Different Extension Methods. *Indian Journal of Agronomy,* 1958, *3,* 119-136.
Rather, D., & Gates, G. P. *The Palace Guard.* New York: Harper & Row, 1974.
Renshon, S. A. (Ed.). *Handbook of Political Socialization.* New York: Free Press, 1977.
Repass, D. E., & Chaffee, S. H. Administrative vs. Campaign Coverage of Two Presidents in Eight Partisan Dailies. *Journalism Quarterly,* 1968, *45,* 528-531.
Riccards, M. P. *The Making of the American Citizenry.* San Francisco: Chandler, 1973.
Riker, W. A Test of the Adequacy of the Power Index. *Behavioral Science,* 1959, *4,* 276-290.
Rioux, M. *Quebec in Question.* J. Boake, Translator. Toronto: James, Lewis, & Samuel, 1972.
Rivers, W. L., Miller, S., & Gandy, O. Government and the Media. In S. H. Chaffee (Ed.), *Political Communication.* Beverly Hills: Sage, 1975.
Roberts, D. F., Hawkins, R. P., & Pingree, S. Watergate and Political Socialization: The Inescapable Event. *American Politics Quarterly,* 1975, *3,* 406-422.
Robinson, J. P. Mass Communication and Information Diffusion. In F. G. Kline, & P. J. Tichenor (Eds.), *Current Perspectives in Mass Communication Research.* Beverly Hills: Sage, 1972.
Robinson, J. P. Interpersonal Influence in Election Campaigns: The Two-Step Flow Hypothesis. *Public Opinion Quarterly,* 1976, *40,* 304-339.
Robinson, M. J. Public Affairs Television and the Growth of Political Malaise: The Case of the Selling of the Pentagon. *American Political Science Review,* 1976, *70,* 409-432.
Robinson, M. J. Television and American Politics—1956-1976. *The Public Interest,* 1977, *48,* 3-19.
Robinson, W. P. *Language and Social Behavior.* Baltimore: Penguin, 1972.
Rogers, E. M. *Diffusion of Innovation.* New York: Free Press, 1962.
Rogers, E. M. Communication and Development: The Passing of the Dominant Paradigm. *Communication Research,* 1976a, *3,* 213-240.
Rogers, E. M. New Perspectives on Communication and Development. *Communication Research,* 1976b, *3,* 99-106.
Rogers, E. M., & Shoemaker, E. F. *Communication of Innovations: A Cross Cultural Approach.* New York: Free Press, 1972.
Rosenau, J. *Citizenship Between Elections.* New York: Free Press, 1974.
Rosenau, N. The Sources of Children's Political Concepts: An Application of Piaget's Theory. In D. C. Schwartz, & S. K. Schwartz (Eds.), *New Directions in Political Socialization.* New York: Free Press, 1975.
Royal Commission on Biculturalism and Bilingualism. *Preliminary Report.* Ottawa: The Queens Printer, 1965.
Rubinstein, H. Some Problems of Meaning in Natural Languages. In I. S. Pool, F. W. Frey, W. Schramm, N. Maccoby, E. B. Parker (Eds.), *Handbook of Communication.* Chicago: Rand McNally, 1973.
Runion, H. L. An Objective Study of the Speech Style of Woodrow Wilson. *Speech Monographs,* 1936, *3,* 75-94.
Russell, B. *Power: A New Social Analysis.* London: Allen & Unwin, 1938.
Salter, C., & Teger, A. I. Changes in Attitudes Toward Other Nations as a Function of the Type of International Contact. *Sociometry,* 1975, *38,* 213-222.
Sanders, C. R. The Portrayal of War and the Fighting Man in Novels of the Vietnam War. *Journal of Popular Culture,* 1969, *3,* 553-564.

Sapir, E. Symbolism. In *Encyclopedia of the Social Sciences.* New York: MacMillan, 1934, *492-495.*

Sapir, E. *Culture, Language and Personality: Selected Essays.* D. G. Mandelbaum (Ed.), Berkeley: University of California Press, 1962.

Savard, J. G. *Multilingual Political Systems.* Quebec: Les Presses de l'University Laval, 1975.

Schattschneider, E. E. *The Semi-Sovereign People.* New York: Holt, Rinehart, & Winston, 1960.

Schonfield, W. R. The Focus of Political Socialization Research. *World Politics,* 1971, *23,* 544-578.

Schramm, W. *Mass Media and National Development.* Stanford: Stanford University Press, 1964.

Schramm, W., & Lerner, D. (Eds.), *Communication and Change in the Developing Countries: Ten Years After.* Honolulu: University of Hawaii/East-West Center Press, 1976.

Schramm, W., Lyle, J., & Parker, E. B. *Television in the Lives of Our Children.* Stanford: Stanford University Press, 1961.

Searing, D. P., Schwartz, J. T., & Lind, A. E. The Structuring Principle: Political Socialization and Belief Systems. *American Political Science Review,* 1973, *67,* 415-432.

Sears, D. O. Political Socialization. In F. I. Greenstein, & N. W. Polsby (Eds.), *Handbook of Political Science: Micropolitical Theory.* (Vol. 2). Reading, Mass.: Addison-Wesley, 1975.

Shain, R. E. Hollywood's Cold War. *Journal of Popular Film,* 1974, *3,* 334-350.

Shannon, C. W., and Weaver, W. *The Mathematical Theory of Communication.* Urbana: University of Illinois Press, 1949.

Shaw, D. L., and McCombs, M. E. *The Emergence of American Political Issues.* St. Paul, Minn.: West, 1977.

Shils, E. A., & Janowitz, M. Cohesion and Disintegration in the Wehrmact in World War II. *Public Opinion Quarterly,* 1948, *12,* 280-315.

Sigal, L. V. *Reporters and Officials.* Lexington, Mass.: D.C. Heath, 1973.

Silberger, S. L. Peers and Political Socialization. In S. A. Renshon (Ed.), *Handbook of Political Socialization.* New York: Free Press, 1977.

Simmel, G. *Conflict and the Web of Group Affiliations.* New York: Free Press, 1955.

Simon, H. A. Notes on the Observation and Measurement of Power. *Journal of Politics,* 1953, *15,* 500-516.

Simon, H. A. *Administrative Behavior.* (2nd ed.). New York: MacMillan, 1957.

Sinclair, J., & Levin, R. *Music and Politics.* New York: World Publishing Co., 1971.

Singer, B. Mass Media and Communication Processes in the Detroit Riots of 1967. *Public Opinion Quarterly,* 1972, *34,* 236-245.

Sniderman, P. M. *Personality and Democratic Politics.* Berkeley: University of California Press, 1975.

Steeper, F. T. Public Response to Gerald Ford's Statements on Eastern Europe in the Second Debate. In G. F. Bishop, R. G. Meadow, & M. Jackson-Beeck (Eds.), *The Presidential Debates: Media, Electoral and Policy Perspectives.* New York: Praeger, 1978.

Stein, M. L. The Secrets of Local Government. In N. Dorsen, & S. Gillers (Eds.), *None of Your Business: Government Secrecy in America.* New York: Penguin, 1975.

Stempel, G. The Prestige Covers the 1960 Presidential Campaign. *Journalism Quarterly,* 1961, *38,* 157-163.

Stempel, G. The Prestige Press in Two Presidential Campaigns. *Journalism Quarterly,* 1965, *42,* 15-21.

Stempel, G. Prestige Press Meets Third Party Challenge. *Journalism Quarterly,* 1969, *46,* 699-706.

Stene, E. O. Newspapers in the Campaign. *Social Forces,* 1937, *2,* 213-215.

Stewart, J. Congress on the Air: Issues and Alternatives. *Journal of Communication,* 1974, *25,* 82-90.

Stinchcombe, A. L. *Constructing Social Theories.* New York: Harcourt, Brace, & World, 1968.

Stycos, J. M. Patterns of Communication in a Rural Greek Village. *Public Opinion Quarterly,* 1952, *16,* 59-70.

Stycos, J. The Potential Role of Turkish Village Opinion Leaders in a Program of Family Planning. *Public Opinion Quarterly,* 1965, *29,* 124-125.

Teune, H. The Learning of Integrative Habits. In P. E. Jacob, & J. Toscano (Eds.), *The Integration of Political Communities.* Philadelphia: Lippincott, 1964.

Tipton, L., Haney, R. O., & Basehart, J. R. Media Agenda-Setting in City and State Election Campaigns. *Journalism Quarterly,* 1975, *52,* 15-22.

Toch, H. *The Social Psychology of Social Movements.* Indianapolis: Bobbs-Merrill, 1965.

Tonkin, H. Equalizing Language. *Journal of Communication,* 1979, *29,* 124-133.

Troldhal, V. C. A Field Test of a Modified Two-Step Flow of Communication Model. *Public Opinion Quarterly,* 1966, *30,* 609-623.

Troldhal, V. C., & Van Dam, R. Face to Face Communication About Major Topics in the News. *Public Opinion Quarterly,* 1965, *29,* 626-632.

Tuchman, G. Objectivity as a Strategic Ritual: An Examination of Newsman's Notions of Objectivity. *American Journal of Sociology,* 1971, *77,* 660-670.

Tuchman, S., & Coffin, T. E. The Influence of Election Night Broadcasts on Television in a Close Election. *Public Opinion Quarterly,* 1971, *35,* 315-326.

Turner, R., & Killian L. (Eds.). *Collective Behavior.* Englewood Cliffs, N.J.: Prentice-Hall, 1957.

Vose, C. Litigation as a Form of Pressure Group Activity. *The Annals,* 1958, *319,* 20-31.

Walzer, M. On the Role of Symbolism in Political Thought. *Political Science Quarterly,* 1967, *82,* 191-204.

Weiner, N. *Cybernetics.* New York: Wiley, 1948.

Weiner, N. *The Human Uses of Human Beings.* Garden City, New York: Doubleday, 1955.

Weissberg, R. *Political Learning, Political Choice and Democratic Citizenship.* Englewood Cliffs, N.J.: Prentice-Hall, 1974.

Wellford, H. Rights of People: The Freedom of Information Act. In N. Dorsen, & S. Gillers (Eds.), *None of Your Business: Government Secrecy in America.* New York: Penguin, 1975.

Westin, A. F. (Ed.). *Information Technology in a Democracy.* Cambridge, Mass.: Harvard University Press, 1971.

Whisenand, J. D. Florida's Experience with Cameras in the Courtroom. *ABA Journal,* 1978, *64,* 1860-1864.

White, D. M. The Gatekeeper: A Case Study of the Selection of News. *Journalism Quarterly,* 1950, *27,* 383-390.

Whitehead, A. N. *Symbolism: Its Meaning and Effect.* New York: MacMillan, 1927.

Whiting, J. W., & Child, I. L. *Child Training and Personality.* New York: MacMillan, 1953.

Wilson, G., & Wilson, M. *The Analysis of Social Change.* Cambridge: Cambridge University Press, 1948.

Wirsing, R. Political Power and Information: A Cross Cultural Study. *American Anthropologist,* 1973, *75,* 153-170.

Wright, C. R. *Mass Communication: A Sociological Perspective.* (2nd ed.). New York: Random House, 1975.

Wolfarth, D. L. John F. Kennedy in the Tradition of Inaugural Speech. *Quarterly Journal of Speech,* 1961, *47,* 124-132.

Zald, M. N. Politics and Symbols: A Review Article. *Sociological Quarterly,* 1966, *7,* 85-91.

AUTHOR INDEX

Page numbers in *italics* indicate where complete references are listed.

SUBJECT INDEX